# Improving AI Self-Driving Cars

Practical Advances in Artificial Intelligence and Machine Learning

Dr. Lance B. Eliot, MBA, PhD

Disclaimer: This book is presented solely for educational and entertainment purposes. The author and publisher are not offering it as legal, accounting, or other professional services advice. The author and publisher make no representations or warranties of any kind and assume no liabilities of any kind with respect to the accuracy or completeness of the contents and specifically disclaim any implied warranties of merchantability or fitness of use for a particular purpose. Neither the author nor the publisher shall be held liable or responsible to any person or entity with respect to any loss or incidental or consequential damages caused, or alleged to have been caused, directly or indirectly, by the information or programs contained herein. Every company is different and the advice and strategies contained herein may not be suitable for your situation.

 First Edition.

ISBN: 978-1-73-630318-4

# DEDICATION

To my incredible daughter, Lauren, and my incredible son, Michael.

*Forest fortuna adiuvat* (from the Latin; good fortune favors the brave).

# CONTENTS

# ACKNOWLEDGMENTS

I have been the beneficiary of advice and counsel by many friends, colleagues, family, investors, and many others. I want to thank everyone that has aided me throughout my career. I write from the heart and the head, having experienced first-hand what it means to have others around you that support you during the good times and the tough times.

To Warren Bennis, one of my doctoral advisors and ultimately a colleague, I offer my deepest thanks and appreciation, especially for his calm and insightful wisdom and support.

To Mark Stevens and his generous efforts toward funding and supporting the USC Stevens Center for Innovation.

To Lloyd Greif and the USC Lloyd Greif Center for Entrepreneurial Studies for their ongoing encouragement of founders and entrepreneurs.

To Peter Drucker, William Wang, Aaron Levie, Peter Kim, Jon Kraft, Cindy Crawford, Jenny Ming, Steve Milligan, Chis Underwood, Frank Gehry, Buzz Aldrin, Steve Forbes, Bill Thompson, Dave Dillon, Alan Fuerstman, Larry Ellison, Jim Sinegal, John Sperling, Mark Stevenson, Anand Nallathambi, Thomas Barrack, Jr., and many other innovators and leaders that I have met and gained mightily from doing so.

Thanks to Ed Trainor, Kevin Anderson, James Hickey, Wendell Jones, Ken Harris, DuWayne Peterson, Mike Brown, Jim Thornton, Abhi Beniwal, Al Biland, John Nomura, Eliot Weinman, John Desmond, and many others for their unwavering support during my career.

*And most of all thanks as always to Lauren and Michael, for their ongoing support and for having seen me writing and heard much of this material during the many months involved in writing it. To their patience and willingness to listen.*

# INTRODUCTION

This is a book that provides the newest innovations and the latest Artificial Intelligence (AI) advances about the emerging nature of AI-based autonomous self-driving driverless cars. Via recent advances in Artificial Intelligence (AI) and Machine Learning (ML), we are nearing the day when vehicles can control themselves and will not require and nor rely upon human intervention to perform their driving tasks (or, that allow for human intervention, but only *require* human intervention in very limited ways).

Similar to my other related books, which I describe in a moment and list the chapters in the Appendix A of this book, I am particularly focused on those advances that pertain to self-driving cars. The phrase "autonomous vehicles" is often used to refer to any kind of vehicle, whether it is ground-based or in the air or sea, and whether it is a cargo hauling trailer truck or a conventional passenger car. Though the aspects described in this book are certainly applicable to all kinds of autonomous vehicles, I am focused more so here on cars.

For this book, I am going to borrow my introduction from those companion books, since it does a good job of laying out the landscape of self-driving cars and my overall viewpoints on the topic.

## INTRODUCTION TO SELF-DRIVING CARS

This is a book about self-driving cars. Someday in the future, we'll all have self-driving cars and this book will perhaps seem antiquated, but right now, we are at the forefront of the self-driving car wave. Daily news bombards us with flashes of new announcements by one car maker or another and leaves the impression that within the next few weeks or maybe months that the self driving car will be here. A casual non-technical reader would assume from these news flashes that in we must be on the cusp of a true self-driving car.

We are still quite a distance from having a true self-driving car. A true self-driving car is akin to a moonshot. In the same manner that getting us to the moon was an incredible feat, likewise, is achieving a true self-driving car. Anybody that suggests or even brashly states that the true self-driving car is nearly here should be viewed with great skepticism. Indeed, you'll see that I often tend to use the word "hogwash" or "crock" when I assess much of the decidedly ***fake news*** about self-driving cars.

Indeed, I've been writing a popular blog post about self-driving cars and hitting hard on those that try to wave their hands and pretend that we are on the imminent verge of true self-driving cars. For many years, I've been known as the AI Insider. Besides writing about AI, I also develop AI software. I do what I describe. It also gives me insights into what others that are doing AI are really doing versus what it is said they are doing.

Many faithful readers had asked me to pull together my insightful short essays and put them into another book, which you are now holding.

For those of you that have been reading my essays over the years, this collection not only puts them together into one handy package, I also updated the essays and added new material. For those of you that are new to the topic of self-driving cars and AI, I hope you find these essays approachable and informative. I also tend to have a writing style with a bit of a voice, and so you'll see that I am times have a wry sense of humor and poke at conformity.

As a former professor and founder of an AI research lab, I for many years wrote in the formal language of academic writing. I published in referred journals and served as an editor for several AI journals. This writing here is not of the nature, and I have adopted a different and more informal style for these essays. That being said, I also do mention from time-to-time more rigorous material on AI and encourage you all to dig into those deeper and more formal materials if so interested.

For those of you that are reading this book and have a penchant for writing code, you might consider taking a look at the open-source code available for self-driving cars. This is a handy place to start learning how to develop AI for self-driving cars. There are also many new educational courses spring forth. There is a growing body of those wanting to learn about and develop self-driving cars, and a growing body of colleges, labs, and other avenues by which you can learn about self-driving cars.

This book will provide a foundation of aspects that I think will get you ready for those kinds of more advanced training opportunities. If you've already taken those classes, you'll likely find these essays especially interesting as they offer a perspective that I am betting few other instructors or faculty offered to you. These are challenging essays that ask you to think beyond the conventional about self-driving cars.

# THE MOTHER OF ALL AI PROJECTS

In June 2017, Apple CEO Tim Cook came out and finally admitted that Apple has been working on a self-driving car. As you'll see in my essays, Apple was enmeshed in secrecy about their self-driving car efforts. We have only been able to read the tea leaves and guess at what Apple has been up to. The notion of an iCar has been floating for quite a while, and self-driving engineers and researchers have been signing tight-lipped Non-Disclosure Agreements (NDA's) to work on projects at Apple that were as shrouded in mystery as any military invasion plans might be.

Tim Cook said something that many others in the Artificial Intelligence (AI) field have been saying, namely, the creation of a self-driving car has got to be the mother of all AI projects. In other words, it is in fact a tremendous moonshot for AI. If a self-driving car can be crafted and the AI works as we hope, it means that we have made incredible strides with AI and that therefore it opens many other worlds of potential breakthrough accomplishments that AI can solve.

Is this hyperbole? Am I just trying to make AI seem like a miracle worker and so provide self-aggrandizing statements for those of us writing the AI software for self-driving cars? No, it is not hyperbole. Developing a true self-driving car is really, really, really hard to do. Let me take a moment to explain why. As a side note, I realize that the Apple CEO is known for at times uttering hyperbole, and he had previously said for example that the year 2012 was "the mother of all years," and he had said that the release of iOS 10 was "the mother of all releases" – all of which does suggest he likes to use the handy "mother of" expression. But, I assure you, in terms of true self-driving cars, he has hit the nail on the head. For sure.

When you think about a moonshot and how we got to the moon, there are some identifiable characteristics and those same aspects can be applied to creating a true self-driving car. You'll notice that I keep putting the word "true" in front of the self-driving car expression. I do so because as per my essay about the various levels of self-driving cars, there are some self-driving cars that are only somewhat of a self-driving car. The somewhat versions are ones that require a human driver to be ready to intervene. In my view, that's not a true self-driving car. A true self-driving car is one that requires no human driver intervention at all. It is a car that can entirely undertake via automation the driving task without any human driver needed. This is the essence of what is known as a Level 5 self-driving car. We are currently at the Level 2 and Level 3 mark, and not yet at Level 5.

Getting to the moon involved aspects such as having big stretch goals, incremental progress, experimentation, innovation, and so on. Let's review how this applied to the moonshot of the bygone era, and how it applies to the self-driving car moonshot of today.

**Big Stretch Goal**

Trying to take a human and deliver the human to the moon, and bring them back, safely, was an extremely large stretch goal at the time. No one knew whether it could be done. The technology wasn't available yet. The cost was huge. The determination would need to be fierce. Etc. To reach a Level 5 self-driving car is going to be the same. It is a big stretch goal. We can readily get to the Level 3, and we are able to see the Level 4 just up ahead, but a Level 5 is still an unknown as to if it is doable. It should eventually be doable and in the same way that we thought we'd eventually get to the moon, but when it will occur is a different story.

**Incremental Progress**

Getting to the moon did not happen overnight in one fell swoop. It took years and years of incremental progress to get there. Likewise, for self-driving cars. Google has famously been striving to get to the Level 5, and pretty much been willing to forgo dealing with the intervening levels, but most of the other self-driving car makers are doing the incremental route. Let's get a good Level 2 and a somewhat Level 3 going. Then, let's improve the Level 3 and get a somewhat Level 4 going. Then, let's improve the Level 4 and finally arrive at a Level 5. This seems to be the prevalent way that we are going to achieve the true self-driving car.

**Experimentation**

You likely know that there were various experiments involved in perfecting the approach and technology to get to the moon. As per making incremental progress, we first tried to see if we could get a rocket to go into space and safety return, then put a monkey in there, then with a human, then we went all the way to the moon but didn't land, and finally we arrived at the mission that actually landed on the moon.

Self-driving cars are the same way. We are doing simulations of self-driving cars. We do testing of self-driving cars on private land under controlled situations.

We do testing of self-driving cars on public roadways, often having to meet regulatory requirements including for example having an engineer or equivalent in the car to take over the controls if needed. And so on. Experiments big and small are needed to figure out what works and what doesn't.

**Innovation**

There are already some advances in AI that are allowing us to progress toward self-driving cars. We are going to need even more advances. Innovation in all aspects of technology are going to be required to achieve a true self-driving car. By no means do we already have everything in-hand that we need to get there. Expect new inventions and new approaches, new algorithms, etc.

**Setbacks**

Most of the pundits are avoiding talking about potential setbacks in the progress toward self-driving cars. Getting to the moon involved many setbacks, some of which you never have heard of and were buried at the time so as to not dampen enthusiasm and funding for getting to the moon. A recurring theme in many of my included essays is that there are going to be setbacks as we try to arrive at a true self-driving car. Take a deep breath and be ready. I just hope the setbacks don't completely stop progress. I am sure that it will cause progress to alter in a manner that we've not yet seen in the self-driving car field. I liken the self-driving car of today to the excitement everyone had for Uber when it first got going. Today, we have a different view of Uber and with each passing day there are more regulations to the ride sharing business and more concerns raised. The darling child only stays a darling until finally that child acts up. It will happen the same with self-driving cars.

# SELF-DRIVING CARS CHALLENGES

But what exactly makes things so hard to have a true self-driving car, you might be asking. You have seen cruise control for years and years. You've lately seen cars that can do parallel parking. You've seen YouTube videos of Tesla drivers that put their hands out the window as their car zooms along the highway, and seen to therefore be in a self-driving car. Aren't we just needing to put a few more sensors onto a car and then we'll have in-hand a true self-driving car? Nope.

Consider for a moment the nature of the driving task. We don't just let anyone at any age drive a car. Worldwide, most countries won't license a driver until the age of 18, though many do allow a learner's permit at the age of 15 or 16. Some suggest that a younger age would be physically too small to reach the controls of the car. Though this might be the case, we could easily adjust the controls to allow for younger aged and thus smaller stature. It's not their physical size that matters. It's their cognitive development that matters.

To drive a car, you need to be able to reason about the car, what the car can and cannot do. You need to know how to operate the car. You need to know about how other cars on the road drive. You need to know what is allowed in driving such as speed limits and driving within marked lanes. You need to be able to react to situations and be able to avoid getting into accidents. You need to ascertain when to hit your brakes, when to steer clear of a pedestrian, and how to keep from ramming that motorcyclist that just cut you off.

Many of us had taken courses on driving. We studied about driving and took driver training. We had to take a test and pass it to be able to drive. The point being that though most adults take the driving task for granted, and we often "mindlessly" drive our cars, there is a significant amount of cognitive effort that goes into driving a car. After a while, it becomes second nature. You don't especially think about how you drive, you just do it. But, if you watch a novice driver, say a teenager learning to drive, you suddenly realize that there is a lot more complexity to it than we seem to realize.

Furthermore, driving is a very serious task. I recall when my daughter and son first learned to drive. They are both very conscientious people. They wanted to make sure that whatever they did, they did well, and that they did not harm anyone. Every day, when you get into a car, it is probably around 4,000 pounds of hefty metal and plastics (about two tons), and it is a lethal weapon. Think about it. You drive down the street in an object that weighs two tons and with the engine it can accelerate and ram into anything you want to hit. The damage a car can inflict is very scary. Both my children were surprised that they were being given the right to maneuver this monster of a beast that could cause tremendous harm entirely by merely letting go of the steering wheel for a moment or taking your eyes off the road.

In fact, in the United States alone there are about 40,000 deaths per year by auto accidents, which is more than 100 per day. Given that there are about 263 million cars in the United States, I am actually more amazed that the number of fatalities is not a lot higher.

During my morning commute, I look at all the thousands of cars on the freeway around me, and I think that if all of them decided to go zombie and drive in a crazy maniac way, there would be many people dead. Somehow, incredibly, each day, most people drive relatively safely. To me, that's a miracle right there. Getting millions and millions of people to be safe and sane when behind the wheel of a two-ton mobile object, it's a feat that we as a society should admire with pride.

So, hopefully you are in agreement that the driving task requires a great deal of cognition. You don't' need to be especially smart to drive a car, and we've done quite a bit to make car driving viable for even the average dolt. There isn't an IQ test that you need to take to drive a car. If you can read and write, and pass a test, you pretty much can legally drive a car. There are of course some that drive a car and are not legally permitted to do so, plus there are private areas such as farms where drivers are young, but for public roadways in the United States, you can be generally of average intelligence (or less) and be able to legally drive.

This though makes it seem like the cognitive effort must not be much. If the cognitive effort was truly hard, wouldn't we only have Einstein's that could drive a car? We have made sure to keep the driving task as simple as we can, by making the controls easy and relatively standardized, and by having roads that are relatively standardized, and so on. It is as though Disneyland has put their Autopia into the real-world, by us all as a society agreeing that roads will be a certain way, and we'll all abide by the various rules of driving.

A modest cognitive task by a human is still something that stymies AI. You certainly know that AI has been able to beat chess players and be good at other kinds of games. This type of narrow cognition is not what car driving is about. Car driving is much wider. It requires knowledge about the world, which a chess playing AI system does not need to know. The cognitive aspects of driving are on the one hand seemingly simple, but at the same time require layer upon layer of knowledge about cars, people, roads, rules, and a myriad of other "common sense" aspects. We don't have any AI systems today that have that same kind of breadth and depth of awareness and knowledge.

As revealed in my essays, the self-driving car of today is using trickery to do particular tasks. It is all very narrow in operation. Plus, it currently assumes that a human driver is ready to intervene. It is like a child that we have taught to stack blocks, but we are needed to be right there in case the child stacks them too high and they begin to fall over.

AI of today is brittle, it is narrow, and it does not approach the cognitive abilities of humans. This is why the true self-driving car is somewhere out in the future.

Another aspect to the driving task is that it is not solely a mind exercise. You do need to use your senses to drive. You use your eyes as vision sensors to see the road ahead. You vision capability is like a streaming video, which your brain needs to continually analyze as you drive. Where is the road? Is there a pedestrian in the way? Is there another car ahead of you? Your senses are relying a flood of info to your brain. Self-driving cars are trying to do the same, by using cameras, radar, ultrasound, and lasers. This is an attempt at mimicking how humans have senses and sensory apparatus.

Thus, the driving task is mental and physical. You use your senses, you use your arms and legs to manipulate the controls of the car, and you use your brain to assess the sensory info and direct your limbs to act upon the controls of the car. This all happens instantly. If you've ever perhaps gotten something in your eye and only had one eye available to drive with, you suddenly realize how dependent upon vision you are. If you have a broken foot with a cast, you suddenly realize how hard it is to control the brake pedal and the accelerator. If you've taken medication and your brain is maybe sluggish, you suddenly realize how much mental strain is required to drive a car.

An AI system that plays chess only needs to be focused on playing chess. The physical aspects aren't important because usually a human moves the chess pieces or the chessboard is shown on an electronic display. Using AI for a more life-and-death task such as analyzing MRI images of patients, this again does not require physical capabilities and instead is done by examining images of bits.

Driving a car is a true life-and-death task. It is a use of AI that can easily and at any moment produce death. For those colleagues of mine that are developing this AI, as am I, we need to keep in mind the somber aspects of this. We are producing software that will have in its virtual hands the lives of the occupants of the car, and the lives of those in other nearby cars, and the lives of nearby pedestrians, etc. Chess is not usually a life-or-death matter.

Driving is all around us. Cars are everywhere. Most of today's AI applications involve only a small number of people. Or, they are behind the scenes and we as humans have other recourse if the AI messes up. AI that is driving a car at 80 miles per hour on a highway had better not mess up. The consequences are grave.

Multiply this by the number of cars, if we could put magically self-driving into every car in the USA, we'd have AI running in the 263 million cars. That's a lot of AI spread around. This is AI on a massive scale that we are not doing today and that offers both promise and potential peril.

There are some that want AI for self-driving cars because they envision a world without any car accidents. They envision a world in which there is no car congestion and all cars cooperate with each other. These are wonderful utopian visions.

They are also very misleading. The adoption of self-driving cars is going to be incremental and not overnight. We cannot economically just junk all existing cars. Nor are we going to be able to affordably retrofit existing cars. It is more likely that self-driving cars will be built into new cars and that over many years of gradual replacement of existing cars that we'll see the mix of self-driving cars become substantial in the real-world.

In these essays, I have tried to offer technological insights without being overly technical in my description, and also blended the business, societal, and economic aspects too. Technologists need to consider the non-technological impacts of what they do. Non-technologists should be aware of what is being developed.

We all need to work together to collectively be prepared for the enormous disruption and transformative aspects of true self-driving cars.

## WHAT THIS BOOK PROVIDES

What does this book provide to you? It introduces many of the key elements about self-driving cars and does so with an AI based perspective. I weave together technical and non-technical aspects, readily going from being concerned about the cognitive capabilities of the driving task and how the technology is embodying this into self-driving cars, and in the next breath I discuss the societal and economic aspects.

They are all intertwined because that's the way reality is. You cannot separate out the technology per se, and instead must consider it within the milieu of what is being invented and innovated, and do so with a mindset towards the contemporary mores and culture that shape what we are doing and what we hope to do.

# WHY THIS BOOK

I wrote this book to try and bring to the public view many aspects about self-driving cars that nobody seems to be discussing.

For business leaders that are either involved in making self-driving cars or that are going to leverage self-driving cars, I hope that this book will enlighten you as to the risks involved and ways in which you should be strategizing about how to deal with those risks.

For entrepreneurs, startups and other businesses that want to enter into the self-driving car market that is emerging, I hope this book sparks your interest in doing so, and provides some sense of what might be prudent to pursue.

For researchers that study self-driving cars, I hope this book spurs your interest in the risks and safety issues of self-driving cars, and also nudges you toward conducting research on those aspects.

For students in computer science or related disciplines, I hope this book will provide you with interesting and new ideas and material, for which you might conduct research or provide some career direction insights for you.

For AI companies and high-tech companies pursuing self-driving cars, this book will hopefully broaden your view beyond just the mere coding and development needed to make self-driving cars.

For all readers, I hope that you will find the material in this book to be stimulating. Some of it will be repetitive of things you already know. But I am pretty sure that you'll also find various eureka moments whereby you'll discover a new technique or approach that you had not earlier thought of. I am also betting that there will be material that forces you to rethink some of your current practices.

I am not saying you will suddenly have an epiphany and change what you are doing. I do think though that you will reconsider or perhaps revisit what you are doing.

For anyone choosing to use this book for teaching purposes, please take a look at my suggestions for doing so, as described in the Appendix. I have found the material handy in courses that I have taught, and likewise other faculty have told me that they have found the material handy, in some cases as extended readings and in other instances as a core part of their course (depending on the nature of the class).

In my writing for this book, I have tried carefully to blend both the practitioner and the academic styles of writing.

It is not as abstract as is typical academic journal writing, but at the same time offers depth by going into the nuances and trade-offs of various practices.

The word "deep" is in vogue today, meaning getting deeply into a subject or topic, and so is the word "unpack" which means to tease out the underlying aspects of a subject or topic. I have sought to offer material that addresses an issue or topic by going relatively deeply into it and make sure that it is well unpacked.

In any book about AI, it is difficult to use our everyday words without having some of them be misinterpreted. Specifically, it is easy to anthropomorphize AI. When I say that an AI system "knows" something, I do not want you to construe that the AI system has sentience and "knows" in the same way that humans do. They aren't that way, as yet. I have tried to use quotes around such words from time-to-time to emphasize that the words I am using should not be misinterpreted to ascribe true human intelligence to the AI systems that we know of today. If I used quotes around all such words, the book would be very difficult to read, and so I am doing so judiciously. Please keep that in mind as you read the material, thanks.

Some of the material is time-based in terms of covering underway activities, and though some of it might decay, nonetheless I believe you'll find the material useful and informative.

# COMPANION BOOKS BY DR. ELIOT

1. **"Introduction to Driverless Self-Driving Cars"** by Dr. Lance Eliot
2. **"Innovation and Thought Leadership on Self-Driving Driverless Cars"**
3. **"Advances in AI and Autonomous Vehicles: Cybernetic Self-Driving Cars"**
4. **"Self-Driving Cars: The Mother of All AI Projects"** by Dr. Lance Eliot
5. **"New Advances in AI Autonomous Driverless Self-Driving Cars"**
6. **"AV Driverless Self-Driving Cars & AI"** by Dr. Lance Eliot and Michael B. Eliot
7. **"Transformative Artificial Intelligence Driverless Self-Driving Cars"**
8. **"Disruptive Artificial Intelligence and Driverless Self-Driving Cars"**
9. "State-of-the-Art AI Driverless Self-Driving Cars" by Dr. Lance Eliot
10. **"Top Trends in AI Self-Driving Cars"** by Dr. Lance Eliot
11. **"AI Innovations and Self-Driving Cars"** by Dr. Lance Eliot
12. **"Crucial Advances for AI Driverless Cars"** by Dr. Lance Eliot
13. **"Sociotechnical Insights and AI Driverless Cars"** by Dr. Lance Eliot.
14. **"Pioneering Advances for AI Driverless Cars"** by Dr. Lance Eliot
15. **"Leading Edge Trends for AI Driverless Cars"** by Dr. Lance Eliot
16. **"The Cutting Edge of AI Autonomous Cars"** by Dr. Lance Eliot
17. **"The Next Wave of AI Self-Driving Cars"** by Dr. Lance Eliot
18. **"Revolutionary Innovations of AI Driverless Cars"** by Dr. Lance Eliot
19. **"AI Self-Driving Cars Breakthroughs"** by Dr. Lance Eliot
20. **"Trailblazing Trends for AI Self-Driving Cars"** by Dr. Lance Eliot
21. **"Ingenious Strides for AI Driverless Cars"** by Dr. Lance Eliot
22. **"AI Self-Driving Cars Inventiveness"** by Dr. Lance Eliot
23. **"Visionary Secrets of AI Driverless Cars"** by Dr. Lance Eliot
24. **"Spearheading AI Self-Driving Cars"** by Dr. Lance Eliot
25. **"Spurring AI Self-Driving Cars"** by Dr. Lance Eliot
26. **"Avant-Garde AI Driverless Cars"** by Dr. Lance Eliot
27. **"AI Self-Driving Cars Evolvement"** by Dr. Lance Eliot
28. **"AI Driverless Cars Chrysalis"** by Dr. Lance Eliot
29. **"Boosting AI Autonomous Cars"** by Dr. Lance Eliot
30. **"AI Self-Driving Cars Trendsetting"** by Dr. Lance Eliot
31. **"AI Autonomous Cars Forefront"** by Dr. Lance Eliot
32. **"AI Autonomous Cars Emergence"** by Dr. Lance Eliot
33. **"AI Autonomous Cars Progress"** by Dr. Lance Eliot
34. **"AI Self-Driving Cars Prognosis"** by Dr. Lance Eliot
35. **"AI Self-Driving Cars Momentum"** by Dr. Lance Eliot
36. **"AI Self-Driving Cars Headway"** by Dr. Lance Eliot
37. **"AI Self-Driving Cars Vicissitude"** by Dr. Lance Eliot
38. **"AI Self-Driving Cars Autonomy"** by Dr. Lance Eliot
39. **"AI Driverless Cars Transmutation"** by Dr. Lance Eliot
40. **"AI Driverless Cars Potentiality"** by Dr. Lance Eliot
41. **"AI Driverless Cars Realities"** by Dr. Lance Eliot
42. **"AI Self-Driving Cars Materiality"** by Dr. Lance Eliot
43. **"AI Self-Driving Cars Accordance"** by Dr. Lance Eliot
44. **"AI Self-Driving Cars Equanimity"** by Dr. Lance Eliot
45. **"AI Self-Driving Cars Divulgement"** by Dr. Lance Eliot
46. **"AI Self-Driving Cars Consonance"** by Dr. Lance Eliot
47. **"Revelatory AI Self-Driving Cars"** by Dr. Lance Eliot
48. **"Edifying AI Self-Driving Cars"** by Dr. Lance Eliot
49. **"Apprising AI Driverless Cars"** by Dr. Lance Eliot
50. **"Improving AI Self-Driving Cars"** by Dr. Lance Eliot

These books are available on Amazon and at other major global booksellers.

# CHAPTER 1

# ELIOT FRAMEWORK FOR AI SELF-DRIVING CARS

This chapter is a core foundational aspect for understanding AI self-driving cars and I have used this same chapter in several of my other books to introduce the reader to essential elements of this field. Once you've read this chapter, you'll be prepared to read the rest of the material since the foundational essence of the components of autonomous AI driverless self-driving cars will have been established for you.

---

When I give presentations about self-driving cars and teach classes on the topic, I have found it helpful to provide a framework around which the various key elements of self-driving cars can be understood and organized (see diagram at the end of this chapter). The framework needs to be simple enough to convey the overarching elements, but at the same time not so simple that it belies the true complexity of self-driving cars. As such, I am going to describe the framework here and try to offer in a thousand words (or more!) what the framework diagram itself intends to portray.

The core elements on the diagram are numbered for ease of reference. The numbering does not suggest any kind of prioritization of the elements. Each element is crucial. Each element has a purpose, and otherwise would not be included in the framework. For some self-driving cars, a particular element might be more important or somehow distinguished in comparison to other self-driving cars.

You could even use the framework to rate a particular self-driving car, doing so by gauging how well it performs in each of the elements of the framework. I will describe each of the elements, one at a time. After doing so, I'll discuss aspects that illustrate how the elements interact and perform during the overall effort of a self-driving car.

At the AI Self-Driving Car Institute, we use the framework to keep track of what we are working on, and how we are developing software that fills in what is needed to achieve Level 5 self-driving cars.

**D-01: Sensor Capture**

Let's start with the one element that often gets the most attention in the press about self-driving cars, namely, the sensory devices for a self-driving car.

On the framework, the box labeled as D-01 indicates "Sensor Capture" and refers to the processes of the self-driving car that involve collecting data from the myriad of sensors that are used for a self-driving car. The types of devices typically involved are listed, such as the use of mono cameras, stereo cameras, LIDAR devices, radar systems, ultrasonic devices, GPS, IMU, and so on.

These devices are tasked with obtaining data about the status of the self-driving car and the world around it. Some of the devices are continually providing updates, while others of the devices await an indication by the self-driving car that the device is supposed to collect data. The data might be first transformed in some fashion by the device itself, or it might instead be fed directly into the sensor capture as raw data. At that point, it might be up to the sensor capture processes to do transformations on the data. This all varies depending upon the nature of the devices being used and how the devices were designed and developed.

**D-02: Sensor Fusion**

Imagine that your eyeballs receive visual images, your nose receives odors, your ears receive sounds, and in essence each of your distinct sensory devices is getting some form of input. The input befits the nature of the device. Likewise, for a self-driving car, the cameras provide visual images, the radar returns radar reflections, and so on. Each device provides the data as befits what the device does.

At some point, using the analogy to humans, you need to merge together what your eyes see, what your nose smells, what your ears hear, and piece it all together into a larger sense of what the world is all about and what is happening around you. Sensor fusion is the action of taking the singular aspects from each of the devices and putting them together into a larger puzzle.

Sensor fusion is a tough task. There are some devices that might not be working at the time of the sensor capture. Or, there might some devices that are unable to report well what they have detected. Again, using a human analogy, suppose you are in a dark room and so your eyes cannot see much. At that point, you might need to rely more so on your ears and what you hear. The same is true for a self-driving car. If the cameras are obscured due to snow and sleet, it might be that the radar can provide a greater indication of what the external conditions consist of.

In the case of a self-driving car, there can be a plethora of such sensory devices. Each is reporting what it can. Each might have its difficulties. Each might have its limitations, such as how far ahead it can detect an object. All of these limitations need to be considered during the sensor fusion task.

**D-03: Virtual World Model**

For humans, we presumably keep in our minds a model of the world around us when we are driving a car. In your mind, you know that the car is going at say 60 miles per hour and that you are on a freeway.

You have a model in your mind that your car is surrounded by other cars, and that there are lanes to the freeway. Your model is not only based on what you can see, hear, etc., but also what you know about the nature of the world. You know that at any moment that car ahead of you can smash on its brakes, or the car behind you can ram into your car, or that the truck in the next lane might swerve into your lane.

The AI of the self-driving car needs to have a virtual world model, which it then keeps updated with whatever it is receiving from the sensor fusion, which received its input from the sensor capture.

## D-04: System Action Plan

By having a virtual world model, the AI of the self-driving car is able to keep track of where the car is and what is happening around the car. In addition, the AI needs to determine what to do next. Should the self-driving car hit its brakes? Should the self-driving car stay in its lane or swerve into the lane to the left? Should the self-driving car accelerate or slow down?

A system action plan needs to be prepared by the AI of the self-driving car. The action plan specifies what actions should be taken. The actions need to pertain to the status of the virtual world model. Plus, the actions need to be realizable.

This realizability means that the AI cannot just assert that the self-driving car should suddenly sprout wings and fly. Instead, the AI must be bound by whatever the self-driving car can actually do, such as coming to a halt in a distance of X feet at a speed of Y miles per hour, rather than perhaps asserting that the self-driving car come to a halt in 0 feet as though it could instantaneously come to a stop while it is in motion.

## D-05: Controls Activation

The system action plan is implemented by activating the controls of the car to act according to what the plan stipulates.

This might mean that the accelerator control is commanded to increase the speed of the car. Or, the steering control is commanded to turn the steering wheel 30 degrees to the left or right.

One question arises as to whether or not the controls respond as they are commanded to do. In other words, suppose the AI has commanded the accelerator to increase, but for some reason it does not do so. Or, maybe it tries to do so, but the speed of the car does not increase.

The controls activation feeds back into the virtual world model, and simultaneously the virtual world model is getting updated from the sensors, the sensor capture, and the sensor fusion. This allows the AI to ascertain what has taken place as a result of the controls being commanded to take some kind of action.

By the way, please keep in mind that though the diagram seems to have a linear progression to it, the reality is that these are all aspects of the self-driving car that are happening in parallel and simultaneously. The sensors are capturing data, meanwhile the sensor fusion is taking place, meanwhile the virtual model is being updated, meanwhile the system action plan is being formulated and reformulated, meanwhile the controls are being activated.

This is the same as a human being that is driving a car. They are eyeballing the road, meanwhile they are fusing in their mind the sights, sounds, etc., meanwhile their mind is updating their model of the world around them, meanwhile they are formulating an action plan of what to do, and meanwhile they are pushing their foot onto the pedals and steering the car. In the normal course of driving a car, you are doing all of these at once. I mention this so that when you look at the diagram, you will think of the boxes as processes that are all happening at the same time, and not as though only one happens and then the next.

They are shown diagrammatically in a simplistic manner to help comprehend what is taking place. You though should also realize that they are working in parallel and simultaneous with each other. This is a tough aspect in that the inter-element communications involve latency and other aspects that must be taken into account. There can be delays in one element updating and then sharing its latest status with other elements.

**D-06: Automobile & CAN**

Contemporary cars use various automotive electronics and a Controller Area Network (CAN) to serve as the components that underlie the driving aspects of a car.

There are Electronic Control Units (ECU's) which control subsystems of the car, such as the engine, the brakes, the doors, the windows, and so on.

The elements D-01, D-02, D-03, D-04, D-05 are layered on top of the D-06, and must be aware of the nature of what the D-06 is able to do and not do.

**D-07: In-Car Commands**

Humans are going to be occupants in self-driving cars. In a Level 5 self-driving car, there must be some form of communication that takes place between the humans and the self-driving car. For example, I go into a self-driving car and tell it that I want to be driven over to Disneyland, and along the way I want to stop at In-and-Out Burger. The self-driving car now parses what I've said and tries to then establish a means to carry out my wishes.

In-car commands can happen at any time during a driving journey. Though my example was about an in-car command when I first got into my self-driving car, it could be that while the self-driving car is carrying out the journey that I change my mind. Perhaps after getting stuck in traffic, I tell the self-driving car to forget about getting the burgers and just head straight over to the theme park. The self-driving car needs to be alert to in-car commands throughout the journey.

**D-08: V2X Communications**

We will ultimately have self-driving cars communicating with each other, doing so via V2V (Vehicle-to-Vehicle) communications. We will also have self-driving cars that communicate with the roadways and other aspects of the transportation infrastructure, doing so via V2I (Vehicle-to-Infrastructure).

The variety of ways in which a self-driving car will be communicating with other cars and infrastructure is being called V2X, whereby the letter X means whatever else we identify as something that a car should or would want to communicate with.

The V2X communications will be taking place simultaneous with everything else on the diagram, and those other elements will need to incorporate whatever it gleans from those V2X communications.

**D-09: Deep Learning**

The use of Deep Learning permeates all other aspects of the self-driving car. The AI of the self-driving car will be using deep learning to do a better job at the systems action plan, and at the control's activation, and at the sensor fusion, and so on.

Currently, the use of artificial neural networks is the most prevalent form of deep learning. Based on large swaths of data, the neural networks attempt to "learn" from the data and therefore direct the efforts of the self-driving car accordingly.

**D-10: Tactical AI**

Tactical AI is the element of dealing with the moment-to-moment driving of the self-driving car. Is the self-driving car staying in its lane of the freeway? Is the car responding appropriately to the controls commands? Are the sensory devices working?

For human drivers, the tactical equivalent can be seen when you watch a novice driver such as a teenager that is first driving. They are focused on the mechanics of the driving task, keeping their eye on the road while also trying to properly control the car.

**D-11: Strategic AI**

The Strategic AI aspects of a self-driving car are dealing with the larger picture of what the self-driving car is trying to do. If I had asked that the self-driving car take me to Disneyland, there is an overall journey map that needs to be kept and maintained.

There is an interaction between the Strategic AI and the Tactical AI. The Strategic AI is wanting to keep on the mission of the driving, while the Tactical AI is focused on the particulars underway in the driving effort.

If the Tactical AI seems to wander away from the overarching mission, the Strategic AI wants to see why and get things back on track. If the Tactical AI realizes that there is something amiss on the self-driving car, it needs to alert the Strategic AI accordingly and have an adjustment to the overarching mission that is underway.

**D-12: Self-Aware AI**

Very few of the self-driving cars being developed are including a Self-Aware AI element, which we at the Cybernetic Self-Driving Car Institute believe is crucial to Level 5 self-driving cars.

The Self-Aware AI element is intended to watch over itself, in the sense that the AI is making sure that the AI is working as intended. Suppose you had a human driving a car, and they were starting to drive erratically. Hopefully, their own self-awareness would make them realize they themselves are driving poorly, such as perhaps starting to fall asleep after having been driving for hours on end. If you had a passenger in the car, they might be able to alert the driver if the driver is starting to do something amiss.

This is exactly what the Self-Aware AI element tries to do, it becomes the overseer of the AI, and tries to detect when the AI has become faulty or confused, and then find ways to overcome the issue.

**D-13: Economic**

The economic aspects of a self-driving car are not per se a technology aspect of a self-driving car, but the economics do indeed impact the nature of a self-driving car. For example, the cost of outfitting a self-driving car with every kind of possible sensory device is prohibitive, and so choices need to be made about which devices are used. And, for those sensory devices chosen, whether they would have a full set of features or a more limited set of features.

We are going to have self-driving cars that are at the low-end of a consumer cost point, and others at the high-end of a consumer cost point. You cannot expect that the self-driving car at the low-end is going to be as robust as the one at the high-end.

I realize that many of the self-driving car pundits are acting as though all self-driving cars will be the same, but they won't be. Just like anything else, we are going to have self-driving cars that have a range of capabilities. Some will be better than others. Some will be safer than others. This is the way of the real-world, and so we need to be thinking about the economics aspects when considering the nature of self-driving cars.

**D-14: Societal**

This component encompasses the societal aspects of AI which also impacts the technology of self-driving cars. For example, the famous Trolley Problem involves what choices should a self-driving car make when faced with life-and-death matters. If the self-driving car is about to either hit a child standing in the roadway, or instead ram into a tree at the side of the road and possibly kill the humans in the self-driving car, which choice should be made?

We need to keep in mind the societal aspects will underlie the AI of the self-driving car. Whether we are aware of it explicitly or not, the AI will have embedded into it various societal assumptions.

**D-15: Innovation**

I included the notion of innovation into the framework because we can anticipate that whatever a self-driving car consists of, it will continue to be innovated over time. The self-driving cars coming out in the next several years will undoubtedly be different and less innovative than the versions that come out in ten years hence, etc.

**Framework Overall**

For those of you that want to learn about self-driving cars, you can potentially pick a particular element and become specialized in that aspect. Some engineers are focusing on the sensory devices. Some engineers focus on the controls activation.  And so on. There are specialties in each of the elements.

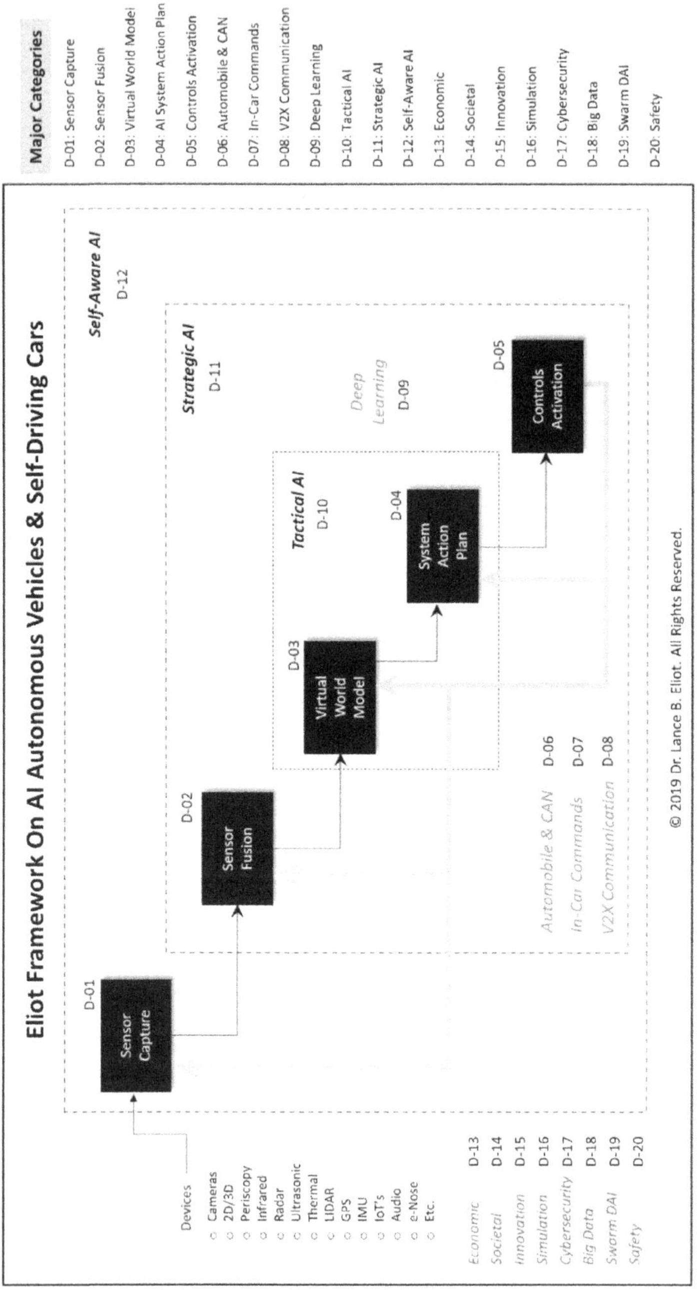
Eliot Framework On AI Autonomous Vehicles & Self-Driving Cars
Self-Aware AI
D-12
Strategic AI
D-11
Tactical AI
D-10
Deep Learning
D-09
D-01
Sensor Capture
D-02
Sensor Fusion
D-03
Virtual World Model
D-04
System Action Plan
D-05
Controls Activation
Automobile & CAN D-06
In-Car Commands D-07
V2X Communication D-08
Devices
Cameras
2D/3D
Periscopy
Infrared
Radar
Ultrasonic
Thermal
LIDAR
GPS
IMU
IoT's
Audio
e-Nose
Etc.
Economic D-13
Societal D-14
Innovation D-15
Simulation D-16
Cybersecurity D-17
Big Data D-18
Swarm DAI D-19
Safety D-20
© 2019 Dr. Lance B. Eliot. All Rights Reserved.
Major Categories
D-01: Sensor Capture
D-02: Sensor Fusion
D-03: Virtual World Model
D-04: AI System Action Plan
D-05: Controls Activation
D-06: Automobile & CAN
D-07: In-Car Commands
D-08: V2X Communication
D-09: Deep Learning
D-10: Tactical AI
D-11: Strategic AI
D-12: Self-Aware AI
D-13: Economic
D-14: Societal
D-15: Innovation
D-16: Simulation
D-17: Cybersecurity
D-18: Big Data
D-19: Swarm DAI
D-20: Safety

# CHAPTER 2

# WEARABLE SAFETY GEAR AND SELF-DRIVING CARS

Pedestrians have a tough life.

When trying to cross the street, you ostensibly are taking your own life into your hands as you dare to go in front of menacing car traffic. Even if a slew of cars is standing still at a red light while you lawfully use the crosswalk, there is still a chance that a driver might mistakenly use their gas pedal and suddenly accelerate forward into you.

Always keep your eyes on those momentarily stationary cars and their drivers, just in case you can miraculously discern that a sudden movement is on the verge of occurring and potentially leap out of the way.

The scariest situations entail a crosswalk that has no traffic signals at all. These uncontrolled wildcard circumstances are a disaster lying in wait.

Will the upcoming cars come to a halt?

Do they see me?

Once they come to a halt, will they remain still until I've completed getting across the street?

We teach children to look both ways. This includes the sage advice to only cross where it is safe to do so. Some youngsters seem to think that if there is a crosswalk in existence, it must axiomatically be a safe place to cross the street. Perhaps these kids assume that those faded painted lines on the street can form a veritable protective barrier that is impervious to being breached by moving cars.

Of course, not all pedestrians necessarily cross the street in a legal and nor prudent manner.

Jaywalkers make a quite dicey decision by crossing at any juncture of a street, doing so at their own peril and upon the belief that they know best about where to properly cross. Sometimes a jaywalker fails to notice oncoming traffic and gets themselves into a dire posture. In other cases, the jaywalker abundantly observes the traffic and yet relies upon their adroit dancing and twisting skills to try and do a Frogger-like escape. Sadly, whichever method a jaywalker opts to use, there is a hefty chance that they will lose this game.

And losing the game of being a pedestrian is very costly.

It seems strange that there are pedestrians that seem to think they will win in a contest with a car and its car driver. The car driver has the multi-ton vehicle at their disposal and can unquestionably be the winner if you are comparing a flimsy human body to the impact destructive forces of a car in motion.

There is no debate that the human will lose, and the car will win.

I'm not suggesting that the car is in the right. The point simply is that if you weigh the physics and forces involved, and merely consider what will happen when a human is struck by a car, the car is going to apply tremendously adverse forces to the pedestrian. Unless you believe in the comic books and superpowers, the odds of a human holding out their hand and bringing the car to a shattering stop, while the human remains standing and happy, well, keep dreaming.

Yet there are daily and plenty of pedestrians that dare cars to come and get them. A pedestrian steps into the street and eyeballs a car driver. The car driver has to decide whether to slow down and possibly stop to let the pedestrian cross. Similar to two gunslingers, they get into a staring contest.

They are unequal gunslingers in terms of how they are armed.

The pedestrian figures that they are nimble and can presumably escape death by pirouetting if the situation so dictates. Perhaps the greater tool that the pedestrian has at their fingertips is the notion that the car driver will be in a lot of trouble, assuming that the car proceeds ahead and rams into the pedestrian.

This is bad news for the driver. The driver will have to deal with repairing the damages done to their car. The driver will undoubtedly have their car insurance rates rise. The driver will possibly have their driver's license suspended or revoked. And the driver could face criminal charges.

The thing is all those special factors that arm the pedestrian seem conceptual and not especially tangible at the time of this life-or-death stare down. The reality there on the ground, in the middle of the street, says that when a human and a car collide, the human is going to be the one suffering the most hurt. Sure, you can argue that the car driver is going to possibly get into deep trouble, but that's long after the split-second instance when the pedestrian loses by getting injured or destroyed.

The outcomes for the pedestrian are to either by the skin-of-their-teeth make it across the street untouched, or possibly get rammed and severely damaged or killed.

The preferred approach to these eye-to-eye contests can differ by locale. Some contend that in New York City, a pedestrian must try to make eye contact with the driver since otherwise, the pedestrian is basically signaling that the driver has the right-of-way and the pedestrian is a goner. Meanwhile, some advise that in Boston the best bet is to purposely not make eye contact with the driver. If a pedestrian does make eye contact, this implies the pedestrian has now lost the street-crossing gambit and the driver is cleared to proceed unabated.

Or maybe it is the other way round.

These norms about being a pedestrian are not very comforting. Suppose the driver is from out-of-town and does not know the expected convention? Another possibility is that a local and well-seasoned driver has decided to buck convention, on that particular day and time, thus they are decidedly not going to play "by the customary rules" known as sacrosanct by pedestrians in that area.

Many towns and cities have been taking proactive measures to try and stem the seemingly rising tide of collisions involving cars and pedestrians. These municipal campaigns are often referred to as Vision Zero or a similar catchy naming. The idea is that by alerting everyone to the pedestrian considerations, hopefully, the number of car collision fatalities involving pedestrians will fall to zero.

It is easy to see that there are two components to the problem.

There are the pedestrians and their desire to cross the street, and there are the cars that are using the street to proceed and wish to do so without disruption or delay. When the two meet there is a high potential for fireworks.

You can try to get pedestrians to be more observant and tread carefully when crossing the street. This is handy but it is not foolproof. People might not retain the thoughtfully urged warnings that have been plastered on billboards and social media. Posting signs at streets is certainly useful, though once again the problem entails having the pedestrian realize the sign is there, having them read the sign, and then in the throes of wanting to cross the street they need to heed the sign.

Don't bet all your chips on that happening.

For car drivers, they are maybe going to see the myriad of signs and billboards about pedestrians and take those warnings to heart. On the other hand, when it comes down to rushing on your way to work or trying to get home to see your children, the reality is that many drivers are not especially tuned to the needs of pedestrians. We already all know that car traffic itself is a dog-eat-dog world, and the feeling extends to the ongoing warfare between cars and pedestrians.

We seem to have landed at a loggerhead of not finding a solution to this problem. Despite extensive attempts to inform and spur pedestrians to be safer, and despite the same being done with car drivers, the sad truth is that the problem fundamentally remains as is. To clarify, we still need to try and do that kind of outreach and it does make a difference, clearly so, but the point here is that the chances of reaching the vaunted zero are a longshot, at best.

What other solutions might be possible, you are likely wondering.

One part of the problem involves making sure that the car driver realizes there is a pedestrian present at the moment in time when the pedestrian and the car are about to intersect in the so-called time-space continuum, as it were.

Pedestrians can be hard to see.

They might be wearing clothes that tend to blend in with the prevailing driving scene. In terms of children, they are smaller in stature and less likely to be readily seen. At nighttime, a pedestrian can be cloaked by darkness. There are a zillion ways that a car driver can fail to spot a pedestrian.

In theory, if a car driver knows in-advance that a pedestrian is there, this would at least reduce the incidents that involve a setting whereby the driver was caught unawares and therefore did not react in time to avoid striking the pedestrian. This is not a cure-all since a driver can opt to not avoid a pedestrian, intentionally striking the pedestrian and knowing full well they are about to do so. That's another slice of the problem and a variant that I'll be covering in a later column.

In any case, there are already various methods used to try and make pedestrians standout such that car drivers will take notice.

Crossing guards wear brightly colored jackets. Some parents use the same kind of garb on their young children when sending them off to school. Another possibility is holding and waving a flag. You've probably seen those triangular-shaped flags that are fluorescent orange and mounted on a lengthy pole. A pedestrian holding the pole in an upright position will aid in being spotted from a greater distance.

Some pedestrians eschew those rather blatant options, especially since those seem to be uncool or otherwise draw the ire of cynics. A more measured approach involves having reflectors on your clothing or perhaps displayed on a hat or cap that you are wearing. These seem to be more acceptable as a form of grabbing the attention of car drivers.

Those are all helpful and certainly are encouraged as a means of startling car drivers out of their zombie-like trances and becoming conscious of pedestrians up ahead of their car. That being said, we can all likely agree that this still, unfortunately, does not guarantee that a pedestrian will be seen (it improves the odds but doesn't push the probability to a complete one hundred percent).

Shifting gears, consider that the future of cars entails the advent of self-driving cars. For AI-based true self-driving cars, there will not be a human at the wheel. An AI-based driving system will be doing the driving.

This brings up the matter of whether self-driving cars will be better at detecting pedestrians than do human drivers. Some worry that self-driving cars might be worse at pedestrian detection. That would be disconcerting, for sure. We would seemingly hope and assume that self-driving cars would be at least as good as humans, and indeed be relishing the possibility that self-driving cars would do even better at the pedestrian detection task.

Human drivers are apt to be distracted while driving. The emergence of now-ubiquitous smartphones has become a key distractor while driving. Some believe that watching cat videos or trying to text while driving is sizable reasons for the increase in pedestrian car-related fatalities. Humans also drink and drive.

AI-based driving systems aren't going to be drinking and driving. Nor will the AI driving systems be driving in a distracted mode akin to how humans lose their focus or opt to look away while at the wheel. In that sense of things, it seems obvious and natural to anticipate that self-driving cars will do a better job at detecting pedestrians.

If self-driving cars can do a better job at detecting pedestrians, this suggests that there will be a lesser number of pedestrian car-related fatalities and striking incidents.

Some wonder whether the wearing of brightly colored jackets and reflectors will still be needed in an era of self-driving cars.

Can we put away those contrivances and just assume that the AI driving systems will be able to properly detect us?

The short answer is no, you cannot ditch those helpful precautions. They will still be useful and recommended for safety purposes.

Some go even further, asserting that you might want to add some new and additional means to be readily spotted by self-driving cars. In other words, there are means of being spotted by human drivers, which can also apply to being spotted by self-driving cars. Also, there are ways to be spotted by self-driving cars that are specific to the nature of self-driving cars (and might or might not apply to human drivers per se).

This is today's intriguing question: *Will the market of pedestrian garb and contraptions for warning human car drivers be spurred toward new products to cope with the inclusion of true self-driving cars on our roadways?*

Before we unpack the matter, let's first clarify what I mean by referring to true self-driving cars.

**Self-Driving Cars And Pedestrians**

For Level 4 and Level 5 true self-driving vehicles, there won't be a human driver involved in the driving task.

All occupants will be passengers.

The AI is doing the driving.

Detecting other cars that are nearby to a self-driving car is somewhat straightforward for the AI driving system. Usually, other cars are relatively sizable, and a self-driving car can make use of its on-board video cameras, radar, LIDAR, ultrasonic units, and other sensory devices to pretty much figure out that a car is in the driving scene of interest.

Pedestrians are another beast altogether.

Trying to detect a pedestrian can be quite tricky.

As I've previously discussed, some AI driving systems are for example at times categorizing a snowman as being a human pedestrian. The point being that pedestrians are not customarily as easy to detect as a car, and yet we are certainly going to be expecting that AI driving systems will treat pedestrians with as much care, respect, and rapt attention as they would nearby cars (maybe that is a somewhat argumentative claim, but you get the gist).

The primary means of detecting pedestrians involves the video cameras of the self-driving car.

Streaming video is being collected while the vehicle is underway. Algorithms inspect the video images and are attempting to discern whether there are any blobs in the imagery that appear to be pedestrians. A pedestrian might be standing behind a light pole or some other obstruction, thus the image might have just a partial indication that a pedestrian is present. It can be arduous for computer-based image processing to do a *Where's Waldo* inspection of video to identify where a pedestrian might be in the cacophony of objects in a busy street scene.

A child might be standing behind an adult, perhaps not seen at all from the vantage point of an oncoming self-driving car and its video cameras.

Imagine that the child opts to suddenly and unexpectedly dart from behind the adult and straight out into the middle of the street. Since the AI driving system did not detect earlier that the child was present (being hidden behind the adult), this means that the appearance of the child will be detected later in the game, so to speak. This in turn might reduce the viable options of trying to come to a halt versus having to veer away from the child that is now within striking distance.

Would wearing a traditional fluorescent vest or jacket help (the kind used to alert human drivers)?

And what about carrying a bright orange flag that was mounted on a tall pole?

Yes, those are still good to go.

Assuming of course that the image processing algorithm being used takes this into account.

Anything that would visually catch the eye of a human driver is likely to be advantageous for being exploited too by self-driving cars. The key is that the automaker and self-driving car developers need to ensure that they are incorporating those telltale clues into the image analysis and pedestrian detection programs that they are using.

This includes the use of Machine Learning (ML) and Deep Learning (DL). To utilize today's ML/DL, you need to train the computational pattern matching algorithms via lots of data. Thus, it would be important to include images of pedestrians wearing the type of "see me" garb that is being used to attract the eye of human drivers. The pattern matching by the ML/DL would hopefully usefully ascertain that those are handy cues signifying a pedestrian is present.

One difficulty with those pattern matching approaches is that they can be either purposefully fooled or inadvertently fooled.

Suppose that a fluorescent jacket is placed on a mannequin. The mannequin is placed on the sidewalk, perhaps outside a store that is selling clothing. It is conceivable that a self-driving car that is passing along that street might misinterpret the mannequin as being a human pedestrian. Why? One possibility is that the pattern matching "learned" that whenever there is a fluorescent jacket on a figure that has the overall shape of a chest and arms, this implies that there is a person there and thus categorized as a pedestrian.

Humans would be less likely to make such a categorization error.

Of course, as previously mentioned, humans make a lot of other kinds of driving errors, thus they do not get a free pass simply because they can usually tell the difference between a mannequin and a real human.

Some have suggested that maybe we ought to come up with a new symbol that can be standardized as a universal "I'm a pedestrian" symbol and then make sure that all self-driving cars would be programmed to look for that symbol. People would then buy clothing with the symbol stitched on it or carry a flag that would display that symbol. This seems on the surface as a nifty idea, but it has numerous drawbacks and likely won't get much traction (see my columns for discussions on that matter).

Another big topic of controversy involves what should happen when the AI driving system does detect a pedestrian. As earlier pointed out, humans will do battle over whether the car proceeds or the pedestrian proceeds. Right now, the default by most of the AI driving systems is that the pedestrian proceeds. Unfortunately, this has already led to some people deciding to leverage this default and thusly jaywalk at will (again, see my coverage).

In any case, keep in mind that the AI driving systems typically use more than just video alone to sense the driving scene. By-and-large, everyone also uses radar, and nearly all are using LIDAR too..

Various research labs and entrepreneurs have been experimenting with using specially adapted clothing and electronics to aid the radar detection of pedestrians. Pedestrians would wear the clothing, such as an adapted jacket or coat, which is lined with materials and electronics to boost the radar detection that is underway by any nearby self-driving car.

In brief, the radar sensors on the self-driving car are transmitting radar signals. Those radar signals reach the objects in the driving scene and bounce back to the radar unit. Based on the time of flight and other factors, the radar is attempting to figure out where objects are, their distance from the self-driving car, and the shape of the object (along with the movement or speed of the object).

Radar is not always going to get a good reading. There are lots of reasons that a radar signal might get stymied or distorted. In that case, if a pedestrian was wearing or holding something that could boost or aid the radar signals, it could enhance the chances of the radar detecting that the pedestrian was present.

At times, during a driving journey, the AI driving system will tend to rely more so or less so on the video camera and more so or less so on the radar. All told, the AI driving system usually has a Multi-Sensor Data Fusion (MSDF) capability that involves trying to combine and reconcile the detections coming from each of the sensors on-board the vehicle.

Another approach entails using a beaconing device that emits a signal to indicate that a pedestrian is present. The beacon could be worn by a pedestrian or possibly handheld. Clothing makers might opt to sew such a beacon into the lining of jackets or perhaps attach the beacon to a hat or cap. Self-driving cars would presumably attempt to detect the beacon signal and then accordingly take into account that a pedestrian might be nearby.

Various questions remain unresolved about the use of pedestrian beacons. For example, would the beacon merely alert that a pedestrian is within some range, or would it provide specifics such as where the person is and other parameters about the pedestrian? Would pedestrians inadvertently become emboldened about crossing the street simply due to possessing a beacon? Would a self-driving car be expected to provide a confirmation response to the wearer of the beacon? Suppose someone placed a beacon on a fire hydrant or light pole, would this confuse the self-driving cars and undermine the value of having beacons? Etc.

Furthermore, a related issue would be whether the sensor suites of self-driving cars would already have the needed facility to detect the beacons. If not, this then raises the issue of having to include additional sensory equipment into self-driving cars, likely raising the costs associated with self-driving cars and creating other concomitant difficulties.

## Conclusion

Some howl at the idea that they might need to purchase and wear some specialized clothing or have a specialized device to forewarn self-driving cars about a pedestrian being nearby.

Outrageous, these clickbait headlines are blaring.

It is a typical reaction when not looking closely at what is actually being proposed. Researchers and entrepreneurs of a responsible nature are not suggesting that you must use these products, just as the same argument can be made about wearing fluorescent jackets or having a bright orange flag. These are simply helpful means of increasing the chances of being detected.

Doomsayers are wanting to immediately decry that this suggests that self-driving cars are inherently flawed and should not be on the roadways until they can *perfectly* detect pedestrians at all times, in all weather conditions, in all manner of driving scenes, etc. That's an expectation that is unrealistic and myopic.

Some are also holding out for the use of V2P (vehicle-to-pedestrian) electronic communication (this is somewhat akin to the earlier discussion related to beacons). The notion is that a pedestrian holding their smartphone can communicate electronically with nearby self-driving cars, and so too the self-driving cars can convey messages to the pedestrian.

In this manner, an approaching self-driving car might send a message to the pedestrian at the street corner and ask them to remain still and not yet enter into the street. This might help, but it certainly won't be the panacea that some are betting on (as I've covered in my columns).

The reality is that pedestrians and cars are still going to be mixing together on our streets. Human-driven cars have the foibles of human drivers. Self-driving cars will be limited by the nature of the sensors being used, the AI capabilities programmed, and the driving scene conditions, along with the nature of the pedestrian in terms of where they are, what they are doing, and what they intend to do.

My prediction is that these pedestrian augmented products spurred into existence to aid in being further detected by self-driving cars will gradually and inexorably be realized as providing value.

This is still a quite nascent market.

There aren't many self-driving cars involved in today's tryouts. There is not much utility in selling and nor someone buying such devices until there is a sufficient volume of self-driving cars on the roadways. That being the case, we can also turn our attention to the Level 2 and Level 3 cars.

They will be likely adorned with the same kinds of sensor suites as used on self-driving cars. As such, the market for these pedestrian-oriented products could arise sooner than the long-awaited emergence of true self-driving cars.

Would a doting parent consider buying a fluorescent jacket that also has a specialized radar reflective array sewn into it, doing so to aid in protecting their child from the vagaries of human drivers and the advent of self-driving cars?

One supposes if those parents are the same ones that buy smart socks for their babies (which monitor heart rate and oxygen levels, plus come with Bluetooth connectivity) and smart diapers (I won't say what those do, you can probably guess), they are bound to want anything that can give their treasured toddler or youngster a decided advantage when crossing the street.

Mark my words, you'll ultimately see these kinds of pedestrian wearables at your big-box retailers and even those neighborhood mom-and-pop stores.

.

# CHAPTER 3

# ZOOM TOWNS AND SELF-DRIVING CARS

By movement, I mean relocating to.

The Zoom Town reference is the catchy new phrase that cleverly brings together the notion of "Zoom" as in being able to work remotely (promulgated by the now-ubiquitous Zoom-like online capabilities), and combined with the homespun "Town" indication. The "Town" part suggests that as a remote worker, you can opt to live wherever you might wish to do so and not have to be residing in a major city for purposes of performing your job.

Many workers have assumed that they were doomed to always work in a big city environment for the entirety of their career. This assumption makes sense because that's where the jobs are. In a sense, this is reminiscent of the old joke about why bank robbers rob banks, and the quippy reply is that they do so because that's where the money is.

For purposes of starting and keeping a career underway, you pretty much had to always be willing to make the trek into a large city.

Consider this typical scenario. Like many such workers, you perhaps daily make that traffic-laden painstaking road-rage spurring drive into the downtown area. You park your vehicle and get charged exorbitant parking rates, which your employer won't cover or does so as pennies on the dollar. Your car is also susceptible to getting stolen or damaged while you are doing your ten-hour grueling job and sitting stoically in your office.

The odds are that you would work in a tall skyscraper. Up the elevator each morning, and then down you come at the end of the workday. Day after day.

As they say, wash, rinse, and repeat.

Due to the commute, you consume a couple of hours a day in the tiresome act of driving a car. Thus, you sadly miss out on all sorts of fun activities and various special moments in life that might have otherwise leveraged your interests and attention. This is the cost you need to bear. Your need to commute is a necessity since it ties directly to your earning a living. And you need to earn a living to put food on the table and pay your rent or cover a hefty mortgage.

It all adds up.

Meanwhile, maybe you have repeatedly and persistently had quiet dreams of chucking the daily grind of being in an office.

Leaning a bit back in your dull and overworn office chair, you thoughtfully reasoned that there was no valid basis for requiring you to come to the office. Couldn't you work from home? This seemed entirely plausible. Today's telecommuting technology is plentiful, inexpensive, and easily utilized, which is a sea change from the way that things used to be (in the past, it was expensive, worked poorly, and unfortunately became a tough barrier to overcome).

Perhaps one of the biggest impediments was the overall perception of remote work and also the downcast view of those that sought to work remotely.

The opportunity to work remotely has nearly always been a slim chance possibility, at least up until the advent of the pandemic. Before the pandemic, very few workers were allowed to do their jobs remotely. Even asking to do so was oftentimes a verboten act and could stall your career. The expectation was that to do your job and also advance your career pursuits, you had to come to the office, and you had to physically interact in-person. That has been the prevailing wisdom.

Of course, times have changed.

Across the board nowadays, there is a realization that working remotely can indeed be productive.

Those that earlier contended that remote workers would be slackers have learned that the opposite oftentimes occurs. Businesses have discovered that remote workers will at times work more than they might have done so while in a normal office environment. They become nonstop workers. No more of those lingering coffee breaks or time spent idly standing around the office cooler. Instead, remote workers do their work, and do their work, and do their work, ad infinitum.

Believe it or not, there are concerns that remote workers are just as likely or more so likely to burnout as are their peers that work in a traditional office setting.

As a result of these qualms, some companies are requiring that their remote workers purposely include some health-inducing time breaks into their online schedules. When in an everyday office you are bound to have various office breaks that happen in a somewhat random fashion, whereby someone stops at your desk to chat, or maybe you go over to grab a pastry, but when at home there is a sense of completely zoning out all interruptions and utterly filling your work schedule with backbreaking meetings one after another.

Another kind of irony is that many remote workers are filling their otherwise normal commute time with doing more of their daily work efforts. In other words, suppose that your drive to work was about an hour in length, thus a daily roundtrip consisted of two hours, during which you were essentially non-functional in any work-related capacity. This meant that you worked an eight or ten-hour day and had that additional two hours of commute time.

Some remote workers are doing the customary eight to ten hours and then tossing the former commute time also into the work rubric routine. In that manner, they are working more like ten to perhaps twelve hours per day. Even though those commutes involved the drudgery of driving, they at least gave some respite from doing work. Now, the commute is gone, but the work time has seemingly expanded (though to clarify, that's not necessarily what the employer intended and nor especially demands, and instead tends to be a choice made by remote workers that are seeking to get as much work done as humanly possible).

In any case, it sure seems like remote work is now a viable option.

Some believe that it might be a fad and will gradually fade away. Others vehemently argue that the business world has now changed, irrevocably, and there is a strident and everlasting realization that remote work is here to stay. Businesses can cut back on those office expenses. Workers generally seem to like the remote working approach. All in all, with the dam having burst, as it were, there is a belief that there is no turning back.

Okay, if remote work is now a widely available option (well, for those types of jobs that remote work is feasible), this also means that the worker does not need to head into a large city downtown area for purposes of doing their job. You can choose to work from anywhere, pretty much, as long as you can establish an electronic network connection and be able to have reliable and relatively stable online access.

The good news is that in the United States, this means that you can essentially work in nearly any town (some exceptions apply, but those are relatively rare).

The newly mobilized professional worker is heading out of the big cities and into the smaller towns across the country. Rather than being jampacked into a metropolis that is teeming with zillions of people, you can live in a rural area or a suburb that you perhaps previously only dreamed of living in. These are places that offer lowered costs of living. You can get more affordable housing, have better schools nearby, and likely be nearer to vast green spaces.

Also, the odds are that the locales you might select are going to have bike lanes, making the act of getting around a lot easier and reducing your reliance on using a car. Neighborhoods tend to be walkable, offering expansive sidewalks, and safer streets all told.

Naturally, many towns would love to attract those mobility freed remote workers. The odds are that such workers will have a reliable paycheck and become local taxpayers. Those workers are bound to revel in living in their chosen Zoom Town, wanting to give back to the community and build their lives and careers in that particular location.

Whereas a worker would usually expect to change jobs every so many years, oftentimes having to uproot their living situation, the thinking now is that those remote workers can likely stay put the preponderance of their working days. As long as they are able to remotely-swing from one remote job to another, during their career progression, there won't be a need to physically relocate to a different city for that next favored career-building opportunity.

To recap, remote workers will be finding their way to Zoom Towns. Those workers will establish local roots and become devotees to that particular town or municipality. There won't be an office that they need to commute to. Instead, they will be working from home.

Working from home, though, doesn't mean that you are somehow homebound and never going to see the light of day. Rather than a commute, you'll likely use a car to get over to the grocery store, perhaps a few times per week. You might use the car for dropping the kids off at the school or for taking them to an extracurricular activity. And so on.

If you look closely at the driving needs, it sure seems that a car becomes less essential and more intermittent in terms of usage for those that are living in a Zoom Town.

Will remote workers that have moved to a Zoom Town even need to own a car?

That's a tough question to answer in today's world.

If you don't continue to own a car, it means that you would undoubtedly become dependent upon the vagaries of getting access to a car whenever a car is needed.

One difficultly entails possibly borrowing someone else's car for those occasions when a car is needed. That can be awkward and there might be a scheduling conflict that means the other car is not readily available. There is also the concern that your driving skills might decay, and you will feel less familiar when at the wheel of the vehicle.

Another approach would be to become dependent upon a ridesharing service.

The problem with that option is that a small town might be constrained in ridesharing availability. In a big city, there are tons of ridesharing options. It seems that at any time of the day or night, you can nearly instantaneously have a ridesharing car fulfill your ride request. In a smaller town, the chances are that there would be long delays in getting a ridesharing car to your home, plus you might personally know the local driver and feel bad about asking them to give you a ride late at night or when it might otherwise seem disruptive to that person.

That's then the conundrum.

Do you continue to own a car, even though you only intermittently need it, and ostensibly requires you to keep your driving skills sufficiently proficient to confidently and safely drive when you need to do so?

Or do you ditch the ownership of a car and opt to rely entirely on ridesharing, but that can be logistically limiting in a smaller town and have other distasteful challenges?

Perhaps the future provides an answer to this dilemma.

Keep in mind that the cars will gradually and inexorably become less dependent upon human drivers. I'm referring to the advent of AI-based true self-driving cars. These are cars that encompass an AI driving system that does all the driving. Humans aren't at the wheel.

That brings us to today's intriguing question: *Will the emergence of AI-based true self-driving cars be welcomed in Zoom Towns, and if so, why might that be the case?*

Let's unpack the matter and see.

**Self-Driving Cars And Zoom Towns**

For Level 4 and Level 5 true self-driving vehicles, there won't be a human driver involved in the driving task.

All occupants will be passengers.

The AI is doing the driving.

Most pundits are predicting that self-driving cars will be owned and operated by large companies and done so as part of a ridesharing money-making enterprise. This means that presumably, the major ridesharing firms of today will likely embrace self-driving cars, and there might be automakers and other corporations that newly jump into the ridesharing fray.

I'm known for my somewhat contrarian viewpoint that there will still be individual ownership of cars, including self-driving cars, and those self-driving cars will not solely be the province of large firms. Furthermore, my prediction is that people will join together in small-sized cooperatives, sometimes referred to as pods, and will collectively buy, own, and operate a self-driving car for the benefit of the group.

In however manner it comes to be, let's assume that self-driving cars will be principally used on a ridesharing basis.

Part of the rationale for using a self-driving car in a ridesharing format is that a self-driving car can generally be used 24x7, meaning that it is available for use at any time. Most people only use their conventional human-driven cars about 5% of the time. In essence, a conventional car sits around 95% of the time, altogether idle and unused. This is to a great extent due to the driver, or more correctly, due to the constraint of requiring that a human driver is available to be at the wheel of the vehicle.

The nice thing about an AI driving system is that it will drive whenever requested to do so. There aren't any rest breaks needed. No need to get some food to continue the driving chore. No sleep is needed. Around the clock, a self-driving car is available to be in-motion and underway (the exception being the act of refueling, and of course for any needed maintenance).

How does this relate to Zoom Towns?

The odds are that Zoom Towns are going to welcome self-driving cars with great eagerness and support.

Here's why.

As mentioned earlier, the remote workers that are moving into Zoom Towns do not need a car per se. They do need to use a car, but not necessarily own a car. Their requirement for a car is that it be available when they need one. In addition, they are either tired of having to drive or their driving skills are gradually decaying.

Into the picture comes the vaunted self-driving car.

You can have a self-driving car come to your home and give you a lift to the grocery store. A self-driving car can provide a ride to the school for you and your kids. Indeed, you can have your children ride in a self-driving car without you being present, assuming you are comfortable with there being no adult-supervision directly in the self-driving car during their driving journey.

Overall, a self-driving car provides the solution to those intermittent needs for having access to a car, plus it relieves the remote professional from having to undertake the driving task. This also means that the remote worker doesn't have to bother the local ridesharing human drivers about giving them a lift at odds hours or for personal chores that one doesn't want the whole town to know about. There is a certain kind of added privacy that can potentially arise due to the use of self-driving cars (well, yes and no, and there are various privacy qualms to keep in mind, see my column coverage).

All in all, self-driving cars are going to be a handy addition to Zoom Towns.

You can anticipate that Zoom Towns will encourage that self-driving cars be available and operated throughout their township. This might include tax breaks or other incentives to get self-driving car operators to put their vehicles in that particular town. Expect too that Zoom Towns will likely advertise that they are embracing the adoption of self-driving cars and therefore showcasing mindfulness about the needs of the locals in their town and illustrate an awareness of meritorious technological innovations.

**Conclusion**

I'd like to end this discussion with that aforementioned upbeat note, but there is, unfortunately, a bit of a rub about the notion of self-driving cars being readily available in Zoom Towns.

Are you ready?

The problem is that the owners and operators might not place their self-driving cars in Zoom Towns.

If you owned and operated a self-driving car, you want it to be used nonstop. For every mile that the self-driving car is transporting someone, dollars are being earned. Given the potential cost of a self-driving (we don't know what it will be, some are asserting it might be high, see my discussions on the pricing aspects), the self-driving car ought to be utilized in a maximum usage manner.

The thing is, a Zoom Town might not entail that kind of use.

Furthermore, a big city is likely to provide a richer opportunity for maximizing the use of a self-driving car. Sadly, the bottom line is that it might not be prudent to put a self-driving car into a Zoom Town and instead place it into a big city environment.

This is especially the case when self-driving cars are first available and relatively scarce.

Over time, assuming that there is a ramping up of the number of self-driving cars, it could be that the big cities become saturated with self-driving cars. At that juncture, which is admittedly quite distant in the future, the ridesharing opportunities might begin to look attractive in the Zoom Towns as an alternative to the no-longer viable and hypercompetitive settings of the big cities.

That does seem to put a damper on the clamoring by Zoom Towns to have self-driving cars in their midst. It could be that self-driving cars are desired, but not made available in the near-term, and those Zoom Towns could end-up being one of the last to see the emergence of self-driving cars. I don't want to end this discussion on such a sour note. And, I don't have to.

Recall the point I made earlier about my belief that self-driving cars might be owned by small groups or pods or collectives. This might be the means for self-driving cars to be included in Zoom Towns. The collectives that join together to get a self-driving car are not necessarily aiming to solely make a buck (that would be a nice bonus). If they can get at least a break-even, the investment into the self-driving car would be worthwhile. Also, the Zoom Town may aid those investors, offering various local incentives to aid them in their quest to make self-driving cars locally available for use.

Will we have self-driving cars in Zoom Towns? Where there is a will, there is a way.

I'd bet that Zoom Towns will become a stellar example of the use of self-driving cars. This will come as quite a surprise to many of the pundits that see self-driving cars as only financially sensible in those big city environs. A retort to that attitude is this: Don't underestimate the earnestness of Zoom Towns and the collective wisdom and grit of the mobility-minded remote workers that will be inhabiting those lovely and to-date undervalued townships.

# CHAPTER 4
# SKEPTICISM IN AI AND SELF-DRIVING CARS

Are you skeptical about most things?

Maybe you are rarely skeptical.

In that case, it might be that you take life as it seems to exist and seldom question what comes your way. Some might say that this puts you at undue risk, namely that you aren't skeptical enough about the world around you. Arguably, this might be construed as being altogether gullible or susceptible to being scammed or falling into untoward traps.

On the other hand, there is a chance that you are the type of person that is skeptical about nearly everything. Doubt continually enters your mind as to whether the things you are seeing, hearing, or otherwise come in contact with are true. The world is composed of falsehoods and it is your natural bent to assume that the whole shebang around you is false. Skepticism runs rampant in your noggin, which some would say is excessive and might undercut the joys of being in the moment and going with the flow of existence.

A healthy dose of skepticism seems to be the usual prescription of how to approach things. In a kind of Goldilocks manner, the notion is to have a sufficient amount of skepticism. Not too much, and not too little.

Of course, a strident argument can be made that skepticism ought to vary depending upon the circumstance or situation at hand. Being middle of the road on skepticism might not be the best course of action in all settings. There are bound to be occasions where the level of skepticism should be ratcheted up or potentially ratcheted down.

Let's use the act of driving a car to help illustrate the applicability of skepticism or the role of being skeptical.

You are driving along and happen to notice a car up ahead that is straying toward the edge of the lane. This car seems to go right up to the lane markers, as though possibly getting ready to change lanes, and then gradually steers back into the midst of the lane. Over and over, this tendency to ever so slightly veer, just a tad, keeps occurring.

One thought is that this is just a random event. The driver perchance is merely moving back and forth in the lane. Nothing to write home about.

If you were a bit more skeptical, perhaps this gingerly act of toying with the lane boundaries is a sign of something deeper. It could be that the driver has had a few drinks at the local bar and decided to take a drive. They are not completely sauced, but nonetheless, the liquor is impacting their ability to drive. Based on this sense of doubt about the driver and their mental state, you opt to stay well behind this moderately weaving car and play it safe by keeping your distance.

Perhaps a hefty dollop of skepticism might lead you to believe that for sure this other driver is out of their gourd. There is no doubt in your mind whatsoever that this is absolutely an intoxicated driver that should not be on the roadways. You quickly dial 911 and report that there is a drunken driver, and the police must stop the car before someone gets badly hurt.

One aspect of the situational aspects of employing skeptical thinking is that the stakes can potentially alter the degree of skepticism seemingly warranted.

When driving a car, the stakes are quite enormous. We take driving as a routine everyday task and don't usually consider it to be particularly risky. The thing is, driving a car and being around other moving cars is decidedly a life-or-death matter. Sadly, there are about 40,000 car crash-related fatalities each year in the United States alone, and approximately 2.5 million crash-related injuries.

Some would assert that being skeptical while at the wheel of a car is assuredly prudent. The old sage line seems to apply, namely that it is better to be safe than sorry.

When discussing skeptical thinking, I usually bring up the notion of directional vectors of skepticism. For example, you can be directing your skepticism at the acts of others. This was evident in the scenario of the car that was somewhat veering within its lane. Your skeptical way of thinking was directed toward the car ahead of you and the driver of that vehicle.

Another directional angle would be to consider skepticism aimed at yourself.

Consider this setting.

Suppose you are driving down a busy street. A lot is going on in terms of pedestrians bustling along, there is a slew of other cars jockeying in traffic around you, some bicyclists are nearby, and so on. The driving scene is hectic.

Out of the corner of your eye, you notice what seems to look like a dog at the side of the street and hiding in some bushes. You only though caught a very brief glimpse. It seemed to be a dog, but you aren't really sure. Maybe it was an object that merely resembled a dog. Could be that there is a child's toy that was shoved into the bushes and the shape perchance made you think about a dog.

You are skeptical that what you saw was truly there.

In that manner, you are expressing skepticism towards yourself.

You are doubting that what your eyes glimpsed was real versus perhaps an optical illusion. Maybe nothing at all was there in the shrubbery and you assumed that there might be, simply based on the overgrowth having a shape and coloring that resembled what a dog looks like. Or perhaps there is some inanimate object in the bushes that approximates the shape of a dog.

The same kind of self-oriented skepticism could occur with your eyes and also with your ears.

Have you ever been driving and thought you heard a siren? You strain to listen carefully and determine if there is a siren in the distance. The sound could indeed be a siren and thus a handy forewarning that an ambulance or firetruck might be coming down the road soon. On the other hand, maybe it was just a whistling sound that was similar to a siren. Then again, there might not have been any noise at all and you entirely imagined that a siren had blared (it was all in your head, one might say).

In each of those instances, you were doubting your sensory capacities. You can also have similar doubts about your mind.

Up ahead is a busy intersection. The light is green. Your mind was momentarily wandering, and you weren't paying close attention to the traffic light. At this juncture, you are unsure whether the light has been green for a while and therefore might soon be changing to yellow and then red. It could be that the light just recently turned green and there is plenty of time to make it through the intersection.

You mull this over in your mind.

The light might be getting ready to switch to yellow. At your current speed and the remaining distance to the intersection, it is going to be dicey to come to a complete stop in time for the red light that will occur after the yellow. Darn it, if you knew that the light had been green for a lengthy time, the odds are that a yellow is imminent and thus it would be best to slow down in anticipation that you'll need to stop at the red light once it appears.

Did you mentally zone out for a fraction of a second, or did you allow several seconds to lapse while somewhat daydreaming and not concentrating fully on the roadway? There are no easy means to know.

In any case, you are skeptical about your own frame of mind. The directional vector of your skepticism is now being directed at yourself and your mental facility.

Before we proceed into the reasons why the topic of skepticism is being noted in this discussion, I can relieve your anxiety by saying that the bushes did not contain a dog (it was a small tricycle that at a glance could be construed as a dog), the driver in the car that was weaving amidst the lane was, in fact, DUI, and the green light stayed green long enough that it was possible to safely proceed through the intersection. Just wanted to tie-up those loose ends, else I realize that some of you might be on the edge of your seat for the rest of the discussion.

Shifting gears, the future of cars will consist of self-driving cars.

These are cars that have an AI-based driving system at the wheel. There isn't a human driver involved.

Let's contemplate how well the AI driving systems will be able to drive a car. The hope is that self-driving cars will drive at least as safe as human drivers. Indeed, the assumption is that a self-driving car will be safer overall due to the aspect that the AI driving system won't be drinking and driving, nor will the AI driving system be distracted by watching cat videos. The human foibles of driving are potentially going to be wrung out and the AI will achieve a safer driving record accordingly (that's the dream).

Here is today's intriguing question: *Will AI-based true self-driving cars be utilizing skepticism or a variant thereof while driving, such that the AI driving system will invoke a semblance of doubt as an aid in performing the driving task?*

Let's unpack the matter and see.

**Self-Driving Cars And The Role Of Skepticism**

For Level 4 and Level 5 true self-driving vehicles, there won't be a human driver involved in the driving task.

All occupants will be passengers.

The AI is doing the driving.

One aspect to immediately discuss entails the fact that today's AI is not sentient.

In other words, the AI is altogether a collective of computer-based programming and algorithms, and most assuredly not able to reason in the same manner that humans can. I mention this aspect because many headlines boldly proclaim or imply that AI has turned the corner and become equal to human intelligence. As if that wasn't bad enough, the outsized headlines seek to amp further the matter by contending that AI is reaching superhuman capabilities.

Why this emphasis about the AI not being sentient?

Because I want to underscore that when discussing the role of skepticism as infused into an AI driving system, I am not ascribing human qualities to the AI. Please be aware that there is an ongoing and dangerous tendency these days to anthropomorphize AI. In essence, people are assigning human-like sentience to today's AI, despite the undeniable and inarguable fact that no such AI exists as yet.

In a moment, I'll explain how skepticism (or its variant), which we would normally consider an intrinsic human trait, can be programmatically rendered into an AI system. There isn't any magic or mystery involved. This is something that can be tangibly measured and quantified.

As a side note, readers of a philosophical bent might argue that skepticism must only be a human quality and cannot ever exist in any other manner or form. Some might even claim that no other creature on earth can embody skeptical ways of thinking, other than humans alone. I'm not going to get bogged down in that debate herein.

The assumption here is that being skeptical is a quantifiable factor of incorporating doubt into a matter at hand and that this can be overtly taken into account when devising a computer-based system. Not everyone will agree with this assumption, so I thought it important to let you know that your mileage may vary on whether anything other than humans can exploit or employ skepticism.

Okay, with that foundational setting, let's jump into the fray.

A self-driving car will have an abundance of sensors that are the proverbial eyes and ears for the AI driving system. The typical sensor suite consists of video cameras, radar, LIDAR, ultrasonic devices, and the like. These sensors are continually collecting data about the driving scene and the data is then mathematically analyzed to try and ferret out what the surrounding driving environment consists of.

Suppose that a video camera on the front of the car is aimed at the road ahead. The video images are being streamed into the on-board computer processors. There are image processing algorithms that computationally examine the imagery. This is done to try and figure out where the roadway is, where other cars are, where the sidewalk is, and so on. There are numerous challenges in doing so, and you cannot falsely think that the image processing capability is going to be perfect and unerringly ascertain all aspects of the driving environment.

Have you been driving your car and suddenly had a glare of light from bright sunshine that momentarily obscured your vision?

We all have had that happen. The same lighting effect can adversely impact a video camera. Perhaps you've used the video camera on your smartphone and had occasions whereby the images were hard to make out because a shiny ray of light blotted out what was able to be seen.

Tying these aspects together, imagine that a video camera being used on a self-driving car provides images that are oversaturated with light due to a sunny spot that the vehicle just encountered. The image processing tries to nonetheless use various filters and mathematical models to recover whatever might be within that driving scene as available via the somewhat confusing images.

Upon mathematically analyzing the scene, the image processing software identifies what seems to be a possible dog, hiding in a set of bushes next to the street. The lighting though is impacting the computational task of identifying the objects in the driving scene as embodied in the video imagery collected.

Should the rest of the AI driving system assume that indeed there is a dog there, and as such perhaps start to slow down the car because the dog might suddenly rush into the street?

Perhaps you recognize that this is similar to the earlier scenario. There might be a dog in those nearby bushes, there might not be.

Mull over the ramifications. The rest of the AI driving system might be programmed to assume that whatever the image processing algorithms indicate is the unvarnished truth. If the video camera image analysis is reporting that a dog might be there, it must be there (a seemingly most-safe assumption).

In a manner of speaking, one might hope that the AI driving system would be somewhat "skeptical" about the image processing report.

If the AI driving system of the self-driving car is going to slow down the vehicle or bring the car to a halt because there might or might not be a dog present, realize that this is going to likely impact the rest of the traffic. A human-driven car behind the self-driving car might not realize why the self-driving car is slowing down, and the human driver could become irked accordingly or caught off-guard, possibly rear-ending the self-driving car.

I realize that this particular example seems relatively benign, ostensibly in this scenario it indubitably seems to make sense to have the AI driving system be extremely cautious. Let's though ramp up this notion. Suppose the AI driving system is constantly taking the most extreme cautious approach to the act of driving. All the time. Incessantly. Would a self-driving car in that mode be viable on our public roadways? Overall, such a design would likely only be able to proceed at a crawling speed, and it would have to do repetitive starts and stops, never proceeding at a full and uninterrupted pace.

We would find such self-driving cars to be impractical as anything that could viably be used in our everyday world of having to deal with the uncertainties associated with driving a car.

How is a semblance of "skepticism" rendered into an AI driving system?

Revisit the earlier point that skepticism can have a directional vector.

The AI driving system ought to essentially employ doubt about itself, incorporating probabilities and uncertainties, along with having cross-checks and computational resiliency purposely built into the system.

Are the sensors working correctly? Is a sensor misreporting something? Can the results of one sensor be compared to another sensor to try and resolve what might be in the driving scene (this is referred to as MSDF, or multi-sensor data fusion)? Etc.

Another realm of self-doubt would entail the on-board computer processors. Are the computer processors working correctly? Is the internal computer memory corrupted? And so on.

And there is the matter of raising doubt or questioning of the AI system by the AI system.

Has the AI driving system encountered an internal error or bug? Is the AI driving system not responding on a timely basis to the roadway conditions? I've covered these kinds of issues in my column and they are all important as integral to a sound and reliable AI-based driving system.

Refocusing the directional vector, consider the skepticism aimed at others.

A self-driving car comes upon a car up ahead that is not quite staying in its lane. The car is straying toward the edges of the lane.

An AI driving system that is not devised with a kind of skeptical programmatic method will not especially notice that another car is weaving like this. Only once the other car dramatically swings out of its lane will such an AI driving system ostensibly take notice of what the other car is doing.

**Conclusion**

The problem facing the developers of self-driving cars is somewhat similar to the earlier point about how much skepticism is healthy to adopt.

We obviously want AI driving systems that are double-checking what is taking place. Perhaps we want them to be triple checking and quadruple checking. This seems warranted given that the act of driving a car involves life-or-death matters.

How far though should this kind of multitudes of checking be extended? You could devise the AI driving system to be spinning its wheels (metaphorically) by checking and repeatedly rechecking to the nth degree.

This might lead to the AI driving system not proceeding at all.

Though I am loath to draw a seemingly direct comparison to a human driver per se, perhaps you've helped a teenage newbie driver learn to drive a car (I am not suggesting that a teenage driver is somehow the equivalent of an AI driving system!). I recall that one teen got into the car, sat at the wheel, and after contemplating all the possible things that could go awry, became racked with doubt and seemed to conclude that it was too dangerous to take the car for a drive.

By whatever wording you wish to use, whether skepticism is a fitting choice or maybe not, an AI driving system has to have a healthy dose of it, ensuring that the self-driving car is calculating the chances that whatever is seen or detected might be false or misleading, and that other drivers might be going askew, and that the AI system itself might oddly veer and go awry.

Unless you are stridently skeptical, it seems little doubt that this kind of doubt is a necessity when driving a ca

# CHAPTER 5
# BYOA AND SELF-DRIVING CARS

I'm sure that you are familiar with BYOB.

Some say that BYOB stands for bring your own beverage. Alternatively, the popular saying refers to bring your own booze, or maybe bring your own beer, or ostensibly just alludes to bring your own bottle.

To each their own.

A less well-known acronym is BYOD.

Have you heard that one?

Anybody in the tech field probably has. This BYOD refers to bring your own device and popped up in the last several years. The idea is that when you go to work for a company, one approach to outfitting you with a smartphone and a laptop consists of issuing those devices to you (owned by your employer), while an alternative approach entails letting you use your own personal devices instead (you own them).

Some employees prefer to use their own equipment rather than have to carry for example another cell phone around merely because it is intended for work phone calls. Thus, firms decided that they would sometimes allow employees to use their own devices, typically getting reimbursed for the portion of use devoted to work versus personal matters (this is a somewhat controversial topic, venturing into privacy issues and the like).

Okay, we've now covered the extremely popular BYOB and the rather tangentially popular BYOD.

Do you know about BYOA?

That's a new one, so don't feel downbeat if you don't know what it refers to.

The BYOA stands for bring your own algorithm.

That's right, the last part of the saying encompasses the notion of algorithms. It seems like everyone these days is talking about algorithms. Businesses are being told that they will someday be run entirely by an algorithm and there won't be much for humans to do. Some naysayers are warning us to be on the watch for sneaky and underhanded algorithms. Those kinds of algorithms are devised to fool humans or cheat humans out of one thing or another.

Algorithms, algorithms, algorithms.

Now, the latest way to think about algorithms involves arming yourself with algorithms that are on your side, acting as your algorithmic protector. In this dog-eat-dog world, if businesses and others are going to use algorithms to come at you and try to manage you or take your money, it seems altogether logical and outright prudent to arm yourself with algorithms to fight back at the onslaught.

Would you go unarmed into a knife fight? Of course not. You would want to have a sharp knife in your belt that could be brandished and used when necessary. The thing is, in terms of algorithms, by-and-large all that you are armed with is your noggin, and you don't have any computer-based algorithms that are tuned and sharpened to be an armament just for you.

Until now.

Let's assume that you nearly always are carrying your smartphone with you, wherever you go (I'd wager that's a pretty good bet and that your smartphone is nearly like an added appendage). Suppose you could load some algorithms onto your smartphone that would be used by you as a means to go toe-to-toe with any outsider algorithms that you encounter throughout your daily efforts. This makes a lot of plain sense and you would seemingly be eager to have those algorithms loaded and ready to bear.

Consider for example the BYOA that is emerging in the healthcare and medical realm.

Follow along on this scenario of a healthcare-related BYOA.

One day, you go to see your physician about a pain that you've been experiencing in your shoulder. The doctor takes a look, asks you to move your arms, and carefully studies the shoulder area. After a few moments of contemplative thought, the doctor tells you that you likely have arthritis in your shoulder. You are then told that you should take it easy on that shoulder for a few days, including using ice on it for about a half-hour a couple of times per day. Also, once you've done that for about a week, you are to let the doctor know how things are coming along, and a potentially new prognosis might be devised.

So far, this seems like an everyday ordinary visit to the doctor.

Let's mull over the situation. Unless you happen to know something about arthritis, you might not have any clear thoughts about how to respond to the doctor about the recommendation being made. The instructions seem to be sensible and therefore maybe you ought to do as the doctor has prescribed. Normally, you would likely thank your physician, pay the bill, and get ready to head home.

But it just so happens that you have pre-loaded a BYOA for healthcare and medical uses onto your smartphone.

While sitting there in the doctor's office, you started the algorithm. When the doctor explained that it might be arthritis, you entered that diagnosis into the algorithm. At this juncture, the algorithm tells you that you should ask the doctor whether the use of a corticosteroid injection might be suitable to aid in reducing the pain and inflammation that you are feeling in your shoulder.

You begin to chat now with the doctor about this added facet, which notably covers something that you would not otherwise have known by your own divines to bring up. In addition, the algorithm next tells you to ask about whether you can take nonsteroidal anti-inflammatory medications (NSAIDs), which are widely used in such circumstances, and a reference to medicine such as ibuprofen or aspirin.

The doctor already has in their mind a kind of healthcare and medical "algorithm" based on many years of medical training and experience. You don't have that in your head, but you do have a smartphone and you do have a BYOA that can help you when discussing healthcare and medical matters.

One aspect of a BYOA is that it might be relatively generic and cover a topic such as healthcare in a general manner. You can liken this to having used an online search to find medical websites that could clue you about arthritis.

An even better BYOA would be customized to you. Perhaps your entire medical history is loaded onto your smartphone and the BYOA can tap into that data. Thus, the algorithm might note that you have special dietary issues that could get in the way of taking aspirin, which is a matter specific to your health and not something that necessarily would come up when looking generically for details about arthritis aspects.

I think you likely get the gist of BYOA.

You arm yourself with an algorithm and it can aid in various situations. The outsider algorithms that it will be used to carry on discourse with might be a human-based algorithm, such as the medical knowledge of the doctor, or it could be used in instances wherein the other side is a computer-based algorithm. For example, maybe you are applying for a mortgage loan and do not know what this entails, so an online application form that is asking you mortgage application questions could be "confronted" by your using a BYOA that has to do with mortgages.

You are bringing a knife to a knife fight.

In fact, it could be that your BYOA is better than the algorithm that you are going head-to-head with. In that case, you are bringing a gun to a knife fight. For the mortgage example, perhaps the BYOA has some nifty tricks up its sleeve about how to get the mortgage application systems to give you discounts that it would not normally grant, but your BYOA has some special ways to squeeze you into those lowest prices.

Not everyone is necessarily enthusiastic about the advent of BYOA.

The company that does mortgages is not especially thrilled that you have a means to readily fill-out your mortgage application and potentially do so to your advantage over their advantage. The medical doctor that is your physician is potentially going to be a bit irate that you are using a machine to question the medical advice that you are being given. And so on.

As an aside, this can easily devolve, such as your medical doctor arguing that your BYOA is wrong or fouled-up, in which case you might challenge the physician about that contention, and the next thing you know, the physician might say "darn it, I'm a doctor, not an engineer" (just had to include that Star Trek-like pun here, sorry).

Whether you like BYOA or not, the odds are that it will gradually take off and become relatively big business. People are going to want to have algorithms at their fingertips that know about all sorts of things. Going to the doctor? Use your medical-oriented BYOA. Buying a new car? Use your BYOA devoted to automobile purchasing and aim to get a solid deal on that hefty purchase.

Speaking of cars, I'm guessing that you know that the future of cars consists of self-driving cars.

Yes, I am shifting the topic of this discussion and taking you down the path of talking about self-driving cars. Why so? Because there is a role for BYOA when it comes to riding in self-driving cars.

Not many are yet thinking about BYOA and self-driving cars, so you can be the first on your block to be well-informed on the topic.

Here's an intriguing question: *Will there be any basis for using BYOA when it comes to the emergence and use of AI-based true self-driving cars?*

The straight-ahead answer is a resounding yes.

Let's unpack the matter and see.

**Self-Driving Cars And BYOA**

For Level 4 and Level 5 true self-driving vehicles, there won't be a human driver involved in the driving task.

All occupants will be passengers.

The AI is doing the driving.

One aspect to immediately discuss entails the fact that today's AI is not sentient.

In other words, the AI is altogether a collective of computer-based programming and algorithms, and most assuredly not able to reason in the same manner that humans can. I mention this aspect because many headlines boldly proclaim or imply that AI has turned the corner and become equal to human intelligence. As if that wasn't bad enough, the outsized headlines seek to amp further the matter by contending that AI is reaching superhuman capabilities (for why the use of "superhuman" as a moniker is especially misleading and inappropriate, see my discussion at **this link here**).

Why this emphasis about the AI not being sentient?

Because I want to underscore that when discussing the role of algorithms as infused into an AI driving system, I am not ascribing human qualities to the AI. Please be aware that there is an ongoing and dangerous tendency these days to anthropomorphize AI. In essence, people are assigning human-like sentience to today's AI, despite the undeniable and inarguable fact that no such AI exists as yet.

With that clarification, you can envision the AI driving system as an algorithm. It is highly complex and has lots and lots of algorithms within it, yet still, it is an algorithm and not somehow sentient.

When you go for a ride in a self-driving car, the AI driving system will determine how to drive the car and take you on your specified driving journey. All that you would usually do is specify the destination and the AI driving system would take care of the rest.

Currently, most of the AI driving systems are relatively narrow in that they focus almost entirely on going from point A to point B. You get into the vehicle, indicate you are heading to the grocery store, and the self-driving car whisks away, taking you there. It is assumed that you will sit quietly and merely enjoy the ride.

Of course, that's not what happens in real life when using a human-driven ridesharing option.

Think about the last several instances of your going in a ridesharing vehicle. I don't know how talkative your drivers have been, but mine seem to be chatty cats, as it were. Besides talking about the weather and sports, there is definitely some discussion devoted to the ride itself.

For example, the driver might sometimes ask if you are in a hurry or not. Some drivers will try to expedite the ride if they can. Others don't like bringing up such a topic because it could imply that they are going to drive dangerously if you say you are in a hurry.

Another facet that sometimes arises is the route that the driver is going to take. Most of the time, probably you don't care what the routing consists of. Assuming that the driver is using a GPS mapping system, the odds are they are going to be leveraging whatever is the best route to your destination.

That being said, if you've ever been to New York City, you probably know that when the traffic is snarled, there are tricky ways to get from point A to point B. A typical GPS navigation system is not necessarily going to reveal those insider-only driving sneaks. As such, if you are a local New Yorker, you might tell the driver that a faster way to proceed involves taking a route that you suggest, rather than relying on the GPS system.

What has any of this got to do with BYOA?

I'm glad you asked.

When you opt to use a self-driving car, the AI driving system is a type of algorithm and it is empowered to drive the car and get you to your destination. Unlike a human driver of today's ridesharing, the AI driving systems are not generally prepared to cope with the interaction between the "driver" and the passenger.

In the future, this will undoubtedly change.

Passengers inside self-driving cars are not going to put up with AI driving systems that are unresponsive. Sure, at first, simply riding in a self-driving car is going to be exciting and people will fall in line with whatever way the system was designed. Gradually, riders are going to wise up. They are going to favor an AI driving system that can be interactive and adjust to the requests or needs of the passenger.

Some of the automakers and self-driving tech firms will accommodate this added need, while others will be slow to do so. Eventually, on a competitive basis, they will all need to pretty much meet the same desired capabilities, else those self-driving cars not so outfitted are going to be avoided by the paying public.

Assume that eventually, the AI driving systems are interactive with their passengers.

You have now opened the door to BYOA.

Let's take a glance at a typical scenario.

You get into a self-driving car and are going from your home to the doctor's office (hey, maybe you have a sore shoulder and want to go see your physician, but that's an entirely different story). You are in a hurry. Also, you know that there are some streets on the way that have some rutty potholes and others that have speed bumps. Going down any of those streets is going to make the car heave up and down, which is going to cause you added pain due to your aching shoulder.

Keep in mind that by the normal convention, you would simply provide the doctor's office address, and the rest of the ride is then upon the shoulders of the AI driving system (well, that was a sore pun, for sure). You would be nothing more than a lifeless lump of baggage or luggage that just so happens to be sitting inside the self-driving car.

Imagine instead that the AI driving system can be interactive. You might tell the AI driving system to avoid the specific streets that you know will cause the car to bounce around. Also, you are aware that the fastest way at this time of the day entails avoiding the school grounds since the kids are getting out of school for the day and the traffic near there will be clogged.

Away the self-driving car goes, driving to the doctor's office while abiding by those preferences.

Or you could have simply used your BYOA.

Yes, on your smartphone you might have loaded an algorithm for dealing with AI driving systems and self-driving cars. The smartphone would electronically transmit to the AI driving system your riding preferences. A type of handshake and electronic dialogue would take place. Your smartphone would then let you know how the electronic negotiation went.

This specific scenario was just a taste of the types of driving preferences someone might have. There are plenty of driving aspects that will be favored by one person over another. For example, maybe you prefer a smooth ride without any bumps or shimmering. Then again, some people relish being in a car that feels the road and gives the impression that you are on rough roads.

Another aspect would be related to your normal routines. For example, perhaps on the way to work each day, you like to swing through the local drive-thru coffee shop to get a honey oat milk latte. The moment that you get into a self-driving car for your morning commute, the BYOA would instruct the AI driving system to include the drive-thru excursion on the way to the office.

**Conclusion**

Some are bound to react to the BYOA for self-driving cars as a horrible idea and one that is destined for grave dangers.

Here's why they would (mistakenly) think this. Suppose the BYOA told the AI driving system to go at superfast speeds, such as 120 miles per hour. On top of that, imagine if the BYOA instructed the self-driving car to run over any pedestrians that got in the way of the vehicle, such as jaywalkers that might wander into the street when the self-driving car is coming along.

That would be terrible. But that's not what the BYOA would be able to pull off. In other words, the AI driving system is not going to undertake illegal or stupid driving moves simply because the BYOA asks to do so. The AI driving system would presumably be programmed to allow for accommodating passenger requests that are considered reasonable and feasible. That applies whether the human passenger directly makes the request, perhaps using a Natural Language Processing (NLP) interactive feature similar to an Alexa or Siri, or whether the BYOA does the same via electronic messaging.

You might liken this to the medical doctor that isn't going to suddenly book you for surgery on your shoulder simply because you ask for surgery to be immediately undertaken. The doctor would push back at such a request. Please note that I'm not likening the AI driving system to what a human might do, but only emphasizing that there are usually limits within which the BYOA is going to "win" in what it might request or suggest.

So, the fears of a BYOA that makes the self-driving car become a wild ride like at a theme park is quite unfounded. Assuming that the automaker or self-driving tech firm has devised the AI driving system adequately, there will be flexibility toward accommodating the requests of riders but bounded by what is suitable for a proper way of driving a car.

# CHAPTER 6
# BATHROOM BREAKS AND SELF-DRIVING CARS

Sometimes, something that might seem inconsequential can be a rather daunting problem.

Have you ever been driving your car and suddenly had your toddler announce that they have to go the bathroom? For most parents, this has happened at least once in their parental lives, if not many times. Indeed, parents that go through this circumstance are bound to repeatedly in the future admonish their children to go to the bathroom before any long road trip gets underway.

I know it sounds like a trivial matter, but when dealing with a crying youngster that is insisting that they need to find relief, any caring parent is going to realize this is rather important stuff to deal with. Of course, movies and TV shows have often utilized such scenarios for comedic purposes. Though not occurring within a car, there is a quite famous scene in the movie *Liar Liar* in which attorney-portraying actor Jim Carrey tells a judge during a courtroom trial that he just has to go to the restroom, for which the judge questions whether the matter can wait or not. The ensuing dialogue is precious, that's for sure.

I suppose the point too is that the urgent need to gain relief is not solely apt to occur only for children. Adults can find themselves mired in the same problem.

Perhaps you are driving on the freeway to work and had consumed an entire cup of coffee that morning, plus you are sipping from a second full cup that is in your car with you. Traffic is snarled. The drive to the office is taking a lot longer than you anticipated.

Regrettably, you begin to feel the need for finding a nearby restroom. The problem is that there aren't any exit ramps up ahead. Even if you were to do a timely exit from the freeway, you aren't sure where you would find a suitable place that has a clean and safe restroom. It used to be that gas stations prided themselves on offering such a handy service, aiming to bring in customers that would then buy petrol and purchase some merchandise at the convenience store. Nowadays, it seems that many gas station bathrooms are oftentimes so deplorably kept that it is the last place you'd ever consider visiting, even in a time of dire crisis.

It used to be that you had to randomly hope for some establishment to be off the next exit up ahead of your vehicle. The good news is that nowadays with GPS and mapping systems, you can usually peek at the digital map and see what kinds of businesses might be at the next series of exits. A rule of thumb seems to be that if there is a well-known eatery such as a McDonald's or similar, those usually have a restroom that is sanitary and safe enough to use in a pinch.

In any case, the driver of the car is on the hot seat, as it were, in the sense that when a request occurs for seeking relief, the driver needs to ascertain where, when, and how to find a reasonably suitable place to stop. You can't just hit the brakes and miraculously have a solution at the door of your vehicle. It will take some amount of additional driving and precious, ostensibly nerve-racking, time to navigate to and arrive at a locale that will resolve the matter appropriately.

As mentioned, that's why any seasoned driver usually considers such conundrums *before* getting behind the wheel of a car. If a drive is going to require any significant amount of time, the odds of a request for urgent aid is going to increase with each mile driven. The potential ensnarement can be an obvious one when taking a vacation trip that goes across many miles of open desert or through vast farmlands. You know beforehand that there won't be viable options during the driving journey. Meanwhile, it is easy to get caught off-guard by those shorter trips that take place on highways or freeways and you get jammed into backed up bumper-to-bumper traffic, thus unexpectedly prolonging the time in the vehicle.

With today's ridesharing, you don't usually hear about situations of this nature arising in a ridesharing context. The chances are that a ridesharing trip is going to be short and sweet. Furthermore, ridesharing typically occurs in cities and populated areas that would allow for cutting a trip short, to utilize a location that seems suitable for the pressing matter. There are instances of ridesharing drivers that have been asked to find a restroom, though such cases are relatively uncommon.

We are back to the notion that the driver is going to be a key determiner of how fate will play out. A passenger that has a request will need to convey the request to the driver. The driver then has to try and figure out a means to accommodate the request. The classic "hold it" is often used by parents, though this can be a stress-inducing instruction and not especially satisfactory to all parties.

Speaking of drivers, the future of cars will consist of self-driving cars, meaning that the driver is an AI-based driving system. Rather than having a human sitting at the steering wheel, there won't be any steering wheel at all, and nor will there be a human driver involved in the driving task.

This raises an intriguing question: *How will AI-based true self-driving cars cope with requests involving an urgent bathroom break as expressed by a passenger inside the vehicle?*

Before we leap into the answer, one might be doubtful that such a question is worth posing at this time. Surely, of all the issues facing the advent of self-driving cars, this particular dilemma has got to be pretty low on the priority list.

You'd be right that the focus of the automakers and self-driving tech makers is more so on the challenges of technologically making AI driving systems that can safely drive from point A to point B. That has to happen for self-driving cars to make any substantive progress in terms of being readily accepted and utilized on our public roadways.

There are plenty of so-called edge or corner cases that will gradually and inexorably need to be worked out. Certainly, the matter being addressed in this discussion could be placed onto such a future-topics list to be resolved at a later date. Nonetheless, there is no getting around the fact that this is an aspect that happens in the real world of driving, at least concerning human drivers, and we would expect that eventually, the full gamut of self-driving cars ought to be able to contend with the same trials and tribulations that occur to human drivers.

All told, this topic is assuredly worth giving some modest consideration toward, and also provides interesting fodder for thinking about how self-driving cars will need to be programmed or adapted to handle the vagaries and nuances of carrying around human riders.

Let's unpack the matter and see.

### Self-Driving Cars And Bathroom Breaks

For Level 4 and Level 5 true self-driving vehicles, there won't be a human driver involved in the driving task.

All occupants will be passengers.

The AI is doing the driving.

One aspect to immediately discuss entails the fact that today's AI is not sentient.

In other words, the AI is altogether a collective of computer-based programming and algorithms, and most assuredly not able to reason in the same manner that humans can. I mention this aspect because many headlines boldly proclaim or imply that AI has turned the corner and become equal to human intelligence. As if that wasn't bad enough, the outsized headlines seek to amp further the matter by contending that AI is reaching superhuman capabilities.

Why this emphasis about the AI not being sentient?

Because I want to underscore that when discussing the matter of concern herein, it is important to not ascribe human qualities to the

AI. Please be aware that there is an ongoing and dangerous tendency these days to anthropomorphize AI. In essence, people are assigning human-like sentience to today's AI, despite the undeniable and inarguable fact that no such AI exists as yet.

In short, if a tearful child inside a self-driving car were to suddenly blurt out to the AI driving system that there was an urgent need to find a restroom, the AI is not somehow sentient and going to instantly respond with a caring reply. The AI driving systems are currently pretty much very limited in any kind of interaction with the passengers of the vehicle. Other than finding out the desired destination, most of the AI driving systems do nothing else as interaction and will simply and silently drive the car to the indicated address.

You can expect that the use of Natural Language Processing (NLP) akin to an Alexa or Siri will step-by-step be included in AI driving systems. This will allow a limited range of discourse with the AI driving system. For example, you might want to change your destination indication, so you speak-up, saying a wake-up keyword for the NLP, and then in short and clear-cut commands would state that you wish to go to a different address.

In theory, this NLP could encompass a capability associated with the bathroom break conundrum.

The NLP would have to be programmed accordingly. A passenger would need to indicate that they are requesting that the AI driving system reroute to a suitable locale that would have a restroom. Presumably, the AI driving system would examine the digital maps being used and proffer potential choices for the passenger, of which the rider might then select one that seems suitable.

Let's mull that over.

Have you ever changed your driving path and came to a nearby restroom that upon actually seeing the locale it became evident that stopping there would unwise?

I'm sure that you have.

The same could happen when rerouting the self-driving car. Even once you arrive at the seemingly nearest option or one that you otherwise designated, upon seeing the nature of the place and where it resides, you might change your mind and desire a secondary choice instead. This means that you would need to instruct the AI driving system to try and go to the next possibility.

These kinds of interactions with a human driver are quite easy and we do not put much thought toward carrying on such conversations. A human driver might instantly realize when they pullup to a filthy gas station that the place does not look safe to stop at. At that juncture, a tough battle can ensue over whether it is worth a chance at using the locale or opting to proceed further.

Meanwhile, one might say the clock is ticking.

Do not expect the NLP capabilities to be as fluid and seemingly able as what you would experience with a human driver. On the other hand, it is sometimes the case that a human driver is recalcitrant and will either refuse to stop, even though the need has reached a crucial level, or will stop at a place that is patently scary and just say that you ought to get out of the car and proceed accordingly.

Hopefully, a well-crafted NLP would not be set up in the same manner.

Some wonder whether self-driving cars might be outfitted with accommodations within the vehicle itself, thus obviating the need to stop anywhere for the pressing need.

This is an interesting idea.

First, let's clarify that self-driving cars will potentially be redesigned beyond what a conventional car currently consists of, especially altering the interior of the vehicle. Right now, a car has to have a driver's seat and driving controls, all of which take up a blocked area in the interior. Without any need for human-accessible driving controls, the entire interior is suddenly openly available and can be reimagined accordingly.

Some futuristic designs showcase that there might be swivel seats inside a self-driving car. This would allow the passengers to face in whatever direction they wished. At one point during a driving journey, perhaps everyone is facing forward, just like in a conventional car. During a trek, perhaps all those seats are swiveled to face each other, allowing for direct face-to-face interaction.

There is also a design approach that involves seats that recline, allowing for taking a nap or outright snoozing while letting the AI do the driving. This makes abundant sense. If you are taking a long road trip, you might as well catch some winks on the way to your destination. That morning commute to work can even provide an opportunity for catching some shuteye, making you ready and refreshed when you reach the office.

Given those redesigns, some wonder whether a form of a "portable potty" might be included in the interior of a self-driving car. This would certainly be handy when the time arises. On the other hand, this would indubitably open other problems and make for a can of worms. You can imagine the logistics difficulties that would underpin having such a capability.

Returning to the more likely options, namely rerouting the self-driving car, you won't necessarily need to interact with the AI driving system to do so. Most of the self-driving cars are going to be equipped with a telecommunications link that will allow you to speak with a remote agent, kind of akin to an OnStar-like feature. You could press a button and have a remote agent, a human, available to speak with about your need to find a restroom.

One aspect that has some controversy involves what the remote agent can and cannot do concerning the AI driving system. There are some automakers and self-driving tech firms that are going to allow a remote human agent to take over the driving controls from the AI driving system.

Some believe that a more prudent approach involves the remote agent being able to provide advice to the AI driving system, rather than being able to directly control the vehicle. For example, the remote agent in this instance might look-up in an online database whether there are any suitable restrooms nearby to your present driving location, and then send an indication to the AI driving system to reroute to that location. Notice that the remote agent is not taking over the driving controls and instead merely changing the destination address.

All told, the options seem to be that the passenger might instruct the AI driving system to go to a location that will provide the needed accommodations, or the rider might make use of a remote agent to assist in altering the course of the self-driving car. The AI is not likely to play an active role in solving the dilemma per se, unlike a human driver that would potentially aid in reasoning about how to deal with the situation. There is also an off chance that some self-driving cars might have a built-in restroom-like option, though this is unexpected and seemingly unlikely.

**Conclusion**

There is an added twist to this. It is conceivable that waystations for self-driving cars might be established. These would be set up to enable the recharging or refueling of self-driving cars. There might also be a maintenance and cleaning crew at those spots. Since self-driving cars are potentially going to be on-the-go 24x7, this implies that there will need to be relatively frequent efforts to keep the vehicle clean and in proper shape for driving and for carrying passengers.

Okay, it is also conceivable that those might be locales that a rider could use a restroom. Similar to the notion of using a restroom at a gas station, these newer kinds of waystations might provide the same facility. On top of that, one supposes that these specially devised waystations might be expanded to include a convenience store capacity too. Nobody can say whether those kinds of waystations will be established. At this time, there are so few self-driving cars being tested on the roadways that we don't know for sure what will be needed to scale-up the volume of self-driving cars for full deployment.

# CHAPTER 7
# GUNSHOT DETECTION AND SELF-DRIVING CARS

Shots fired!

It is certainly startling when you hear a loud bang that sounds like a gunshot.

Imagine sitting in your living room and from outside comes that blaring sound. It seemed like gunfire, but you aren't quite sure. There was a very loud noise, it was a sharp popping sound reminiscent of a gunshot, and it was close enough to be heard.

Luckily, the sound wasn't so close that it might have been gunfire directed at or particularly nearby your home.

Should you call the police to notify them about the apparent gunfire?

That's an interesting question.

Sometimes, people that think they might have heard a gunshot are reluctant to report that they heard the sound. One form of reluctance is due to their being unsure of what the sound really was. You don't want to officially claim that there was a gunshot if the sound turns out to be fireworks, or maybe a car that backfired making an abrupt boom. No sense in wasting the time of the authorities to track down something that was relatively innocent and unnoteworthy.

Another form of reluctance is based on the belief that others will report the incident, therefore there is no need for you to do so. The irony here is that oftentimes nobody at all reports the gunfire because they all assume that certainly someone else is or has already done so. Police indicate that they will frequently find out after-the-fact that many people heard the noise and yet opted to not report it since they "naturally" assumed that someone else would.

According to some nationally reported statistics, supposedly only about 20% of overheard gunfire is being reported. One supposes that some don't report gunshots if they believe that there is little valuable information that they can provide.

For example, people are unlikely to be able to definitively identify how far away the gunfire was. The glaring sound of a gunshot can carry for a lengthy distance. Perhaps the gunfire that you thought you heard is not anywhere close to your neighborhood.

Besides the distance away, there is also the matter of where or at least in what direction did the gunfire come from. Anyone that hears such a sound while quietly sitting in their home is bound to have trouble trying to provide a reliable indication of where the origin of the gunshot was. Maybe it came from somewhere far in the distance in front of your house, or perhaps it was more so toward the back of the domicile. Any shot that is far away will also likely echo around and it might be tough to pin down where it started.

Perhaps surprisingly, some people report gunfire and can even indicate that they can discern what type of gun was likely being used. These tend to be people that served in the military or that own a gun or otherwise have an interest in guns. For them, the instant they hear a gunshot, they can pretty much ascertain what type of weapon was used. Their ears are tuned to what gunshots sound like and how they differ by the type of gun involved.

You might be wondering why it would make any difference whether people opt to contact the authorities to report hearing a gunshot.

It makes a big difference in terms of protection for everyone and can demonstrably aid law enforcement efforts.

Somebody willing to shoot a gun while in a normal everyday neighborhood or community is endangering the lives of those that live there or that perchance happen to be there. We've all read the headlines about knuckleheads that fired a gun on July 4th as a celebratory act, and sadly the bullet or bullets came raining down and injured or killed someone. The shooter didn't seem to be intending to produce such an outcome and got carried away at the moment, nonetheless, the act of wantonly shooting a gun is usually illegal and ill-advised.

Of course, the gunshot could also be associated with a heinous crime underway. Maybe a carjacking is taking place and the criminal has shot at the driver of a car. Perhaps a gang is having some form of a shootout. And so on.

Shots fired reporting by the public can significantly make a difference in many crucial ways. The police might otherwise not be aware of the criminal activity taking place. By being made aware, they can respond accordingly, possibly stopping the crime and preventing mayhem. Also, ambulances can be put on alert in case someone has been shot and medical assistance is urgently needed.

Okay, so it usually makes sense to report promptly when you hear a gunshot and provide as much detail as you can muster. When the police receive a multitude of such reports from the public, they can use the info to try and triangulate where the gunfire might have originated from. In addition, they can compare and contrast the reporting, using the bits and pieces of what people believe they heard to try and piece together a more robust picture of the likely particulars.

In other words, suppose a bunch of houses all have someone that opts to report a gunshot sound. If the preponderance of the reporting indicates that the gunfire came from the west, this is probably a telltale indication that indeed that's the direction of origin. One house might say the sound was very close, and another might say it was faraway. By using those indications, it might be feasible to pin down a relatively specific location.

One facet that comes to play involves time.

People start to call about a gunshot after say a minute or two of hearing one. Some wait longer, some call sooner. Meanwhile, the clock is ticking. By the time that the calls are all reported, and the info assembled and analyzed, this means that the shooter has had an opportunity to scoot away or hide. Thus, the sooner that the reporting can occur and the faster that the analysis can occur, the more likelihood of being able to find and stop the gunfire activity.

This gunshot detection is a recurring problem in some cities.

To cope with the matter, there are technological capabilities that can aid in performing detecting gunshots. Here's the way that it usually works (note that different forms of tech can be used, depending upon the circumstances at hand).

One approach consists of placing special devices at key spots around an area that gunshots are potentially expected to occur. These devices are typically acoustical, meaning that they listen for sounds and can measure the impulse sound waves produced by a gunshot.

In addition to listening for the gunshot, sometimes these devices will also use an optical sensor, seeking to detect the muzzle flash of the gun that produced the gunfire. You don't usually think about the muzzle flash as a clue about a gun being fired. You might be surprised to know that the muzzle flash can create quite a bright light that can be seen from a large distance, especially for an optical sensor that is solely focused on detecting such a sudden burst of light.

Besides acoustical detection and possibly an optical detector, there is the possibility of using infrared sensors. Furthermore, some of the latest devices also include a video camera. The video camera is ostensibly used to either video the act of firing the gun or more likely is usually used to figure out license plates and the cars in a given area. The notion is that whoever might have fired the gun might attempt to escape the area in a car, and the video can provide a record of the cars that were in the area at the time of the gunshot.

The placement of these devices is a notable aspect of their utility.

Usually, the devices are mounted onto existing telephone poles, light poles, power poles, and similar structures. The device has to be high enough to be kept clear of obstructions and also not readily toyed with by someone that wants to bust the devices or muck with them. The devices are considered stationary and remain in their static position for however long their use is anticipated to be needed.

The devices also would include an electronic telecommunications capability. This allows the devices to immediately report when a notable sound has been detected (or muzzle flash, etc.). There might be software running on a processor of the device that analyzes the sounds and tries to determine the distance, direction, and whether it was a gunshot or something else that made the noise.

In short, these devices serve to report suspected gunfire. By having many of them, the reporting from the devices can be triangulated, similar to how the same effort is undertaken when people call to report gunfire. Of course, the beauty of the devices is that they are ready, willing, and able to report whatever they detect, doing so 24x7, and can do so with the kind of accuracy as feasible via the sensory units being used.

All told, the deployment of an array of these sensors can quicken the time of detection, which can then demonstrably improve the response time to a scene. This can also cut down on potentially wasted resources whereby the police and ambulances are sometimes sent to respond to the sound of a car that merely backfired, and for which the devices are unlikely to misreport that kind of noise as a gunshot.

The data collected by the devices can also possibly be used in criminal prosecution. When trying to tie the shooter to a scene involving gunfire, there might be few witnesses available. The devices can potentially provide needed evidence to showcase what took place and who was involved.

Not everyone necessarily welcomes these gunshot detection systems.

One concern is the potential privacy intrusions that might occur. Suppose the microphones of the devices pick-up the conversations of people that perchance are walking near the devices or live in the vicinity of them. Also, the video cameras are presumably going to capture the license plates of all vehicular traffic, and this might seem disturbing to those that live in the area. Etc.

Communities that seek to put up a gunshot detection system will oftentimes wrestle with the benefits of the capabilities versus the downsides of using such tech. There are ways to try and mitigate the privacy qualms, though there are tradeoffs involved. In any case, there is no denying the aspect that the gunshot detection system is likely going to do a good job of detecting gunfire, albeit with other caveats surrounding the use of such a system generally.

If a community wants to use a gunshot detection system, they will need to either purchase the devices or license their use. There is a cost involved. The devices need to be posted at the respective locations identified as suitable. There is a cost involved in posting them. Over time, assuming the devices are kept in place, there will be maintenance possibly needed, or units replaced if they get damaged by accident or on purpose. There is a cost for that too. Eventually, it is conceivable that the devices will no longer be needed, and there might be a cost involved in taking them down.

I bring up this point to merely indicate that there is no free lunch about using a gunshot detection system. There are various costs involved, naturally so. That being said, communities that are living under the specter of gunfire are likely to do a cost-benefit analysis and ascertain that the potential for saving lives and turning the community back toward one of safety is worth the cost.

Suppose there was another means to potentially detect gunfire, doing so in a manner that might not seem readily apparent.

Get ready and sit down for this one.

In the future, we will inevitably have self-driving cars (for my coverage see **the link here**). These are cars that are driven by an AI driving system. There isn't a human at the wheel. The belief is that we will eventually have self-driving cars that are serving as ridesharing vehicles, proffering rides at a fraction of the cost of today's human-driven ridesharing options.

One vision of the future is that there will be self-driving cars relatively commonly cruising around, waiting for someone that needs a lift to make a request. Unlike a human driver that might be roaming around and awaiting a ridesharing customer, the AI driving system can easily drive 24x7 and just keep going and going. There aren't any rest breaks or food breaks needed.

Self-driving cars are loaded with state-of-the-art sensory devices. Those sensors are used to figure out the driving scene. Via sensors such as video cameras, radar, LIDAR, ultrasonic units, thermal imagining, and the like, the AI driving system collects the detected data and tries to mathematically calculate where to drive.

Here's where I am going with this.

Imagine if we could leverage those self-driving cars to become a kind of gunshot detection system. This might be a handy means to rapidly identify when gunfire occurs. In that manner, you are getting two birds with one stone. The self-driving cars are already roaming for use as passenger transportation, and they could potentially do double duty as a gunshot detector.

Today's intriguing question is this: *Would it be feasible to leverage the advent of AI-based true self-driving cars in a quest to undertake the detection of potential gunfire?*

Let's unpack the matter and see.

**Self-Driving Cars And Gunshot Detection**

For Level 4 and Level 5 true self-driving vehicles, there won't be a human driver involved in the driving task.

All occupants will be passengers.

The AI is doing the driving.

One aspect about self-driving cars that I keep pressing on is the notion of what I refer to as the roving eye. Essentially, self-driving cars are going to capture on video and via their other sensors the everyday world around us. When a self-driving car goes down your block, it will video and collect data about the homes, the cars parked in driveways and on the streets, and even video that shows you and your kids are playing in your front yard.

This data is sometimes being immediately discarded by the on-board processors and only used from moment-to-moment for purposes of determining the driving aspects of the vehicle. In other cases, the data is collected into an internal database on-board the car. Furthermore, the data is at times uploaded via OTA (Over-The-Air) electronic communications into the cloud being used by the fleet operator or the automaker.

It would make sense to collect the data and make use of it. For example, the data could be utilized to potentially improve the driving capability of the AI driving system. I've also pointed out that the data could be used in a myriad of other very positive ways, such as providing ongoing and timely info about real estate in a given area, and so on.

The use of the data could also be used as a crime deterrent. If a criminal tries to commit a crime, there is a chance that a roaming self-driving car might have caught them on video. It could be that a multitude of roving self-driving cars each caught the crook in different stages of the crime, and the pieces of that puzzle could be put together to tell the whole story.

Could self-driving cars be used for detecting gunshots?

Yes, there is a possibility of doing so.

The sensors could be used to visually detect the gunfire and possibly detect the shooter. In terms of listening for the sound of gunfire, that's something that would take a bit of an extra step. Allow me a moment to briefly explain.

Some self-driving cars do not yet have microphones on-board that are aimed outside of the vehicle. Gradually, this is happening, since the automakers and self-driving tech firms are realizing that hearing the sounds of an area can be handy for driving purposes. For example, the siren sound of a fire truck or an ambulance can be quite important when driving a car.

Whether the acoustical detection of the types of external-facing microphones being used would be sufficient for also reliably detecting gunshots is something that would depend upon how a maker has outfitted their self-driving cars.

Also, the software stack of the AI driving system is not going to natively have a gunshot detection capability. This is something that isn't on the list of nearly anyone that is focusing on right now getting self-driving cars to safely drive from point A to point B. At best, the idea of developing a gunshot detection capacity is on an edge or corner case list, meaning it has very low priority at this time and might at some future point surface as something worthy of pursuing.

One of the toughest aspects of using self-driving cars for this purpose is the vagaries involved.

By vagaries, I mean that, unlike sensors that are bolted to a light pole or other fixture, the sensors of the self-driving car are integral to the vehicle and therefore are going to be in pretty much continual motion. They aren't planted in a fixed position.

Furthermore, if self-driving cars aren't perchance cruising around in your neighborhood when a gunshot occurs, they won't be useful to the gunshot detection. This implies that the chances of self-driving cars serving as a useful tool in gunshot detection would be based on whether they frequent the area where gunshot detection is desired.

Some believe that we will ultimately have self-driving cars everywhere and at all times. In that case, we will be saturated with self-driving cars and they might perchance be in the right place at the right time to aid in detecting gunfire. That's a long time from now, and so don't hold your breath waiting for this to soon arise.

Nonetheless, it is an interesting consideration. We could potentially leverage the presumed ubiquitous nature of deploying self-driving cars and find another handy aid in doing gunshot detection.

There are plenty of added twists.

For example, there will be a multitude of brands of self-driving cars. This suggests that trying to get them to coordinate their gunshot detection would be logistically challenging. On the other hand, one supposes that they would each include a feature that reported directly to a central authority and left the analysis aspects to others. In that way of thinking, the self-driving cars are solely acting as data collectors and not doing the rest of the gun detection effort.

**Conclusion**

Some argue that it would make little sense for the automakers and fleet operators to enter into this gunshot detection realm. Those firms might be accused of serving a form of Big Brother that is doing the legwork for the authorities. Also, if their collected data was utilized for gunfire detection, it might end up being used in criminal cases and the automaker or fleet operator would get dragged into legal matters that seem quite afield of their emphasis on self-driving cars per se.

Another possibility would be for those specialized firms that are devoted to gunshot detection systems to pair with a self-driving car operation. In a sense, you could use the static sensors as one layer of detection, and leverage the self-driving cars as an additional layer of detection. It is easy to see that this might provide added coverage.

That last point is important because some might be thinking that the days of those that today provide gunshot detection systems are being counted down as the rise of self-driving cars looms ahead. Not so. There is a much greater likelihood of the two joinings together, rather than self-driving cars somehow driving them out of business (a bit of a rough pun there).

# CHAPTER 8
# KEEPING INSIDE OF SELF-DRIVING CARS

Here's an important announcement: Please keep your hands, feet, and head inside the vehicle at all times.

That's something you've undoubtedly heard countless times when taking a ride on a roller coaster or perhaps when going on a tourist bus that is taking you on a safari. The notion is quite simple. For your safety, keep within the confines of the vehicle. This is not only for your safety, but as they emphasize, it also can entail the safety of others too.

Prudent advice, which sometimes goes in one ear and out the other.

It seems as though there are invariably some violators that think they are an exception to the rule about staying inside the vehicle. They frantically put their arms outside the window and wave as though the world is their oyster. They are willing to stick their head out as far as a giraffe, or perhaps if on a safari allow their head to butt heads with an actual giraffe.

Admittedly, these violations are generally benign and nothing adverse comes from them. Even on a thrilling roller coaster, most ride designs ensure that someone with outstretched legs, feet, arms, hands, and head are going to survive and not get hurt. There is a sufficient gap, usually, between however far outside the vehicle you can reach and any kind of structures that might ding you or do worse damage to your appendages and your noggin.

I don't want to seem to be a sour doomsday admonisher, but betting your limbs on the assumption that someone has made sure you are going to be okay when violating the outstretching rules is quite a gamble. The cost to you is going to be extraordinarily high. There are plenty of news reports of people that got badly hurt upon the act of getting some part of their body smushed (or bitten) as a result of extending beyond the expected reach.

The same principle about staying within a vehicle can readily apply to riding in an everyday automobile.

You might have seen videos of frustrated ridesharing drivers that have had to gently and then severely berate some passengers that have gone hog wild while inside the ridesharing car. This seems to especially happen during the infamous spring break and when those carefree college kids are on their joyous vacation. They get into the car that has come to pick them up, and nearly instantly they roll down the windows and start flailing out to whoever will look at them. Party, party, party.

I suppose this seems innocent enough. Shouldn't they be able to enjoy their time off from taking exams and having to hit the books? Yes, having a good time seems fair, though perhaps after a few too many drinks, they are amping up their chances of getting hurt.

How so?

There are numerous ways to get your hands, feet, or head into a really rotten situation. For example, the traffic might be so tightly squeezed together that one of your appendages gets banged against the side of another vehicle or perhaps clipped by an outcropped side-view mirror. If driving in an area with a lot of trees, there is the oft chance that a tree branch is close enough to the roadway that you could bang against it.

Probably the more likely untoward scenarios involve what will happen if the driver of the car has to suddenly and unexpectedly hit the brakes. The odds are that extending yourself out of a window will involve foregoing your seatbelt or at least pulling beyond the proper standard lengths. Upon the powerful forces of physics when rapid braking occurs, you are going to not have the full safety associated with the seatbelt. On top of that, your exposed limbs could rock back and forth and potentially get pinned or otherwise banged up.

None of that goes through the mind of those that are having a good time. Until they should ever experience the downsides of having part of their precious body outside and get severely harmed, the odds are they will not mentally calculate the dangers involved. It is all fun and games. Anyone that has seen or directly experienced what can go wrong is likely to be worried on the behalf of those that naively don't know what potentially awaits them.

The driver of the vehicle is usually tasked with the unenviable chore of trying to coax people to get back within the requisite and appropriate confines.

Any ridesharing driver or tourist bus driver is somewhat hesitant to play the role of the bad guy in terms of scolding riders that have gone beyond the limits of what is reasonable. The driver doesn't want to upset the passengers. The driver is hoping to get a nice monetary tip. The driver wants the riders to feel like they are having a grand old time. Nonetheless, the driver is ultimately going to be held responsible for the unsavory deeds of their riders.

Some drivers try to establish the rules at the get-go and add some humor or other clever form of emphasis to make sure the rules about staying inside the car are properly grasped. You might liken this to those flight attendant briefings about safety while on an airplane. Most passengers do not pay attention to the briefing. On the other hand, if the flight attendant tries to make the briefing somewhat memorable, the hope is that the passengers will pay attention and then also abide by the rules so conveyed.

To some degree, warning riders about not extending outside the windows or the allotted safe space can be especially handy for those that might have taken such an act by accident of sorts. We can find ourselves impulsively waving our arms or sticking out our necks, doing so without giving much thought to the matter. A rider is oftentimes feeling as though they are not directly responsible for what happens while someone else is doing the driving. Drivers tend to feel the weight of responsibility for their "crew" upon the ship that they are sailing (one could suggest that the driver is the captain, as it were).

When I've been referring to windows, there is also the opportunity to extend beyond a sunroof or moon-top of a car. Those are windows that are aimed at the stars above are pretty common these days. You can open the roof and allow the wind to gush into the vehicle, giving a sense of truly being on the roadway. At the same time, it is quite possible that a passenger might stick their head outside of the rooftop opening. I don't need to tell you what could go wrong, it seems relatively self-evident.

Now that we've covered that groundwork, let's consider the future of cars. The plain fact of things is that the future of cars consists of self-driving cars. AI-based true self-driving cars are driven by an AI driving system and there isn't a human driver at the wheel.

Without a human driver, one serious concern that can arise (after giving the matter some soulful thought) is that the passengers might become even more careless and "carefree" about what they are doing while inside the vehicle. As mentioned earlier, the driver is usually the caretaker of making sure that the riders won't get themselves into dire postures.

Today's intriguing question: *Will the advent of AI-based true self-driving cars include having the AI driving system warn riders about keeping their hands, feet, and head within the vehicle and if so, what will make this admonishment have any substantive teeth to it?*

Let's unpack the matter and see.

**Self-Driving Cars And Rider Admonishments**

For Level 4 and Level 5 true self-driving vehicles, there won't be a human driver involved in the driving task.

All occupants will be passengers.

The AI is doing the driving.

One aspect to immediately discuss entails the fact that today's AI is not sentient.

In other words, the AI is altogether a collective of computer-based programming and algorithms, and most assuredly not able to reason in the same manner that humans can. I mention this aspect because many headlines boldly proclaim or imply that AI has turned the corner and become equal to human intelligence. As if that wasn't bad enough, the outsized headlines seek to amp further the matter by contending that AI is reaching superhuman capabilities is inappropriate.

Why this emphasis about the AI not being sentient?

Because I want to underscore that when discussing the role of the AI driving system, I am not ascribing human qualities to the AI. Please be aware that there is an ongoing and dangerous tendency these days to anthropomorphize AI. In essence, people are assigning human-like sentience to today's AI, despite the undeniable and inarguable fact that no such AI exists as yet.

With that clarification, you can envision the AI driving system doesn't natively somehow "know" that people are apt to extend their hands, feet, or head outside the windows or confines of the car. The AI doesn't "know" that the riders can get physically hurt and possibly severely damaged by taking such action. And so on.

Those are all facets that need to be programmatically devised by the automaker or self-driving tech firm that makes the AI driving system. If they aren't considering those facets, there won't be anything somehow innately in the AI driving system that will "realize" that humans are foolish or foolhardy when it comes to such practices.

Right now, most riders in any of the self-driving cars that are doing these experimental tryouts are taking the ride as a quite serious matter. They are excited to be inside a self-driving car. They are unsure of what to do. They act as though they are in a veritable delicate store or shop of glassware and crystal, wanting to avoid touching anything that might upset the ride or get themselves into trouble.

Once self-driving cars become prevalent, you can toss that timidity out the window. Indeed, you can fully expect that riders will decide that they can really let loose while inside a self-driving car. They know that a human driver is not there to boss them around. This means that they can presumably do whatever they wish. Wild times are at hand.

In short, if the AI driving system is not augmented to act as a parental-like influencer in this particular matter, riders are going to be giddy and feel that they are being given a free license to have a rowdy time.

You can readily imagine the extensive lengths to which some riders might go. With today's world of wanting to have selfies and gain your own bit of fifteen minutes' worth of fame, there are assuredly going to be some that will carry things a bridge too far. One shudders to think of how people might dangerously even attempt to crawl out a window or ride on the trunk or hood of the vehicle. There is also the crazy possibility of trying to shake hands with someone in a car next to you or other nutty approaches.

The lack of a human driver opens the door to some rather frightening antics. Those antics can produce extremely unfortunate consequences. As they say, it might be sensible to try and close the barn door before the animals get loose. This means that the AI driving systems should caution riders about staying within the confines of the vehicle.

Of course, that seems a pretty simple thing to do. Just have a prerecorded message that plays each time that someone gets into a self-driving car. There, that's all you need to do.

Would that be sufficient?

Not really.

It is akin to those flight attendant briefings. People would probably listen intently the first time they heard or saw the precautionary warning. By the second or third time of riding in a self-driving car, they likely would be already sticking out their feet, hands, and head, doing so either by outright ignoring the droning cautionary words or maybe by being reminded about what they aren't supposed to do (and, therefore, ironically, opt to do that very thing).

There needs to be more than just the telling of what to not do.

A human driver would watch for misbehaviors of riders and then sternly inform them to stop their antics. If the driver felt that things were going overboard (a bit of a pun!), they would have ways to try and assure compliance. This might involve stopping the ride and telling the riders that they are on their own and cannot continue the driving journey. Another possibility entails informing the riders that they will be placed onto a "banned" list that means they won't be able to use that ridesharing service again. Etc.

These are all feasible actions for an AI driving system too.

Again, this would need to be programmatically devised and won't happen merely by an amorphous hope of sentience. Let's dig a bit further into these rider dunning modes.

First, how will the AI driving system detect that passengers are going outside the confines of the vehicle?

Keep in mind that self-driving cars are outfitted with a slew of sensors, including video cameras, radar, LIDAR, ultrasonic units, thermal imagining, and the like. These are sensors that are usually aimed away from the vehicle. This makes sense because the idea is that the sensors are trying to detect the driving scene that surrounds the vehicle.

That also tends to imply that those sensors are not going to be especially helpful when trying to figure out what the riders are doing. The usual sensor suite is intended to figure out what pedestrians are doing, what other cars are doing, and not necessarily paying any attention to the interior of the self-driving car.

There are though likely to be additional video cameras that are pointed inward. This allows for providing a Skype-like capability that would enable passengers to do interactive online activities, such as conferring with people at work while commuting in a self-driving car or perhaps taking an interactive online class for some added training.

The AI driving system could be augmented by using those inward-facing cameras and do so to detect misbehaviors of those within the self-driving car. Woefully, some people might be tempted to mark graffiti for tear-up the interior, thus the use of video cameras would hopefully curtail that kind of miscreant activity.

One aspect of the video cameras that are pointing inward is the fact that you are being recorded. This implies that at some later time there is a record or proof of something that you did wrong. That doesn't though deal with the real-time aspects of someone attempting to reach outside the windows of the car. Thus, the AI driving system or its augmented component would presumably be continually monitoring the riders and be programmed to figure out when someone tries to outstretch. A form of facial recognition that applies to the body and appendages would generally be capable of making these types of detections.

You might be thinking that the AI driving system should just deny anyone from being able to open any of the windows. In essence, lock the doors and lock closed the windows. That solves the problem entirely. Yes, it might, but the odds are that passengers are not going to favor a self-driving car that won't let them roll down a window. People are still going to want the "thrill" of having the wind blowing on them and the sensation that they are riding inside a moving car.

Okay, so people are going to be able to open windows of self-driving cars. The AI driving system or its augmented component will be mathematically scanning the video camera images to detect if someone is reaching outside the windows. If someone does so, the AI will produce a verbalized alert and inform the transgressor to please pull back into the car. And if the violator continues to be unwilling to abide, the AI would presumably indicate that the ride will be safely brought to a halt, and the passenger is going to be placed on a banned-rider list.

That's all part of the normal playbook of a human driver.

In case you are concerned that people will feel upset that a piece of automation is telling them what to do, another possibility would be for the AI to contact a remote agent of the fleet operator. The remote agent, a human, would come online and tell the rider to please obey the instructions given. In this manner, it is a fellow human being that is doing the chaperoning, as it were, rather than the AI system.

Will people be concerned that they are under constant surveillance by the AI driving system via the use of those inward-facing cameras (a potential privacy intrusion of some magnitude)?

You might try to argue that this is no different than a human driver watching their passengers. One supposes that there is a bit of a difference, namely that the rider is being videotaped in the case of the self-driving car. Their every move and activity is being diligently recorded. That can be disturbing. At the same time, many of the ridesharing services have their human drivers doing the same thing right now, and thus you are not necessarily avoiding the video capture by simply taking a human driver rather than using a self-driving car.

With all of these potential controls in a self-driving car, there is admittedly a chance that those that are purposely aiming to have an "outstretched" ride (wherein they can stick most of themselves outside the car) are going to gravitate back toward a human driver rather than using a self-driving car. The odds are that a human driver can be swayed into allowing that kind of craziness.

**Conclusion**

Additional caveats are involved in this matter.

For example, just because someone inches out their fingers and hands, this doesn't seem to warrant getting the fifth degree and being excessively harangued. Indeed, that kind of policing would certainly make riders decide they don't want to use self-driving cars. The point is that the programming of the AI that is going to be doing the real-time video analysis will need to be devised to allow for some *reasonable* amount of going out-of-bounds.

Assuming that the AI is devised to provide a bit of latitude, you can just hear the glowing review by a rebellious teenager that took a ride in a self-driving car and was allowed to wave at their friends, saying that the AI was a cool driver, and they ended up giving the ride a stellar five-star rating.

The parents would undoubtedly showcase a knowing grin, realizing that fortunately their beloved teen has all their limbs still intact, and be appreciative that the boundaries of riding inside a self-driving car were being judiciously observed.

Somebody, or something, has to make sure that those hands, feet, and head remain whole and are kept safely inside the vehicle at all times.

# CHAPTER 9
# ROUTING BIASES AND SELF-DRIVING CARS

Which way to go?

During a recent ridesharing lift, the driver offered that my trip from the airport to my home could either be undertaken via an inland route that would take about 25 minutes, or alternatively the route could primarily be scenic via a beach-going route that would require nearly 35 minutes of travel time. The driver was entirely willing to take whichever of the two routes that I preferred.

If I was in a hurry, certainly I would have chosen the shorter-timed trip. This choice might not have been as breathtaking, but it would at least get me to my destination in a 10-minute sooner timeframe. On the other hand, for just a pittance of an added 10 minutes, the trip via seeing the waves and long stretches of sandy beaches seemed alluring and irresistible.

Yes, I opted for the ocean view and figured that the totality of selecting the longer ride was probably better for my overall mental health and psychic well-being anyway.

The fact that I was given a choice is somewhat unusual, I would assert. It seems that most occasions of taking a ridesharing journey are usually pre-ordained by the use of today's marvelous GPS systems. The computer algorithms doing the routing are amazingly good at what they do. In days past, the algorithms were somewhat crude and simplistic, oftentimes solely based on the distance involved to try and determine which was the "best" route to take.

Humans know that distance is not the only determining factor of how long a driving trip will take.

You can readily pick a shorter distance that will get bogged down in gnarly traffic. You inch along at a snail's pace. Another route that was longer in miles driven could easily be much shorter in terms of time consumed during the travel effort. The point is that you need to consider not just the distance since that's only one perspective on the problem. What kind of traffic might be encountered? Are there lots of stop signs or traffic signals? Are the streets being torn-up for roadway repairs? Etc.

Selecting the right routing can be a bit of a chore.

Of course, modern-day routing algorithms have a myriad of factors that they take into account nowadays. This means that human drivers do not need to put much thought into the routing aspects anymore. Just bring up the GPS, enter the destination, and you'll quickly get a quite sound travel path laid out for you.

Easy peasy, as they say.

The GPS that the ridesharing driver was using for my trip from the airport did not encompass the notion of a scenic trip versus a drabber inland trek. That wasn't part of the algorithmic properties. This was something that the driver knew first-hand, having driven in the area for many years and by living generally in the nearby vicinity. Also, the driver indicated that prior riders had sometimes explicitly requested a beach-going path, so he regularly brings up the matter on an upfront basis rather than waiting for passengers to ask about it.

The motivation didn't seem to be about money, though that was perhaps on the mind of the driver. Imagine that if a rider reached their destination and found out from a friend that they could have taken the scenic route, yet the driver didn't mention the possibility, perhaps the tip or rating of the driver would get dinged accordingly. That's the version wherein the driver failed to be proactive and gets penalized accordingly.

Another result could be that by informing riders of the choice of possibilities at hand, the driver might get a larger tip. You see, even if someone selects the inland route, they are likely to be appreciative that an additional option was offered. This might spur the rider to give an extra tip. Meanwhile, if the rider does take the scenic path, the odds are ostensibly heightened that the passenger will leave a boosted tip, doing so because of the joy involved in seeing the spectacular views.

All in all, the driver seems to come out a winner.

Drivers that don't consider the notion of providing an option are going to lose out. They are either blissfully unaware of the alternative path or perhaps they are just willing to abide by whatever the GPS indicates. Since the rider might also have the GPS mapping available, the driver might also figure that it is easiest to simply drive as the GPS instructs, otherwise, the rider might question what kind of underhanded trickery the driver is up to.

That's why this particular driver was seemingly astute enough to ask.

Had the driver chosen to take the scenic route and let's say opted to not mention this rerouting to me, I might have gotten suspicious. We've all experienced those shady taxi rides wherein the driver goes half-way around town to stretch out a driving trip, bolstering the meter charges astronomically. A ridesharing driver doesn't want to get into that type of dicey predicament and possibly lose their privileges with the ridesharing network service that they were dispatched on.

Anyway, this specific example dealt with the choice of going inland versus taking an ocean view route. There are certainly other criteria or characteristics that could lead to a similar situation. In other words, there might be something about a GPS proposed routing that is not necessarily the end-all in terms of which way to proceed. A driver might have in their mind additional factors worthy of potential attention.

Let's try a somewhat akin use case.

Suppose the driver told me that there were two potential routes.

One that would take me through parts of town that were extremely unseemly, and the other route that would be a kind of everyday route with nothing unusual or untoward along the way.

What might the unseemly categorization consist of? Perhaps some areas are covered with graffiti. Maybe there is a ton of trash all over the streets and sidewalks. Such an area might have known gang activity and frequent shootings. There might be a slew of statistics that showcase the area to be a high crime locale and altogether dangerous to be in.

If you were given such a choice, which route would you pick?

You might be wondering what the difference in the driving time might be. It could be that you'd be okay with the blighted route if it cut down demonstratively on the time for the journey. Or you might insist that no amount of saved time would be worthwhile in exchange for driving in the sordid area. Another consideration might be the time of day for the ride. If the ride is in the middle of the daytime, perhaps the risks are lessened. A ride through that part of town at say midnight might be an entirely different consideration.

To recap, we have ridesharing drivers that might or might not mention to passengers that there are alternative routes to a given destination. A typical computer-based GPS might not take into account all of the factors that a human driver might consider and instead optimize solely on driving time and distance. A ridesharing driver might choose a preferred route without necessarily informing the passenger or might let the passenger know what their choices are and have the rider decide which route they prefer.

To some extent, this routing question is on the shoulders of the driver.

Sure, there is the GPS system that is providing the most likely route. We can pretty much assume that by-and-large the ridesharing drivers will just go ahead with whatever the GPS indicates. No sense in fighting city hall, as it were. Furthermore, there is a slight chance that asking a passenger about their route preferences might cause some riders to get upset, feeling as though this is something the driver ought to know, and they are wasting the time of the rider in dealing with a straightforward matter.

Shifting gears, let's consider the future of cars and the advent of self-driving cars. The emergence of AI-based true self-driving cars will entail the use of computer-based AI driving systems. This means that there will not be a human driver at the wheel.

How might that impact this routing conundrum?

The simplest answer is that the AI driving system will stridently perform or execute the GPS algorithm indicated routing. Whatever the GPS spits out, that's what the AI driving system is going to undertake. If this means going the inland route, so be it. If this means going the unsightly route, so be it. There won't be any semblance of challenging what the GPS instructs.

Well, actually, that is an overly simplistic way of thinking about the situation.

There is a lot more to this.

Time to dig a bit deeper.

First, be aware that right now the automakers and self-driving tech firms are putting the preponderance of their focus toward getting a self-driving car to safety go from point A to point B. For this focus, there isn't much of a care about which way the GPS says to go. Assuming that the GPS is providing drivable paths, the rest of the matter is up to the AI driving system being able to navigate and maneuver along those designated streets and highways (well, as long as the Operational Design Domain or ODD is also being observed).

Flash forward to the future and imagine that self-driving cars are relatively prevalent.

The odds are that self-driving cars are going to be organized into fleets. A fleet operator will have numerous self-driving cars in a particular area and make those vehicles available for ridesharing purposes. For example, having self-driving cars roaming around an airport is likely to be a smart thing to do. Flying travelers arriving at the airport are going to undoubtedly need a ride to somewhere in town.

Okay, so we've got a slew of self-driving cars that are meandering around near the airport, waiting for requests. The thing is, there might be numerous fleets all competing for that same passenger business. I've got my fleet of self-driving cars near the airport, and you've got yours there, and likewise so do other fleet operators.

Why would a potential passenger choose one of the self-driving cars over another?

We'll make the somewhat obvious assumption that all of the self-driving cars are generally equal, namely, they are driving at the same level of safety, they are indistinguishable one from the other. I'm not saying they are all the same models or brands of vehicles, only that from the perspective of wanting a ride, they are nearly the same as a convenient form of ground transportation (we can also assume the cost is about the same too).

Presumably, I want people to select my fleet over your fleet. This makes sense since I want to try and maximize my revenue and keep my self-driving cars busy. An empty roaming self-driving car is pretty much going to be losing money while wandering. When a passenger is riding in a self-driving car, this generally means that someone is making money by that activity. The moment that a prospective passenger chooses your fleet over mine, I am saddened and there is a hole in my pocket (the money being lost to you).

I've got to come up with some other means to attract passengers. The vehicle itself is not going to be the differentiator.

Aha, the routing might be a handy way to make my self-driving cars more attractive.

We know that human drivers are apt to provide those tailored insights about which path to take. A standard GPS might not be imbued with those kinds of particulars. Thus, for my fleet, a specialized GPS is devised, one that leverages what human drivers know about a region and therefore can accordingly provide a wider or more introspective selection of routes.

Here's the envisioned future. A fleet operator advertises that their self-driving cars are using a super-duper enhanced GPS routing algorithm. This algorithm will ensure that you never end up getting routed through the bad parts of town. No worries when you get into their self-driving cars since their chosen routes will always avoid the unseemly or unsightly areas.

Guaranteed, or your money back.

Some would say that this is a useful and an above-board way of doing things. Others though would decry this kind of routing and the flagrant and abdominal advertising that goes with it (I'll explain why, in a moment).

Here's then an intriguing question: *Will the advent of AI-based true self-driving cars potentially include skirting around the bad parts of town, automatically so, and what makes that a potentially controversial concern?*

Before we unpack the matter, it will be useful to clarify what is meant by referring to an AI-based true self-driving car.

### Self-Driving Cars And Routing Aspects

For Level 4 and Level 5 true self-driving vehicles, there won't be a human driver involved in the driving task.

All occupants will be passengers.

The AI is doing the driving.

For fleet operators that are in charge of running a slew of self-driving cars, there is something they will especially delight in and altogether not miss at all. As tough as it is to say this aloud, the beauty for fleet operators is that there be won't be any human drivers involved in the fleet. All the driving is being undertaken by AI driving systems.

Human drivers need rest breaks. They need food breaks. They need bathroom breaks. All told, they are humans.

They also drive in ways that utilize human foibles. Human drivers are at times driving in a distracted manner. The distraction can be readily apparent such as watching a cat video when their eyes should be on the roadway, or the distraction can be nearly impossible to discern such as a driver that just had a fight with their boss and therefore mentally become preoccupied when now behind the wheel of a moving car.

Despite these qualms about human drivers, as per the discussion earlier, there is the possible advantage of them knowing the local area. This can make a big difference in terms of where they drive and where passengers will be taken.

The individualistic aspects of driving are going to be weaned out of the act of driving.

Human drivers are each of their own driving mores and mannerisms. Within the bounds of driving lawfully, there is a tremendous amount of latitude about driving. For self-driving cars, of a specific brand or model, will generally drive in the same manner, assuming that the street scene is the same (in other words, a self-driving car going down a street that has a dog on the loose is going to be driving somewhat differently from a similar self-driving car in a case where there isn't a dog loose on that street).

If a fleet operator wants to instruct all of their human drivers to avoid a certain part of town, this is somewhat problematic to do but assuredly straightforward and extremely quietly possible via the use of an AI driving system.

Why does this possibility get the dander up by those that eschew the notion?

They argue that this kind of across-the-board consistency and ease of avoiding certain parts of a town or city is going to be bad for everyone. People taking rides in self-driving cars will never realize that a certain part of town is in rough shape and needs bolstering. The act of skirting that area is tantamount to denying that there are issues there that need to be dealt with and resolved. Furthermore, this could also lead to few if any riders every getting dropped off in that part of town. This in turn could depress the business activity in that area. There is less opportunity for businesses to set up shop there, knowing that self-driving cars are not likely to be dropping people off in those locations.

In essence, the mass routing of self-driving cars to avoid a given area of town could have the adverse indirect consequence of turning that part of town into a kind of isolated desert, cornered off from the rest of the city or county that it resides within.

Some pundits point out that there might be new regulations needed to try and overcome this kind of outcome.

Perhaps there would be legally imposed restrictions that self-driving cars could not be programmed to avoid specific parts of town. If a route to a given location went through a "bad" part of town, this could not be routed around. Whatever is the optimal path, regardless of where it goes and assuming that optimum is based solely on time and distance, that's how the self-driving car must operate.

Others express that this would seem overhanded. Why place the burden on the backs of the self-driving cars and the fleet operators? If a part of town is being avoided, the city or town authorities ought to take this as a sign that they need to do something to rectify that situation. Turn around that part of town and make it thriving, such that self-driving cars and fleet operators will gladly route into those areas.

Another idea is that those areas that are being avoided ought to potentially offer incentives to the fleet operators, trying to get self-driving cars to come into those areas. Of course, the counter-argument is that those areas might not be able to come up with those incentives, by the very fact that they are already in bad shape, to begin with.

## Conclusion

This issue will not yet appear until we have a greater prevalence of self-driving cars on our roadways. The number of experimental tryouts is much too small to make this kind of conundrum noticeable at this juncture of the self-driving car advancement.

Some various twists and turns will further arise. For example, consider this chilling notion. We know and already accept that if a human driver is menaced by a pedestrian in the middle of the street that is brandishing a weapon, the car driver will likely take evasive driving action. The human driver might try to drive away from the person, or possibly even drive toward the person, using the vehicle as a means of deterring the threatening act.

Self-driving cars are assumed to be programmed to never threaten a pedestrian. If a human opts to walk out in front of a self-driving car, we naturally hope that the AI driving system will bring the self-driving car to a stop. A human driver might not do so in the case of a pedestrian that is armed and the driver believes that the most prudent action entails a battle of car versus human.

The point is that when a self-driving car goes into an area that might have a lot of crime, presumably the criminals would know that the self-driving car and the AI driving system will always back down. In that case, it would potentially be relatively effortless for such crooks to try and stop and carjack those self-driving cars (or take other horrific actions).

Overall, there is going to be a lot of handwringing and new issues to be dealt with as our society experiences the advent of self-driving cars. Some mistakenly or naively believe that there is nothing societally different about whether a car is being driven by a human versus an AI system, but that kind of thinking is going to have a rude awakening.

Seems prudent to be considering these matters now, rather than waiting for the day that the horse has already gotten out of the barn, such that those wonderous self-driving horseless cars have already become ubiquitous as our primary form of vehicular travel

# CHAPTER 10
# BLURRING DATA AND SELF-DRIVING CARS

Have you ever taken a picture and realized that a person in the snapshot appears blurry due to your camera being out of focus?

I'm sure you have.

In some cases, the blur happens by accident, whereby you should have set the focus but failed to do so. It was merely an oversight. If you perchance discovered the issue right away, hopefully, you were able to quickly take another photo and delete the remiss one. Problem solved.

There are also situations involving the use of a blur for intentional purposes.

Perhaps you have a few friends that want their pictures taken. Behind them are people partying and making quite a scene. You don't want the background to overtake the attention to the foreground, namely the gaggle of your best friends that are aching to have a quality shot taken. So, you set the focus to make the background blurry and ensure that the foreground is nice and sharp.

Suppose that you indeed take such a picture and keep it around on your smartphone. A few weeks later, someone asks you if George or Samantha were in attendance at the event. You are pretty sure they were, though your memory is a bit hazy (potentially due to the numerous margaritas that you had).

Wait for a second, they might have been in the background of that photo that you took of your dearest friends. You go ahead and pull-up the picture to check it out. Unfortunately, the blur is overwhelming and there are no easy means to discern who else was captured in the snapshot.

Why all this discussion about blurs in images?

The use of a blurring technique can potentially be useful as a means of trying to attain a level of privacy for those that might be captured on an image or a video. This might entail blurring the face of someone. It could involve blurring their entire body and whatever kinds of motions they made. The blur is obscuring information and making it difficult to ascertain what was in the image or video. That can be a good thing if you are aiming to provide privacy to those caught on tape.

As with most things in life, there is also a downside involved too. In the example about trying to ferret out whether George or Samantha was at the party, the blurred portion of the photo was unable to help in answering the question about their presence. There are likely lots of instances whereby a blurred aspect makes some potentially useful information only marginally handy and possibly entirely unusable.

Your mileage will vary, as they say, depending upon whether you are desirous of having blurs or are downtrodden that blurs are at hand.

Shifting gears (I promise to come back to the blurs in a moment), let's talk about cars.

The future of cars consists of self-driving cars. These are cars that have an AI driving system at the wheel of vehicle. The driving actions are undertaken by the AI. No human driver is making use of the driving controls.

An important element of self-driving cars is the use of various sensors to detect the driving scene. These sensory devices are the veritable eyes and ears of the AI driving system. For most self-driving cars, the types of sensors encompass video cameras, radar units, LIDAR units, ultrasonic devices, and the like. The array of sensors are mounted on the vehicle and are used to figure out where the roadway is, where other cars are, where pedestrians are standing, and so on.

This seems relatively innocuous and there isn't much attention being given to the plethora of sensors that self-driving cars contain. No big deal, it seems, since the sensors are logically required to sense the world that surrounds the vehicle. Without those sensory devices, the AI driving system would be blind to what is happening around the car.

Here's the rub.

Those sensors can capture a lot more than you might at first imagine that they do.

Envision that you put a video camera on the top of your conventional car. You turned it on and set it to record, doing so continuously. You then decide to drive from your home to the local grocery store.

What happens during that rather routine drive?

Your video camera is capturing all the activity that you perchance come across. For example, after backing down your driveway, you drive down the block to the corner. Turns out that your neighbors next door were in their front yard. They were tossing a baseball back and forth with their children. That seemingly everyday activity is now captured onto your video camera recording.

I believe you get the gist of the matter.

The point being that with that merely one video camera mounted on your conventional car, it will be collecting videos about the daily lives of anyone that you happen to drive past. Let's up the ante. Suppose that all of your neighbors put video cameras on the rooftops of their cars too. They will also now be recording anything that they encounter while on any driving journey.

Welcome to the emerging world of self-driving cars.

Those seemingly heralded self-driving cars are going to be

capturing imagery and other data about whatever they detect, wherever they go, all of the time that they are underway. Keep in mind that there is an assumption that eventually, we will predominantly have zillions of self-driving cars on our roadways, and very few conventional cars.

Returning to your neighborhood and the idea of video cameras mounted on a few neighborhood conventional cars, ratchet this up to assume that all cars that come down your street will have a full suite of state-of-the-art sensors (because they are self-driving cars). Those advanced vehicles will be amassing a lot of information about the comings and goings on your block.

If self-driving cars were empty and simply roaming the community to be available for any ride requests, they would be capturing daily activity.

Whenever someone takes a ride in a self-driving car, it will capture the surroundings that are along the path to the stated destination. By riding in a self-driving car from your home to the local store, the self-driving car will record video and other data about whatever was taking place during that time period.

Please sit down for this next shocker.

I don't want to get you on the edge of your seat, but imagine that this massive amount of data was collated and assembled to try and piece together the daily efforts in a city or town. In theory, you could pull together the data from all of the self-driving cars and pretty much recreate a semblance of where people were, when they were there, what they did while there (assuming they were outside or otherwise visible), etc.

I've referred to this as the roving eye of the coming era of self-driving cars.

You could say that this roving eye will be a marvelous addition to our society. There are numerous positive uses. For example, you want to see the latest real estate in an area that you are considering buying a home. It is conceivable that the data from self-driving cars could be used to see exactly what the homes look like, nearly up to the minute.

This can also be used for crime-fighting. A burglar tries to break into someone's house. The crook scoots away before being caught. Turns out that there were self-driving cars that happened to be along that street during the time period of the criminal activity. The sensory data is examined, and the identity of the thief is figured out.

There are some notable downsides too.

Do you want just anyone to know where you were on last Monday or Tuesday? Presumably, an inspection of data from self-driving cars might show that you were in front of your house, mowing the lawn, on Monday morning. You then left your house and walked down the street to visit a friend at another house. You stayed there for about two hours. And so on.

Some people are worried about privacy intrusion from video cameras that are mounted on telephone poles or that are used by people as they carry their smartphones. Those are peanuts in comparison to the magnitude of video and other sensory data capturing those self-driving cars will undertake.

The more we adopt and utilize self-driving cars, the greater the amount of observing of our daily lives that will occur. It's as simple as that.

Are we doomed to come under the crush of a Big Brother dystopian world by accepting self-driving cars as our preferred mode of transportation?

Sadly, not many are considering this issue and it won't visibly arise until there are enough self-driving cars that the kind of overlapping and semi-continuous recording rises to a level of noticeability. Until then, we will be laying the seeds for the future that will seemingly catch us by "surprise" about what we have done to ourselves over time.

Shucks, you might be thinking, if this is a looming problem, perhaps something ought to be done, sooner rather than later. There must be some means to keep from digging a hole that appears to be a quite disturbing abyss.

Aha, allow me to bring up an old friend of sorts, namely the blur.

The earlier discussion about the blurring of information was in fact the "answer" before I had presented you with the question at hand.

Similar to how a blurring effect was able to mask whether George or Samantha was at the wild party, the same kind of notion and capacity could be used for dealing with the data that the roving eye detects and collects.

Here is an intriguing question to ponder: *Will the advent of AI-based true self-driving cars and their roving eye be potentially made more societally palatable via the use of blurring?*

Let's unpack the matter and see.

**Self-Driving Cars And Roving Eye Blurring**

For Level 4 and Level 5 true self-driving vehicles, there won't be a human driver involved in the driving task.

All occupants will be passengers.

The AI is doing the driving.

One aspect to immediately discuss entails the fact that today's AI is not sentient.

In other words, the AI is altogether a collective of computer-based programming and algorithms, and most assuredly not able to reason in the same manner that humans can. I mention this aspect because many headlines boldly proclaim or imply that AI has turned the corner and become equal to human intelligence. As if that wasn't bad enough, the outsized headlines seek to amp further the matter by contending that AI is reaching superhuman capabilities.

Why this emphasis about the AI not being sentient?

Because I want to underscore that when discussing the role of the AI driving system, I am not ascribing human qualities to the AI. Please be aware that there is an ongoing and dangerous tendency these days to anthropomorphize AI. In essence, people are assigning human-like sentience to today's AI, despite the undeniable and inarguable fact that no such AI exists as yet.

With that clarification, you can envision the AI driving system doesn't natively somehow "know" that the sensors are capturing a lot of information that might be considered intrusive.

Those are facets that would need to be programmatically devised by the automaker or self-driving tech firm that makes the AI driving system. If they aren't considering those facets, there won't be anything somehow innately in the AI driving system that will "realize" that society doesn't want that kind of pell-mell collecting of our daily activities.

With that important context, let's dig into how this might work.

Recall that when discussing the act of taking a picture, one point made was that the background could be out of focus and thus blurry, and likewise the foreground could be out of focus and blurry.

There's not much debate that the foreground of any sensory detection by a self-driving car is going to be crucial for the driving of the vehicle. As such, the foreground is ostensibly going to have to be kept in focus.

The more open-ended question is whether the background needs to be kept in focus too. In other words, suppose that the sensors were calibrated to ensure that anything in the background was blurry. This might help to overcome the otherwise wanton avid capturing of daily activities that are not particularly crucial to the driving of the vehicle.

Of course, you can readily argue that this dividing line between the foreground and the background is altogether untenable.

Suppose that a dog is running around in someone's front yard. We probably would want the self-driving car to detect that a dog is up ahead, and though currently inside a yard, the dog might decide to dart into the street once the self-driving car comes along.

If there is a purposeful blurring when the sensors are trying to detect the driving scene, it could be that vital clues about the surroundings would no longer be readily usable. This in turn could mean that the AI driving systems will not be able to drive as safely as we would hope for.

Some would assert that it makes absolutely no sense to intentionally undercut the capabilities of the sensors. Indeed, those proponents would undoubtedly contend that we need even stronger sensors that have increasingly piercing capabilities, being able to do detection that is far above that of what humans might be able to do.

Under that rather strident thinking, we might wish to momentarily herein set aside the notion of trying to prevent the sensors from capturing whatever they can potentially detect. Assume that the sensors are going to be allowed to detect as much as they can.

The sensory data flows into the on-board processors of the self-driving car. At that juncture, the data is mathematically examined for purposes of driving the car. The AI driving system tries to computationally interpret the data to figure out the driving scene. Upon doing so, the AI driving system figures out the driving action to undertake and emits commands to the vehicle accordingly.

You could suggest that the data from the sensors could now be discarded since it has been used for its primary purpose. In that way of thinking, there is no need to worry about what is contained in the data. Just dump it out, after it has been used for the driving act. Ergo, the data cannot now presumably be used for any nefarious purposes since it isn't sitting around anymore. The moment that the sensory data has been analyzed for driving purposes, make sure it gets deleted.

That is the end of the road for the sensory data.

Well, that presents a couple of challenges.

First, it means that you can't potentially use the data for the other augmentable upside possibilities that were mentioned earlier. The data won't be around and therefore it can't be used to figure out the latest aspects of real estate or be used to catch those despicable criminals. Some would argue that you are possibly tossing out the baby with the bathwater (an old-time expression).

Secondly, you cannot necessarily guarantee that the data will be deleted. Once you've let the data into the onboard systems, this is like letting the horse out of the barn, or the cat out of the bag. Sure, you might believe that the data is going to be deleted, and the system might be programmed accordingly. Nonetheless, the data can potentially be kept, despite the otherwise desired notion of deleting it.

In that viewpoint, you either are going to not capture the data at all, or you are going to capture it and need to do something with it.

This is where an intentional blurring comes to play.

One approach consists of taking the data after it has been examined for driving purposes and then blurring the data so that those elements that are generally considered irrelevant to the driving act can no longer be readily discerned. You don't necessarily delete those aspects, you blur them.

A difficult question arises about when the right timing is to do the blurring.

If you do so while the data is fresh and just brought into the on-board systems, this means that you need the computational resources on-board to do this type of blurring action while the car is underway. Some would argue that whatever computational processing you've got ought to go entirely towards the driving act. Do not usurp those precious processing cycles from the life-or-death matters of driving the vehicle.

Okay, in that perspective, we might have some background process that does the blurring when the self-driving car is parked and not underway. Or basically whenever there is spare processing time available.

Another notion is that you could do the blurring once the data has been uploaded into the cloud. You see, it turns out that self-driving cars are going to be using OTA (Over-The-Air) electronic communications to connect with the cloud of the fleet operator or automaker of the self-driving car. This would be used to readily push down crucial updates to the AI driving system. It can also be used to upload data from the self-driving car and into the cloud.

Thus, some would say that you shouldn't use any processing on-board the self-driving car for the blurring and instead let it happen in the cloud. The self-driving car would upload whatever data it has collected. This data would be in its rawest form. The cloud processing by the fleet operator or automaker would be programmed to then blur the data.

Sorry to report that this chain of where the data is going and what its status consists of will open a bit of Pandora's box.

For example, suppose that the raw data in its entirety is being kept on-board the self-driving car. Once it gets loaded up into the cloud, perhaps at that juncture it is deleted from the on-board processors (a copy now exists in the cloud). Unfortunately, this does mean that for some length of time, the data is sitting there in the vehicle, in all its glory. There is nothing blurred as yet. This leaves open the chance that the data could be somehow siphoned or copied and now be made available with everything it has to show.

That's why some vehemently argue that the data ought to be blurred at the soonest possible opportunity.

Of course, there are other matters intertwined. The data is likely in an unencrypted format upon first flowing into the on-board systems. Some would urge that the data be right away encrypted. In that manner, you don't necessarily need to worry about the blurring, since anyone that could surreptitiously get the data won't have anything useful due to the encryption.

This brings up that there are two camps typically at logger's heads here. One camp says that the full and unblurred data should never be allowed to leave the car. In that sense, it should not be allowed to be uploaded to the cloud. Only once it has been blurred, and possibly encrypted too, can it be uploaded. The other camp says that it is fine to upload the whole shebang, and as long as it is encrypted, you just blur it after getting into the cloud.

**Conclusion**

There are a lot more monkey wrenches that can be thrown into this thorny matter.

Let's suppose that the data does get blurred. We are presuming this implies that there is no longer the qualm about being able to detect that your neighbors were playing catch with their kids in their front yard.

Sometimes, that which can be blurred can, later on, be unblurred.

This means that the blurring might be undone. If the images or video is allowed to be copied, you could use all sorts of unblurring techniques to try and turn the blurred aspects into something discernible. It might not be recast into its original pristine state, but at least given sufficient definition that perhaps it once again is intruding on privacy.

The cat and mouse gambit of the blurring algorithms is an ongoing battle. Someone comes up with a newer and better blurring routine. Someone else then comes out with a new-and-improved unblurring approach. Round and round, it goes.

At this time, few are worrying about the roving eye of self-driving cars.

Over time, perhaps my exhortations will only become a blur, though I am really hoping they become unblurred in time for appropriate thought and action to be taken about this mesmerizing and rather clear-cut dilemma.

There really is no blur about it.

# CHAPTER 11
# AUTONOMOUS VEHICULAR CLOUDS

Any farmer will tell you that sometimes a planted seed takes a while to grow.

In the field of autonomous vehicles (AVs), there has been ongoing talk about the advent of the *vehicular cloud,* which is gradually and inexorably going to take root.

Let's take a deep dive into the expanding ways of how this specialized form of cloud computing is arising. Someday, mark my words, the vehicular cloud will be a mighty redwood tree in the sense of altogether existent and standing tall, and we'll likely look back at the amazing aspect that it all began in such modest ways.

As I've previously indicated in my columns, the use of cloud computing and the inclusion of the cloud as integrated into the emergence of autonomous vehicles portends a quite vital match. When I refer to autonomous vehicles, perhaps a more commonly used vernacular would be to mention self-driving vehicles (note that today's headlines usually refer to self-driving rather than using the somewhat formalized and academic-sounding AV moniker). For purposes of this discussion, consider that the notion of self-driving and the notion of autonomous vehicles are generally the same.

There will be self-driving cars, self-driving trucks, self-driving motorcycles, self-driving drones, self-driving submersibles, self-driving planes, self-driving ships, and so on. These are everyday forms of transportation that will entail an AI-based driving or piloting system that is at the wheel of the craft. The basis for garnering the acclaimed banner of being autonomous will be because the vehicle will be entirely operated by machine and without the need for any human-guided effort.

An especially notable intertwining of self-driving vehicles in conjunction with the cloud entails the capability of using OTA (Over-The-Air) electronic communications. The vehicle will have various on-board computer processors and hard drives or similar electronic-oriented memory technology, along with sensors for detecting the outside world, and will be equipped with communication devices for connecting with the cloud.

The OTA will allow for software updates to be downloaded into the vehicle, providing a remote updating facility. In addition, data collected by the vehicle can be uploaded into the cloud. There is continuing debate about how much data should be kept in the vehicle versus pushed up into the cloud, along with strong viewpoints about the implications of having these "roving eyes" amid the plethora of data that will be collectible.

Okay, so there are these self-driving vehicles, and they are going to be leveraging the use of the cloud.

The cloud can provide a place to store data that was first obtained via self-driving vehicles. Also, the cloud can make use of vast and powerful computing resources that are otherwise not readily encompassed within the vehicles themselves. The computational processing capabilities within the vehicle are focused on the self-driving activity, plus they are not of the outsized supercomputing realm that can be found within the cloud.

A typical high-tech cloud-based setup for autonomous vehicles involves taking conventional cloud computing and marrying the access to and use of self-driving vehicles into the normal elements of the cloud. Various customized components are likely needed to ensure that the conventional cloud aspects are tailored to the specifics of autonomous vehicles.

You might be leaping ahead mentally and perhaps be assuming at this juncture of the discussion that perhaps this conventional cloud is therefore a presumed *vehicular cloud* because it has been honed toward the nature of autonomous vehicles.

Sorry, that's not quite accurate and there is still a bit more to the story. Please continue reading.

First, be aware that there is another variant of the cloud that not many people generally are aware of, something referred to as the mobile cloud.

The mobile cloud is kind of a reverse version of what you might normally associate with traditional or conventional cloud computing. I'm betting that you think of conventional cloud computing as computer resources that are available online and are variously collected together as though somehow centralized in their configuration.

Well, here's a bit of a twist for you.

Imagine that the mobile devices that we carry around are miniature variants of available computing resources. Your smartphone is handy for purposes of texting with others and can store all your favorite vacation pictures and those spectacular selfies that you've taken. That smartphone in your pocket is a computing device that has computational capabilities and also can store data.

Suppose that you asked a friend to keep some of your photos on their smartphone, perhaps due to your smartphone getting low on available memory. You could send those prized photos to your friend and they would (hopefully) dutifully keep them on their smartphone. At some later time, you might ask your friend to send them back over to you.

This is essentially the underpinnings of a mobile cloud.

You could ask all of your many friends to do likewise with each other, in the sense of every one of them sharing their computational resources with one another (via their respective smartphones). These are mobile devices. They are being treated as though they are part of a larger collective or cloud. As such, the appropriate name for this phenomenon would be to call it a mobile cloud.

Alright, there is the conventional cloud and there is also the potential for a mobile cloud. Two types of clouds.

Some mistakenly think that these are perhaps bitter enemies, as though they are competing for the royal crown of being the true cloud. That's nonsense. These are appropriate variations of the "cloud" and they are perfectly able to coexist and work hand-in-hand. No bickering cats and dogs, as it were.

Trying to successfully pull off a mobile cloud is a tougher row to hoe.

Consider even the simplest case of you sharing your photos with your friend, and they now have a responsibility of making sure that they don't inadvertently delete those photos or perhaps let someone else see them. The mobile cloud can have a semblance of the wild west associated with it. This is partially why you don't see that much heralding the advent of the mobile cloud.

In any case, we have now established the basis for bringing up the *vehicular cloud.*

Are you ready?

Those emerging autonomous vehicles that are self-driving cars, self-driving trucks, and the like, can be characterized as computers-on-wheels. This makes indubitable sense since to bring about autonomous or AI-based driving requires an impressive amount of computing capabilities. When a human does the driving, you don't necessarily need gobs of computers on-board. For an AI-based driving system, you have to put into the vehicle a cavalcade of computing capabilities.

Self-driving or autonomous vehicles are inherently mobile. That's what they do. We use them to get around and traverse from point A to point B. In that manner of thinking, you could say that self-driving vehicles are mobile devices. Just as your mobile smartphone gets carried around from place to place, an autonomous vehicle carries you around from place to place.

The significance of this realization is that potentially we could leverage the computers within the vehicles for purposes beyond that of driving the vehicle. This seems a mental stretch for some people. Perhaps this will help. You likely store in the trunk of your car some goodies, such as spare bottles of water, a jacket, some camping gear, and so on. In that manner, you are using the vehicle as a storage medium.

Autonomous vehicles will have a lot of computer memory on-board. You could potentially store your photos in that onboard computer memory. When you needed to retrieve the photos, you merely connect with the vehicle via an electronic means and grab those photos that you had stored there. This is somewhat similar to the mobile cloud notion that was described earlier.

With all of that in mind, the definition of the *vehicular cloud* is a form of a cloud that consists of a combination of the mobile cloud, the conventional cloud, and vehicles.

Simply stated: *Vehicular cloud = Conventional cloud + Mobile cloud + Vehicles*

The reference to vehicles is usually intended to be autonomous vehicles. The reason for defaulting to autonomous vehicles is that they are chockfull of computing. That being said, there is certainly room in this realm to include semi-autonomous vehicles too (they also have extensive computing resources).

We'll clarify that: Vehicles = *Autonomous vehicles + semi-autonomous vehicles*

In case you are wondering what constitutes autonomous versus semi-autonomous, a quick indication about the levels of autonomy associated with self-driving cars might help to provide needed clarity.

**Delving Into Vehicular Clouds**

Returning to the points made about the vehicular cloud, there is this ingenious combining of the conventional cloud, along with the notion of a mobile cloud, along with the inclusion of vehicles that range from semi-autonomous to autonomous.

Some wonder why in the world would you seek to make use of the computing available on the vehicles.

This seems entirely counterintuitive at first glance. Just let the vehicle do its thing, performing the self-driving, and call it a day.

One answer that is perhaps smarmy, relates to why people climb mountains, namely because the mountains are there (an old joke, for sure).

Today's use of cars is a rather wasted or enormously under-utilized economic and societal asset. Most cars sit around for about 95% to possibly 98% of their available usage time. You drive your car to work and park your car. It stays there unused during your eight-hour shift or longer workday. You drive home and park your car in your garage. It stays there unused during the nighttime and until used the next morning.

As a form of transportation, your car is woefully untapped.

Toss a slew of state-of-the-art computing resources into a vehicle. You've just added an additional resource, one that is not exclusively for bringing about transportation (the computers can be used for other purposes, though admittedly some of the computing is specific to the self-driving function).

As such, a vehicle that is jampacked with handy computing resources and if it is going to sit in a parking lot or your garage for the preponderance of its time, those are sadly wasted or underutilized computing resources that could be put to use.

As a form of available computing, a self-driving vehicle could end-up being woefully untapped.

We could put that computing to other useful purposes. The thing is, to do so would require somehow connecting them and being able to harness that immense array of computing, doing so sensibly and systematically.

Welcome to the *vehicular cloud.*

Yes, that does make sense.

It is economically and societally sensible to leverage the computing available in modern vehicles.

You can straight out utilize the raw computing horsepower. The collective available computing will eventually be enormous. There are about 250 million conventional cars in the United States alone, and predictions are that those will eventually give way to self-driving cars. This won't happen overnight. Gradually, conventional cars will be mothballed, and the prevalence of self-driving cars will increase over a decades-long period.

We don't yet know how many self-driving cars will be required to achieve the equivalent transportation needs availed by the existing 250 million conventional cars.

Some pundits assert that we will need a lot fewer self-driving cars to cover what today is a primarily idled set of conventional cars. Other pundits anticipate that we will witness a huge surge in the use of ground transport whence self-driving cars become available, and thus it could be that we might need as many or even more self-driving cars due to the factor of induced demand.

Besides the raw computing power, there is also the use of the sensory devices that will be on autonomous vehicles (and, to some degree, also included on semi-autonomous too). In theory, it would be possible to tap into using the sensory devices, or at least perhaps using the data that the sensory devices provide.

### Conclusion

There are of course challenges that come with the vehicular cloud.

Some worry that tapping into the computing of an autonomous vehicle would cause a "distraction" during the driving or piloting task.

Trying to compute the value of pi to the zillionth digit is a lot less important than making sure that the vehicle safely makes its way in the world. Those that are developing autonomous vehicles would need to ensure that the computing resources for driving are given the highest of priority and perhaps even block-off or turn away any other requests while the vehicle is underway.

Another concern is whether this leveraging of the computing resources in a vehicle might enable the implanting of a computer virus by a cybercriminal. One shudders to consider the implications of what an evildoer virus might achieve while inside an autonomous vehicle.

The answer there is that this is already something that has to be at the forefront of autonomous vehicle developers. Adding a vehicular cloud to the mix does not somehow imply that without the vehicular cloud there is no risk.

Via the OTA that self-driving vehicles are going to include, there are plenty of ways to try and usurp the on-board systems. The point is that the proper security provisions for autonomous vehicles need to already be included.

There is an interesting aspect too about whether autonomous vehicles will have much available "extra" computing anyway.

Here's the logic.

Human-driven vehicles are subject to the needs of human drivers. A human driver indubitably gets tired and must stop driving else they will be driving erratically and dangerously. Human drivers need breaks for food, for using the restroom, for whatever. Self-driving vehicles don't need those kinds of breaks in the action. Presumably, a self-driving vehicle could be going 24x7, subject to the limitations of refueling and maintenance. The general assumption is that self-driving cars will be operating continuously, driving around while awaiting a passenger request for a ride.

If that's the case, we no longer need to be concerned about vehicles that are unused for the preponderance of their available time. And, the logic follows that the computing resources will also be utilized to the same extent, namely that they will be focused on the driving chores and not be available for any other purposes.

Of course, we don't know that this belief or assertion that self-driving vehicles will always be on the go is valid. Maybe they will be, maybe they won't. Even if they are on the go, this does not necessarily imply that all of the computing resources are soaked up toward the driving chore.

This all told hopefully provides you with some intriguing food for thought about the future of transportation, and likewise the future of computing and the cloud. Some refer to this as the Vehicular Cloud (VC), others call it Vehicle Cloud Computing (VCC), and some prefer to use the phrasing of the Autonomous Vehicle Cloud (AVC) as the signature naming.

Whatever you might like to call this, the odds are that it is going to be big. Just like those majestic redwood trees that grow to gargantuan sizes, the future of the *vehicular cloud* looks equally exalted.

# CHAPTER 12
# EDGE CLOUDS AND SELF-DRIVING CARS

Cats versus dogs.

Wrong!

Instead of saying cats *versus* dogs, it would be better to emphasize cats and dogs.

Anyone that has watched online videos about cats and dogs would certainly see that these two beloved animals can get along. There is nothing more endearing than to see an excitable dog and an effervescent cat that opt to play together, plus sharing a hard-earned nap side-by-side, and otherwise relishing jointly their coexistence on this planet.

Yes, they can coexist and even become BFFs (best friends forever).

What tends to tear them apart in non-domesticated settings amid the wilds of nature involves the bitter fight for survival and having to battle over scarce food that they both are seeking desperately to obtain. One can certainly understand how being pitted against each other for barebones survival purposes might get them into fierce duals when keystone nourishment is on the line.

Some distinctive animalistic behavioral differences enter into the picture too. For example, dogs delight in chasing after things, and thus they are prone to chasing after a cat that they might perchance spy and seek to play with. Cats aren't necessarily aware that the dog is giving chase for fun and are apt to therefore react as though the pursuit is nefarious.

Another aspect of a notable difference is that dogs tend to wag their tails when they are happy, while cats usually whisk their tails when they are upset. From a dog's perspective, the cat's tail wagging might seem like a friendly gesture and an indication that all is well. From a cat's perspective, the dog's tail whipping back-and-forth might be interpreted as a sign of an angry beast that ought to be avoided. In that sense, you could conjecture that the difficulty of having cats and dogs get along is based on everyday miscommunication and misunderstanding of each other.

Why all this discussion about cats and dogs?

Because there is another realm in which there is a somewhat false or at least misleading portrayal of two disparate entities that supposedly don't get along and ergo must be unpleasant adversaries. I'm talking about edge computing and the cloud.

Some pundits claim that it is edge computing *versus* the cloud.

Wrong again!

The more sensible way to phrase things entails striking out the "versus" and declaring edge computing <u>and</u> the cloud (for those of you that prefer that the cloud get first billing, it is equally stated as the cloud and edge computing; you are welcome to choose whichever order seems most palatable to you).

The point is that they too can be BFFs.

Let's consider a particular context to illustrate how edge computing and the cloud can work together hand-in-hand, namely within the realm of autonomous vehicles (AVs).

As avid readers of my column are aware, I've emphasized that we are on the cusp of some quite exciting days ahead for the advent of autonomous vehicles. There is a grand convergence taking place that involves high-tech advances, especially in the AI arena, along with continued miniaturization of electronics and the ongoing cost reduction of computing that is inexorably making AI-based driving systems efficacious.

When I refer to autonomous vehicles, you can generally interchange the AV moniker with a reference to self-driving, which is the somewhat informalized and less academic-sounding way to describe these matters. There are autonomous cars, autonomous trucks, autonomous drones, autonomous submersibles, autonomous planes, autonomous ships, and so on that are gradually being crafted and put into use. You can readily recast this by saying there are self-driving cars, self-driving trucks, self-driving drones, self-driving submersibles, self-driving planes, and self-driving ships, rather than using the AV naming.

A rose by any other name is still a rose.

For this discussion about the cloud and edge computing, it will be easiest to perhaps focus on self-driving cars, though you can easily extrapolate the remarks to apply to any of the other self-driving or autonomous vehicle types too.

How does the cloud pertain to self-driving cars?

That's a straightforward question and an equally straightforward answer.

Via the use of OTA (Over-The-Air) electronic communications, it is possible and extremely useful to push new software updates and patches into the on-board AI driving system of a self-driving car. This remote access capability makes the effort to quickly apply the latest software an enormous breeze, rather than having to take the vehicle to a dealership or car shop and physically have the changes enacted.

OTA also provides for uploading data from the on-board systems up into the cloud. Self-driving vehicles have a slew of sensors that are used to detect the surroundings and figure out where to drive. In the case of self-driving cars, this oftentimes includes video cameras, radar, LIDAR, ultrasonic units, and the like. The data collected can be stored within the vehicle and can also be transmitted up into the cloud of the fleet operator or automaker.

You hopefully have a quick gist now of what the cloud and self-driving cars have in common.

Next, consider the nature of edge computing and how it applies to self-driving cars.

Edge computing refers to the use of computer-based systems that are placed at the "edge" or near to the point at which a computing capability is potentially needed. For roadway infrastructure, there is earnest interest in putting edge computing devices along our major highways and byways. The notion is that this computing facility would be able to keep track of the nearby roadway status and electronically signify what the status is.

Imagine that you are driving along on a long and winding road (hey, that's something worthy of making a song about). You are dutifully keeping your eyes on the highway and are trying to drive with abundant care and attention. Unbeknownst to you though is that there is some debris about a mile up ahead, sitting smackdab in the middle of your lane.

Without getting any kind of precautionary alert, you are bound to unexpectedly come upon the debris and react impulsively. Perhaps you swerve to avoid the debris, though this veering action might cause you to lose control of the vehicle, or maybe you slam head-on into traffic coming in the other direction. Had you been tipped beforehand about the debris you could have prepared to cope with the situation.

Assume that an edge computing device has been placed along that stretch of road. The edge computer has been getting info about the roadway and accordingly taking action. Upon getting notified about the roadway debris, the edge computer has contacted the local authorities and requested that a roadway service provider come out and remove the debris. Meanwhile, this edge computing device is also acting as a kind of lighthouse beacon, sending out an electronic message to alert any upcoming traffic about the debris.

A car that was equipped with a receiver that could read the edge computer emitted signals could let a human driver know that there is debris up ahead. In the case of a self-driving car, the AI driving system would be receiving the signal and opt to plan the driving task to deal with the soon to be reached debris.

There are major efforts underway to develop and deploy V2I (vehicle-to-infrastructure) capabilities that would undertake the kind of activities that I've just depicted. We will eventually have traffic signals that are more than simply light-emitting red-yellow-green lanterns. You can expect that traffic signals will be packed with computing capabilities and be able to perform a host of traffic control tasks. The same can be said for nearly all types of roadway signs and control features. The speed limit can be conveyed electronically, in addition to being shown on a signboard.

Since we are discussing V2I, it is worthwhile to also mention V2V (vehicle-to-vehicle) electronic communications.

Cars will be equipped to send messages to other nearby cars via V2V. Returning to the debris scenario, suppose a car came upon the debris and no one else had yet encountered the obstruction. This first car to do so could transmit an electronic message to alert other nearby cars to be wary of the debris. Other cars that are within the vicinity would presumably pick-up the electronic message and then warn the driver of the vehicle accordingly.

One aspect of V2V that comes into question is the longevity of such messages. If there is a bunch of car traffic, they would all be sharing about the debris. On the other hand, if the first car to encounter the debris sends out a message, but there isn't any other nearby traffic, this implies that the debris warning won't be hanging around and able to forewarn others. A car that perchance comes along an hour later on this perhaps somewhat deserted highway will not be within range of the other car and therefore not get the helpful warning.

This is a key point in favor of edge computing as an augmentation to V2V (or, in lieu of V2V if not otherwise available).

An edge computing device could be stationed along a roadway and be scanning the V2V messaging.

By examining the V2V crosstalk, the edge device opts to start beaconing that there is debris on the road up ahead. This now allows for greater longevity of the messaging. Even after that first car is long gone and much further away, the edge computer can continue to make any additional traffic aware of the situation. Note that it is also possible that the car finding the debris might have done a direct V2I to the edge device, in which case that's another means for the edge computer to discover what the status of the roadway is.

Time for a twist in the tale.

I mentioned earlier that some are suggesting that edge computing and the cloud are at logger's heads with each other. You might be puzzled as to how cloud computing and edge computing are rivals when it comes to the self-driving car setting that I've described (they aren't, but some are claiming that they are).

Here's the (vacuous) assertion.

Those pundits are claiming that the time lag of the cloud versus edge computing means that the cloud is unsuitable for self-driving cars, while edge computing is suitable since it is a lessened latency (by-and-large) for electronically communicating with those in-motion self-driving vehicles.

We can unpack that contention and reveal that it is invalid overall.

First, it will be useful to clarify the difference between autonomous vehicles and semi-autonomous vehicles.

**Delving Into Edge Computing And The Cloud**

Returning to the point made about the claimed slowness of cloud access in contrast to edge computing access, you'll see in a moment that this is a generally legitimate distinction but that it is being misapplied and used in a misguided or misleading manner.

As an aside, there are obviously instances whereby the access to a conventional cloud could be slower than access to an edge device (all else being equal, we might expect this), but there are also instances whereby the cloud access might be faster (though, likely rarer, depending upon numerous technological assumptions).

Anyway, do not be distracted by the ploy about the access timing. It is like one of those infamous card tricks or hat tricks, getting you to look elsewhere and not keeping your eye on the ball. The trickery involves an allusion to the idea that an autonomous car is going to be taking active driving instructions from either the cloud or edge computing. To this, I say hogwash. Admittedly, some are pursuing such an approach, but I've previously and extensively argued this is a dubious avenue.

Here's what I mean.

Consider for a moment the role of a human driver when approaching the earlier depicted scenario about debris being in the roadway. A human driver might receive a message, however so received, whether by text message, phone call, etc., letting them know that there is debris up ahead. The human driver then decides to perhaps slow down, getting ready to potentially come to a stop. Upon reaching the debris, the human driver opts to veer into the emergency lane to the right of the roadway, undertaking a means to deftly drive around the roadway debris.

Notice that the driving actions were entirely performed by the human driver. Even if a text message might have said to slow down and get ready to aim to the right of the debris, nonetheless the final choice of how to drive the car was on the shoulders of the driver. They merely received hints, tips, suggestions, or whatever you want to call it. In the end, the driver is the driver.

The reason for covering that seemingly apparent aspect of the driver being the driver is that (in my view) the AI driving system has to be "the driver being the driver" and not be *driven* via some remote outside-the-car entity.

If messages are coming from the edge device about what to do, the AI driving system is still on-its-own, as it were, needing to ascertain what to have the driving controls undertake. The same thing applies to any communications with the cloud. The AI driving system, despite whatever the cloud might be informing the vehicle, should still be "the driver" and undertaking the driving task.

I think you can see why latency would be a crucial matter if the AI driving system was dependent upon an external entity to actually drive the controls of the vehicle. Just imagine that a self-driving car is moving along at say 75 miles per hour, and there is an external entity or being that is controlling the driving (such as a human remote operator). All it takes is for a split-second delay or disruption in the communications, and a calamity could readily result.

Okay, so if the AI driving system is the driver, this also implies that the latency from the edge computing or the cloud should not make a demonstrative difference per se. Just as a human driver cannot assume that something external to the car is always available and always reliable, the driving aspects have to be dealt with by the on-board AI driving system and do so regardless of available externally augmented info.

In the roadway debris example, suppose that there is an edge computing device nearby that logged an indication about the debris, and accordingly is beaconing out an electronic warning. A car is coming along. In a perfect world, the beacon signal is detected and the driver is forewarned.

In the real world, perhaps the beacon is faltering that day and not sending out a solid signal. Maybe the edge device is broken and not working. Furthermore and alternatively, whatever device on the car that picks up the signal might be faulty. And so on.

As long as the AI driving system considers such connections as supplemental, there is not a glaring issue per se, since the AI is presumably going to cope with the debris upon directly detecting the matter. Sure, we would prefer that a heads-up be provided, but the point is that the heads-up is not essential or an incontrovertible requirement to the driving task.

Some might misinterpret this point as though I am suggesting that there should not be any such external information being provided, which is not at all what I am saying. Generally, the more the merrier in terms of providing relevant and timely info to a driver. The key is that the driver, even without such info, must still be able to drive the car.

**Conclusion**

The use of edge computing and the use of the cloud for self-driving vehicles is decidedly not one of a win-lose affair, and instead ought to be considered a win-win synergy. Unfortunately, it seems that some feel compelled to pit the advent of edge computing and the advent of the cloud against each other, as though these two have to be acrimonious enemies. Use the edge, don't use the cloud, because of the claimed latency aspects, these pundits exclaim.

They are making a mishmash that doesn't hold water in this context.

One might (generously) excuse their misguided viewpoint as being similar to misunderstanding the wagging of the tail of a dog and the whisking of the tail of a cat. In any case, trying to rile up a sensible and peaceful coexistence into a seemingly adverse battle or struggle of one over the other is not particularly productive.

A last thought for the moment on this topic.

The remaining and beguiling question is whether the somewhat analogous example entailing the dogs and cats means that the cloud is the dog and the edge computing is the cat, or perhaps the dog is the edge computing and the cat is the cloud. I'll ask my beloved pet dog and cat what they say, and maybe let them duke it out to decide.

Well, then again, I know that will likely take things in stride, gently nudging upon each other as they mull over this thorny question, and they are likely to arrive at an answer that they both find delightful. That's just how they are.

# CHAPTER 13
# LIP-READING AND SELF-DRIVING CARS

Spy movies used to include a pivotal moment involving a secret agent that would surreptitiously read the lips of someone seated at a table while behind a pane of glass such as in a distant restaurant or high-rise building. Upon cleverly deciphering the mouthing words of what the person was saying, the secret agent would finally know the truth about a crucial matter.

Such is the glory of being able to do lip-reading.

The ability to read lips is considered a vaunted skill and one that can be challenging to master. This capability to do speech reading is pretty tricky in a myriad of ways.

First, you need to be able to visually see the lips of the person that you are trying to decipher. That might seem like an obvious requirement, but the point is that sometimes the lips are not particularly easy to see. The person doing the speaking might have their hands up toward their mouth, partially covering their lips from view. You see this happen intentionally in baseball games when the catcher goes out to the mound to chat with the pitcher, and they both cover their mouths with their baseball gloves.

Besides trying to see the lips of a speaker, it really makes quite a difference if you can also see their entire mouth, their teeth, their jaw, their head, their neck, and so on. Turns out that the delivery mechanisms of speaking are apt to entail all of those anatomical elements. Lips alone are somewhat limiting in terms of discerning what someone is saying.

Another vital factor involves the language that the speaker is employing. If you aren't familiar with the language that someone is using, the odds of making any sense from the movement of their lips is not especially high. You generally need to know what language they are using and be fluent in that language, to increase the odds of doing the lip reading with any accuracy.

Adding to the arduous aspects is the potential context of the spoken words. In the case of the baseball players, you ostensibly know that they are talking about the baseball game and what the next pitch is going to be (unless, of course, the players standing out at the mound decided to merely do some gossipy chitchat, an aspect depicted comedically in many baseball-oriented movies). For spy movies, usually, the context is that the speaker is discussing some top-secret plans or divulging a secret code that unlocks an unassailable bank vault.

The available lighting or illumination associated with the person speaking is another key element. If their mouth and head are hidden in darkness, the chances of watching their lips move are low. You could try to use other means such as infrared devices and the like. I don't think most of us lug around those kinds of contraptions, though it is certainly the type of thing that we would expect James Bond to be carrying.

We can add to the daunting list of factors that the distance to the subject of interest can make lip readability harder. Presumably, the further away you are as the lip reader, the less distinctively clear cut can you see the lips of the person. And there is the factor of time that indubitably comes to play. Speaking is an act that plays out over time. You need to watch long enough to see a series of words, and then try to figure out how those words are being used in sentences, and ultimately how it all comes together into some form of an overarching narrative.

Whoa, that's a lot of difficulties and showcases why lip reading is a tough skill to master.

Nowadays, there are automated ways to aid in doing lip reading.

The advent of facial recognition by computers has also led to the emergence of facial speech recognition, also known as digital lip reading (that might seem odd as though referring to the lips as digital, but the meaning is that the computer or a digital-based system is doing the lip-reading, rather than a human doing the lip reading).

This has been specially advanced due to the use of Artificial Intelligence (AI) techniques and technologies.

Computational models of the human mouth have become relatively sophisticated and can make the talk-to-text capabilities rather impressive. Probably one of the biggest leaps has come from the use of Machine Learning (ML) and Deep Learning (DL). The use of ML/DL is essentially a statistical and computational pattern matching that can detect recurring patterns, which in this case consist of the moving of lips.

If we feed into the ML/DL a slew of examples that have a person saying certain words and then have lots of people that also state those words, the mathematical calculations can attempt to ascertain a type of correlation between how the lips moved and the words that were being uttered. A difficulty sometimes though is that the ML/DL can overfit the data being used, becoming only capable of detecting words as spoken by the type of language and speakers chosen for the training data set.

Thus, the AI doing the lip reading might not do well when examining just anybody that is using those same words and might be mathematically constrained toward just those that perchance match to the original training set.

Similar in some ways to the human lip-reading difficulties, there is a semblance of statistical accuracy involved. Maybe a word here or there is not able to be deciphered. Some words are detected but are not completely decipherable and therefore have a probability associated with what the word might be. Throughout a speaking sequence, perhaps the lip reading only gets some percentage of the words and misses or altogether "guesses" at the words that were indecipherable.

That's why the context is vital and also why the time allotted to witness the speaking is significant too. Generally, the lengthier the time of observing the speaker, the likelihood of figuring out the words tends to usually increase, and likewise knowing the context can help in filling in the blanks. For example, back to those baseball players, if one of them says the word "home" you can pretty much anticipate that the next word might be "plate" as in referring to the base where the catcher is going to be.

Something that I want to right away clarify is that the AI-based lip-reading systems are not sentient. I mention this because there are headlines that keep insisting that today's AI is somehow human-like or even superhuman in its capabilities. This is quite misleading, and an unfortunate exaggeration of what AI technology can presently do.

A human that reads the lips of another person will be able to cognitively assess the nature of the discussion or the manner of speaking that the person is undertaking. This cognitive assessment can be a big determiner of making any sense out of the spotty string of words being detected. An AI-based system doing the lip-reading doesn't have that kind of cognition. In that sense, the AI is at a decided disadvantage in performing the talk-to-text task.

That being said, the AI-based system has some keen advantages over a human trying to read lips.

The AI won't tire of the task. A human might be bored waiting to see someone say something, or perhaps might look away or flinch just when the moment arises that the person says a vital word, such as the secret code for opening that ironclad safe loaded with gold bars.

An AI system would be using cameras to observe the person that is speaking. Those cameras can have specialized lenses and be able to see imagery at a great distance, possibly also enhance the focus and deal too with poor lighting. The human eye is a great and amazing thing, yet it is in some ways less capable than souped-up cameras.

Another facet is the possibility of training the AI lip-reading system to decipher across multiple languages. A human trying to read lips might be fooled if the person doing the speaking suddenly switches to another language, attempting to throw-off any observers. It is relatively easy to train an AI-based lip-reading system to encompass a multitude of languages, and potentially be able to analyze nearly any language known to mankind.

There are apps these days that will do lip-reading and can achieve reasonably good results. The odds are that if the talk-to-text can get part of the way there in doing the lip-reading, a human that examines the results can potentially fill in the rest. In other words, suppose the app only gets some of the words, a human that reads the resultant text can apply their own cognitive awareness of the world and potentially divine what the speaker might have been saying overall.

That's why some of these modern-day apps are used by those that are hard of hearing or might be deaf. The app can potentially provide added capability at doing lip-reading. Of course, having to hold a smartphone and point it at someone speaking is considered perhaps somewhat rude in certain circumstances, and therefore you might not readily be able to use such a feature. Do keep in mind though that we are on the verge of having so-called smart glasses, akin to the Google Glasses that were earlier proffered, and in that manner, the use of these kinds of lip-reading apps might be less garish accordingly (since the glasses are already "naturally" aiming at the person speaking).

Besides trying to figure out the lip-reading while in-person and in real-time, another approach involves recording the speaking activity on video and then applying the lip-reading algorithms to the recorded aspects. Using a recording can be especially helpful since the video can be played and replayed, repeatedly doing so, allowing for multiple attempts at discerning the words being spoken.

As movie buffs know, sometimes a secret agent would be sitting in a car and be parked outside a locale where the subject frequented. Nonchalantly sitting in the parked car, the secret agent was fervently glancing over toward the subject and attempting to do the lip-reading.

Being inside the car was a handy cover and a means to not appear to be starkly staring or otherwise out-of-place.

Speaking of cars, the future of cars consists of self-driving cars.

That's a nifty segue into a quite interesting consideration about lip-reading. Self-driving cars will be chockful of electronic sensory devices such as video cameras, radar, LIDAR, ultrasonic units, thermal imagining, and the like.

An intriguing question is this: *Will AI-based true self-driving cars potentially be able to do lip-reading, and if so, what might this portend?*

Let's unpack the matter and see.

**Self-Driving Cars And Lip-Reading**

For Level 4 and Level 5 true self-driving vehicles, there won't be a human driver involved in the driving task.

All occupants will be passengers.

The AI is doing the driving.

One aspect to immediately discuss entails the fact that the AI involved in today's AI driving systems is not sentient (akin to my points earlier on the sentience topic). In other words, the AI is altogether a collective of computer-based programming and algorithms, and most assuredly not able to reason in the same manner that humans can.

Why this added emphasis about the AI not being sentient?

Because I want to underscore that when discussing the role of the AI driving system, I am not ascribing human qualities to the AI. Please be aware that there is an ongoing and dangerous tendency these days to anthropomorphize AI. In essence, people are assigning human-like sentience to today's AI, despite the undeniable and inarguable fact that no such AI exists as yet.

With that clarification, you can envision the AI driving system doesn't natively somehow "know" the meaning of whatever might be said by someone that is the subject of a lip-reading algorithm. The words might be determinable to some degree as though they are blobs of visualized movement that are being mathematically associated with blobs that are words of text. Those blobs can be collected together into sentences. The use of Natural Language Processing (NLP) capabilities can attempt to ferret out the nature of the narrative, though realize this is of the limited capacity that you experience when using Alexa or Siri.

Returning to the focus on self-driving cars, you might be wondering what does lip-reading have to do with self-driving cars.

As noted, self-driving cars will have video cameras, oftentimes of quite high quality and caliber. The video cameras mounted on the vehicle are intended to detect the driving scene and the surroundings of the self-driving car. The AI driving system receives data from those cameras, does various image processing, and tries to figure out where the road is, where pedestrians are, where are other cars are, etc.

That would be the primary reason for the video cameras. Realize though that those video cameras are capturing whatever perchance they happen to see. I've exhorted in my columns that there is an era coming ahead of what I refer to as the roving eye. We will have self-driving cars all around us, roaming and driving here and there, meanwhile, those video cameras can capture our daily activities.

Imagine a self-driving car going down your neighborhood street. The video camera is capturing the street scene, showcasing where cars are parked, whether any dogs are running into the middle of the street, and so on. At the same time, the video is capturing that you and your children are playing catch with a baseball in your front yard. This presumably has little to do with the driving chore of the self-driving car, and merely is part of the overall scene and nonetheless captured by the video cameras.

The data from the video cameras might be retained on-board the vehicle, and then later on uploaded into the cloud of the fleet operator or automaker via the use of OTA (Over-The-Air) electronic communications. How will that video be used? Perhaps it might be analyzed to consider real estate aspects in a given area, such as the look of the homes and the status of the neighborhood. There are numerous ways to potentially monetize that data.

We might also anticipate that there will be privacy-related concerns. Who has control of all that video? To make matters even more imposing, realize that there will be lots of self-driving cars that will go past your home, during the course of any ordinary day. In theory, the video could be cobbled together to give a relatively full accounting of your comings and goings from your home.

Putting aside those qualms herein for a moment, let's consider how the lip-reading aspects enter into the picture, as it were.

A self-driving car is sitting at a red light, waiting for the light to go green. People standing on the sidewalk nearby are chatting quietly, such that they otherwise cannot be overheard. They are though within the eyesight of the video camera.

Presumably, an AI-based lip-reading program could be analyzing their lips and attempting to ascertain what they are saying. This could be instantly converted into text or spoken aloud by the mechanized AI system. A passenger inside the self-driving car could readily "overhear" the conversation of those pedestrians, doing so by leveraging the capabilities of the self-driving car.

I realize that anyone developing an AI driving system is probably getting steamed at this portrayal and they would vehemently be stating that doing lip-reading is not within their job description. Assuredly, the notion of encompassing a lip-reading capability into an AI driving system is either not on the list of projects to be undertaken, or if it does appear on such a list it would be considered an edge or corner case and be quite low on the list.

Indeed, some might insist that there is absolutely no cause to have a lip-reading capability included in the AI driving system.

Well, that isn't entirely the case.

There are in fact ways in which a lip-reading facility might be useful.

For example, suppose a roadway construction worker is up ahead of the self-driving car and standing at the side of the road, directing traffic around a roadway repair activity. The worker might mouth words at a human driver, trying to convey something about which way to drive. They are speaking aloud but cannot be readily heard over the din of the construction work taking place.

A human driver would likely do a variant of everyday lip-reading and gather that the worker is saying to move over to the left and slow down. Likely, the worker might be also holding a sign and waving too, thus there are a variety of visual aspects coming to play. The mouthing of words is not likely the sole form of communicating, and yet it is another mode and one that can contribute to the driver grasping what is going on and what they are supposed to do at the steering wheel of the vehicle.

It certainly seems that we would want the AI driving system to be able to likewise figure out the driving scene in such a scenario. The added feature of doing lip-reading in real-time could be useful. Yes, this is a bit of an edge case, no doubt about that. The point is that to claim that there is no basis for having a lip-reading capability as part of the self-driving car capabilities is immediately undercut by the apparent example that showcases there is some merit (which, you can then argue as to how meritorious or not it is).

We can also somewhat sidestep the argument about the lip-reading being embedded into the AI driving system by looking at the use cases beyond the act of driving per se.

Suppose that the passengers inside a self-driving car are hard of hearing. The self-driving car comes to a parking lot. The passengers roll down the window to chat with a parking lot attendant. Assume that the parking lot attendant tells the passengers that a good drop-off point is over near the front entrance to the mall. Unfortunately, due to their hearing difficulties, they can't make out what the parking attendant is saying.

The self-driving car could have a lip-reading program that would do the talk-to-text and then show the text on a screen inside the vehicle. Those passengers would then read the screen and could instruct the AI driving system to drop them over at the front entrance.

In this example, lip-reading is not necessarily embedded into the AI driving system. It would be outside the realm of the driving aspects and could be likened to other features in a car such as the infotainment systems. The lip-reading app would be for the benefit of the passengers.

**Conclusion**

There are many added twists and turns on this topic.

Rather than the digital lip-reading app being on-board the vehicle, it could be utilized in the cloud.

This means that the video from the self-driving car that has been uploaded into the cloud could be inspected and potentially used to reveal what people nearby the self-driving car were saying. Why would this ever be used? Some point to the potential for crime-fighting. Others worry that this is a bridge too far and will be used in a Big Brother manner.

Here's a final insight for now and one that you might find either extremely alarming or possibly consider as quite helpful and ingenious.

Are you ready?

In addition to video cameras pointed outward, you can expect that self-driving cars will have inward-pointing video cameras too. This can be handy for doing Zoom-like interactive online sessions while you are riding in a self-driving car. The video cameras can also be used to deter people from writing graffiti in the vehicle or tearing up the interior.

Those inward-facing video cameras can also be used to do lip-reading.

We'll start by covering the upside version of this use. There are several passengers inside the self-driving car. Some of the passengers are hard of hearing, and they also are not versed in doing lip-reading. As such, an added service or feature of the self-driving car is that it can attempt to do the lip-reading and enable the passengers to essentially converse with each other, aided by the lip-reading program.

Nice!

The downside is that you might be having conversations in the self-driving car and not be desirous of those conversations ever seeing the light of day. You might think that if you cut off or cover the microphones inside the self-driving car that your chatting will never be discovered. Of course, the video camera, if enabled, would be capturing your conversation visually.

A larger issue will entail what and when those inward-facing video cameras are going to be engaged. Furthermore, what will happen to the video that has been so recorded?

Until now, this is not a noticeable concern since few cars are equipped with inward-facing video cameras. For self-driving cars, you can bet that there will be such video cameras, and the odds are that even conventional new cars will have cameras included too.

There is a quite famous line by President Theodore Roosevelt stating that you should speak softly and carry a big stick. If you don't favor all of this digital lip-reading, perhaps you might abide by his advice and use that stick to cover-up when you don't want your words to be read.

Something to perhaps silently think about, that's for sure).

# CHAPTER 14
# BARRING TINKERING AND SELF-DRIVING CARS

Turn a wrench.

As you might know, that is the customary parlance used to refer to a car enthusiast (they can "turn a wrench" or mechanically work on a car). Such devotees are often characterized as so-called motorheads or in other countries a revered petrol-head (there is an ongoing debate about whether this "petrol" reference is going to be fitting amidst an era of EVs).

In any case, these are clearly aficionados that relish tinkering with automobiles.

You certainly must know this type of person, or you perhaps are an avid member of such a venerated group, proudly so. The moment a car comes down the street, these enthusiasts (fanatics, some insist) are quick to size-up the vehicle and declare it to be either a worthy prize or a potential piece of junk. There is usually no in-between. Someone that prides themselves on knowing about cars is apt to be very ready to make quick and altogether razor-sharp decisions about vehicular worthiness.

There is a famous scene in the popular movie *My Cousin Vinny* in which actress Marisa Tomei is playing the role of Mona Lisa Vito and gets maneuvered by her fiancé Vinny into serving as an expert witness pertaining to "general automotive knowledge" (a memorable line from the movie). When asked why she might be able to serve in such a capacity, she rattles off an impressive list of car mechanic-related experiences, including tune-ups, transmission overhauls, engine work, and so on (you've got to watch the scene if you are car buff or automobile dilettante).

Being able to tear apart and rebuild a car is certainly a notable skill and worthy of admiration. There are about 250 million cars in the United States alone, and we all are pretty much dependent upon the availability of functioning cars in our daily commutes and when running errands. Thankfully, there are those among us that have made a choice to conquer the complexities of knowing how cars work and are able to keep the world flowing accordingly.

There is another segment of society that has a similar aficionado kind of attention, though not necessarily toward cars. I'm talking about technoids, gadget geeks, tech gurus, or those computer nerds (if you will), that love to tinker with computers.

You must know someone like that, or, once again, perhaps you are like that. When a new computer comes into the marketplace, these enthusiasts are eager to read up on the specifications. They can readily assess whether the CPU is any good and will pontificate about how it is slower or faster than some other computer around.

They typically own a slew of computers, many of which are opened up, and the circuit boards are grandly exposed for ease of access. Besides the hardware fascination, these computer whizzes are apt to have an arsenal of software utilities that they like to use. They can readily examine the computer bits and bytes underlying a hard drive and deploy arcane programs to play tricks on the hardware.

Okay, so which of these two types of fans or enthusiasts are regularly referred to as *gearheads*?

That's a bit of a trick question. The moniker of being a gearhead can be applied to those that can turn a wrench and are labeled as motorheads, and likewise, you can say that those computer geeks are gearheads too.

Some pundits would be quite willing to debate which of the two groups ought to be crowned as gearheads. Motorheads might indignantly state that only they are allowed to use that royal plumage.

Of course, you might have those expert technoids that would irately differ and proclaim that they are the true bearers of the gearheads trophy.

Rather than trying to split hairs, perhaps we can all get along and agree that the illustrious gearhead title can be equally shared. Sometimes the gearhead naming can refer to those that tinker with cars. Meanwhile, in the same breath, sometimes the gearhead designation refers to those that tinker with computers.

Why all this discussion about gearheads and their tinkering on the venerable contraptions and devices of mankind?

Because they are about to find themselves faced with a huge deflating disappointment and it could just crush their august gearhead souls right out of their being. Yes, this devastating blow could indeed happen due to the advent of self-driving cars.

Wait for a second, you might be thinking, shouldn't the emergence of self-driving cars be the dream of every gearhead?

A self-driving car is a twofer, as it were. It is a car. And it is a computer, a very state-of-the-art computer that stretches the boundaries of modern-day computing. Self-driving cars seem to be the perfect new toy for gearheads.

It is almost like it is birthday time for gearheads and they are getting their cake and the icing all at the same time. Motorheads would salivate at the car aspects. Technoids would slaver over the computer hardware and software.

This is a match made in heaven.

You can bring together the two groups. They can work hand-in-hand. They can also poke away at which self-driving car is the best, and which is the worst. There is an unexplored mountain here to be first delved into and today's gearheads are front and center. The era of self-driving cars is just beginning to inch into view and now proffers the chance to forge a gearhead specialty that heretofore did not exist.

Sorry, but you'll need to put away those celebratory balloons and confetti. There won't be any tinkering going on with those AI-based true self-driving cars.

Allow me a moment to explain the matter.

You know how your smartphone has a seal on it that says that if you open the thing up, you are voiding the warranty. Well, it is even worse when it comes to wanting to "open up" the innards of a self-driving car.

That's a big no-no.

Self-driving cars are going to strictly off-limits to any kind of tinkering. I realize that many gearheads would say that they don't care whether the manufacturer's warranty gets voided or not. Gearheads would scoff at such a warning and likely proclaim that you don't need and nor want that stupid warranty anyway. If you know what you are doing, you can do a much better job on any tinkering, and the only aspect the manufacturer can do well is to charge you an arm and a leg for something that you can do for pennies on the dollar by yourself.

With self-driving cars, this notion of going beyond the stipulations and restrictions imposed by the automaker or self-driving tech maker is more than just a recommendation. It is a serious and airtight condition.

Why so?

Because if your smartphone gets messed-up by tinkering, it means you are having a bad day, while if a self-driving car gets messed-up and is allowed to get onto the roadway, you are going to have somber and immense consequences.

Self-driving cars are about life-or-death.

You don't probably consider that each time you get behind the wheel of a car, you are facing life-or-death, but it is in fact the case.

While driving a car, you are continually making life-or-death decisions that can impact your life, and the lives of those in other nearby cars, and the lives of pedestrians.

The same can be said for self-driving cars. Every time a self-driving car gets underway on a driving journey, life-or-death is at stake. The passengers riding in the self-driving car are vulnerable to life-or-death circumstances, such as if a human-driven car suddenly rams into the self-driving car.

For some odd reason, some of the general public seems to believe that self-driving cars will never get into car crashes. Perhaps this is partially fueled by those campaigns that claim erroneously that self-driving cars will ensure that we never have car crashes ever again. These are sometimes coined as the aim to achieve zero fatalities. As I've repeatedly stated, zero fatalities is a nice aspirational goal, but it is also misleading and won't be accomplishable.

Anyway, the point overall is that self-driving cars are not going to be amenable to the tinkerers and will have all sorts of safeguards and provisions to try and doggedly prevent any tinkering. You might think that this settles the matter and the gearheads will just have to accept the notion that they won't be tinkering with self-driving cars.

Regrettably, the earnest energies of gearheads are likely to compel them toward trying to do tinkering. You might even suggest that because self-driving cars are going to be extremely locked-down, this perhaps makes them an even more attractive target for tinkerers that believe they have the gosh-darn right to tinker if they wish to do so.

In that sense, it is a dangerous kind of cat and mouse game that might ensue. The automakers and self-driving tech firms will be devoutly trying to prevent tinkering, while some gearheads that won't take no as an answer will be stridently seeking ways to do tinkering.

A somewhat oddball or perhaps ironic basis for the tinkerers to defend their posture is that if they are prevented from tinkering, it is a good sign for self-driving cars. This implies that cybercrooks and evildoers that might want to subvert self-driving cars will also be prevented from performing their malevolent form of tinkering. By essentially forcing the automakers and self-driving tech firms into defending against everyday gearheads, this simultaneously is forging stronger protections against those having sinister intentions.

That's one of those around and around arguments and isn't going to be resolved herein.

The intriguing question for today's discussion is this: *Will AI-based true self-driving cars entirely be off-limits for any gearhead tinkering, and if so, why can't tinkering be allowed?*

Let's unpack the matter and see.

## Self-Driving Cars And Tinkering

For Level 4 and Level 5 true self-driving vehicles, there won't be a human driver involved in the driving task.

All occupants will be passengers.

The AI is doing the driving.

One aspect to immediately discuss entails the fact that the AI involved in today's AI driving systems is not sentient. In other words, the AI is altogether a collective of computer-based programming and algorithms, and most assuredly not able to reason in the same manner that humans can.

Why this added emphasis about the AI not being sentient?

Because I want to underscore that when discussing the role of the AI driving system, I am not ascribing human qualities to the AI. Please be aware that there is an ongoing and dangerous tendency these days to anthropomorphize AI. In essence, people are assigning human-like sentience to today's AI, despite the undeniable and inarguable fact that no such AI exists as yet.

With that clarification, you can envision that the AI driving system doesn't natively somehow "know" when someone decides to tinker with the vehicle. This is something that needs to be programmed as part of the capabilities of the self-driving car.

Look at it this way.

If a human driver walked up to their car, they might be able to discern that someone has messed around with their beloved vehicle (as an aside, obviously, some people don't know much about cars and would be oblivious to any under-the-hood changes). A savvy driver that knows about cars could perhaps start the engine and immediately detect that the revving sounded different, or upon starting to roll forward could discern that the driving controls are reacting differently than normal, etc.

Even the most casual driver would certainly observe if the tires on their car had been changed out (well, most would, hopefully). Those dull-looking tires that are now shiny and a larger-sized set would seemingly be noticeable.

Likewise, most drivers can usually feel the difference in the car when they take it to the automobile repair shop and some significant alterations have been made. Maybe the brakes were on their last legs, and now they are fresh and ready to be used. The moment that the owner takes the vehicle down the street, and upon first using the brakes, they would likely realize that the braking action is much sharper. They also would not have to press as firmly on the brake pedal. And the prior squeaking sound is no longer heard now that the brakes were replaced.

Okay, so those are somewhat common ways that a human driver might realize that their car has been tinkered with.

For self-driving cars, as mentioned there isn't a human driver, and therefore no human driver that is going to be standing around or getting into the car and looking for changes that might have been made to the vehicle.

What about those passengers?

I dare say that most passengers would not have any semblance of whether a car has been tinkered with or not. Unless the tinkering was blatantly obvious, and only if the car was doing some pretty strange things, would most passengers ever detect that something has been altered. When you get into a ridesharing car being driven by a human, you as the rider take at face value that the car is in suitable shape. You assume, rightfully so, that the human driver is aware of the functioning of the car and you are trusting them to ensure that the car is journey viable.

This emphasizes that the AI-based driving system has to include a provision of figuring out whether the self-driving car is in a proper drivable state.

Think carefully about that point.

Someone that does tinkering might be able to alter the car and yet the car is still fully drivable. Imagine that a gearhead decides to soup-up the engine of the self-driving car. The thinking by this enthusiast is that the car itself was limited to going say a max of 100 miles per hour, but it would be nifty if the car was enabled to go 120 miles per hour.

Suppose that such a change was made to the vehicle. The vehicle is still drivable. It will be able to do all the driving functions it could do before the change.

If the AI driving system is only seeking to ascertain whether the car is simply drivable, that is a far cry from ensuring that the car is still the same car that it once was. The AI driving system is usually devised to operate the car in a previously trained and known way (via the use of Machine Learning and Deep Learning). Crucial parameters have been established about how the car takes corners, what its stopping distance consists of, and so on.

Changes made to the self-driving car that impact any of those factors are going to potentially confound the AI driving system. It might assume that the vehicle can be brought to a stop in some X number of feet. If a change has been made that means the vehicle now has to require some Y number of feet, say an amount more than X, this indubitably bodes for grave concern.

Here's why.

Follow me on this driving scenario.

The AI driving system is using sensors to detect the driving scene. Based on the detection, it is plotting out how to safely drive the car. If a pedestrian suddenly steps onto the street in front of the self-driving car, the algorithms involved in determining what driving action to take are going to calculate the appropriate action as based on (for example) the setting related to the stopping distance of that car.

Thus, the AI driving system might inadvertently calculate that the vehicle can be stopped in time, but we are supposing that someone has tinkered with the car and has unfortunately impacted the stopping distance capability. Unbeknownst to the AI driving system, it is using outdated or outmoded parametric values in calculating that the pedestrian can be avoided by simply employing the brakes. The reality might be that once the brakes are applied, a longer stopping distance is needed, and the vehicle "unexpectedly" rams into the pedestrian.

The bottom line is that the self-driving car has to be kept intact in terms of the nature of the car and the nature of the AI driving system. They are paired up. They are on the same dance card. They need to be able to align together in a manner to ensure that safe and sound driving is going to occur.

Any changes made to the car are likely going to require some form of changes to the AI driving system.

Any changes made to the AI driving system might or might not require commensurate changes to the car.

You cannot assume that the AI driving system will somehow spontaneously figure out what changes have been made to the vehicle. This kind of detection of the vehicle status, along with a dynamic real-time fluidity of the AI driving system is not especially being crafted right now.

There is enough on the plate of things to do that involve just getting the AI driving system to safely drive a given car from point A to point B. Trying to infuse into the AI driving system a capability of on-the-fly figuring out the nature of the vehicle, and then adjusting the driving aspects, accordingly, entails a much heavier lift and a vaunted facility of a much greater formation.

Generally, the AI driving systems are being honed for specific makes and models of cars right now. Once the AI driving system has been so tailored, the expectation is that the make and model are going to stay as it is for that particular instance of the AI driving system. If there are any substantive changes to the vehicle, you would need to revisit the AI driving system and make adjustments correspondingly.

You can't just somehow grab the AI driving system from one type of car, and dump it into another car of a different make or model. A human driver would generally have that kind of flexibility, which shows you how amazing humans are, and for which we aren't yet able to devise AI driving systems with that kind of adaptability (I've described how this might occur in the future, see my columns for coverage).

## Conclusion

I'm sure the gearheads are already toying with the idea that if they simply need to adjust one for the other, in the sense that if they change the car they need to change the AI driving system, or that if they change the AI driving system they might need to make changes to the car, and ergo the whole thing is easy peasy. In other words, no big deal. All they need to do is make sure that they make the needed collective set of changes.

Not wanting to be the party spoiler but remember that self-driving cars are about life-or-death consequences.

Is the general public willing to accept the notion that a backyard tinkerer can make a change to a self-driving car, and the self-driving car is then going to roam around on our public roadways, though nobody else necessarily knows what changes were made and what effect they might have on the driving of the vehicle?

The odds are that this is going to be rejected as a way of doing things. The expectation will be that the automakers and self-driving tech firms will tightly lockdown their vehicles. Any tinkering under-the-hood should be immediately detected and an alert should be emitted. The AI driving system should have a double-check that tries to ensure that only if the vehicle is untouched will the AI driving system proceed to take the car on a driving journey.

That's a lot more than merely voiding a warranty.

You can likely also see why there is a heated debate about the ownership of self-driving cars.

Some assert that self-driving cars ought to only be owned and operated by major companies that will ensure that no tinkering takes place. If you put self-driving cars into the ownership hands of individuals, the angst is that they might do all sorts of wild things in an attempt to change up the vehicle and the AI driving system.

A counterargument is that if the proper protections are put in place, which seems like a necessity, it doesn't matter who owns or operates the vehicle. A large company that owns and operates a self-driving car can just as easily have someone that opts to mess around with the vehicle. The protective features should be mandatory and always checking, regardless of who happens to own or operate the self-driving car.

A final twist is the question of maintenance and repairs for self-driving cars (see my analysis about this matter in my columns). Presumably, only bonafide and specially designated maintenance and repair shops will be permitted to work on self-driving cars. Unlike a conventional car, and as extolled earlier, there is concern that if just anyone can tinker with a self-driving car, even an otherwise reputable car repair facility unless they are carefully selected and monitored, the risks associated with self-driving car calamities will rise.

For those gearheads eyeing the emergence of self-driving cars, one might say that curiosity killed the cat. Or perhaps that anything that can go wrong, will go wrong. I have a feeling though that they are already gearing up for the delights of tinkering with these ultimate gears-on-wheels machines and probably thinking to themselves, it is simply elementary, my dear Watson.

Hopefully, gearheads and pretty much no unauthorized "tinkerers" will opt to tamper with self-driving cars. We can aim to sleep well at night by the belief that even the more egregious and zealous of gearheads *auto know better* (yes, that's a bit of a pun, and it assuredly won't buff out).

# CHAPTER 15
# HAULING STORES AND SELF-DRIVING CARS

You look out the window of your home and see what appears to be a fancy store parked temporarily outside in front of your house.

Say what?

Actually, it is pretty exciting that a store has opted to come to you, allowing you to both directly see and physically touch the goodies that are offered by that particular establishment. There is something notably satisfying about being able to be in-person with the merchandise that you are seeking to potentially purchase.

Doing online shopping is perfectly fine as an alternative to visiting a physical store, but you can't directly handle the goods. Of course, you can always order something online and then return it after getting the item into your hands. That is nonetheless still a bit of a hassle and seems enormously wasteful from a logistics perspective.

It sure would be nice to have the store come directly to you.

Heck, ice cream trucks seem to be able to bring their icy scrumptious goodies directly to your block (for my discussion on the future of ice cream trucks and neighborhood delivery, so why can't other purveyors of goods do the same? Makers of clothing, shoes, and the like don't even have to worry about refrigeration and nor the need to heat-up stuff such as those ubiquitous pizza delivery services do.

Your dream of seeing a store parked outside your domicile and alluringly ready to provide a shopping extravaganza is already coming to fruition. This can happen today for example via the highly touted

Louis Vuitton mobile boutique (well, let's call it a mobile *store* if that's okay, though admittedly not quite as fancy-sounding as a *boutique*).

Envision a sophisticated-looking trailer that houses Louis Vuitton merchandise and provides an immersive experience via shimmering glass siding doors, plush crème-colored carpets, and seemingly bathes you in opulence as you examine the treasures within. At your beck-and-call is a sales representative that can skillfully introduce you to the many fine goods now readily available at your fingertips.

Yes, you say to the sales attendant, I'd like that stunning diamond necklace and the matching extravagant handbag. Wait for a second, do you select the handbag first, and then choose the right kind of matching jewelry, or the other way around? No worries since the sales advisor can clear things up for you. Upon making your purchase, the items will be placed adroitly into Louis Vuitton branded bags and you can then briskly carry the valuables to your home as you proudly reenter into your domicile after having gone on a vaunted shopping trip.

A joyous hassle-free shopping trip that took place a few steps away from your home.

You didn't need to drive over to the mall. You didn't need to try and find a place to park your car. You didn't need to burdensomely carry your purchases throughout the mall as you made your winding way back to your parked car. For those that might have opted to use ridesharing rather than driving their own car, the shopping trip still has its tiresome difficulties such as waiting for a ridesharing vehicle to show-up and hoping that the driver won't be a jerk.

One also supposes that going shopping just outside the door of your home is still a means to feel like you have gone elsewhere and have been transformed by the excursion away from your always-at-home existence. Though some believe that stores coming to you won't be needed once the pandemic has subsided, others insist the notion of working from home is now going to be a normal part of life and we will soon realize that being primarily at home is the mainstay for much of your working career.

In short, you can expect that we will see a lot more of these trailers or mobile shopping vehicles that will gradually become commonplace on our roadways and in our communities.

Generally, these will be standalone trailers that are towed and do not have their own self-contained means of locomotion. The handy aspect about being a separate trailer is that the boxcar characteristic allows the facility to be hooked up to any vehicle that is properly capable to haul the on-the-go store. In theory, this lessens the immediate cost of the mobile store itself and reduces the maintenance effort that might be required (no engine to be tuned-up or any similar automotive repairs).

That being said, you ought to expect that there will be a mixture of mobile store contrivances on our highways and byways. Besides the hitched-up trailer variants, there will certainly be vehicles that have been converted into drivable stores. The merchandise of the store is placed within the drivable vehicle, all together as one entire unit. In some instances, this might be a better approach, though tradeoffs exist regarding whether to use the trailers versus the all-in-one method.

One aspect that would seem to be unarguable is that whether using a trailer or an all-in-one, there must be a driver that will haul the store to you. In the case of a trailer, you'll need someone at the wheel of the vehicle that is doing the hauling. For an all-in-one, the same would certainly seem to be the case, namely, someone has to be driving the mobile store.

From the perspective of the store owner, this might mean that there are at least two people needed to carry out this mobile store operation. A driver is needed, plus a store salesperson is needed.

To reduce the labor costs and the logistics headaches, probably handy to have a salesperson that can serve equally as the driver or find a driver that can be trained to be a salesperson. This is a veritable instance whereby one head is better than two if you get the gist (a bit of a reversed pun).

Accomplishing that one-for-the-price of two is not necessarily as easy as it sounds.

Consider that a salesperson has a specialized skill set, being able to perform the sales function and also be dutifully aware of the merchandise being sold. Meanwhile, a driver also has a type of particular skillset, namely being able to drive, doing so safely and properly.

Note that this is not just any kind of driving, this is driving involving a larger-sized vehicular contraption. When a trailer is being towed, the act of driving becomes a lot more complicated. The vehicle doing the towing is one factor of the driving task. The second and integral factor is the thing being towed and how it can be suitably maneuvered on the roadway.

Having your mobile store go into a ditch is not something anyone wants.

Okay, so you wouldn't just hire a salesperson that drives an ordinary car and suddenly expect out-of-the-blue they can adequately drive the mobile store. You would need to train them for that specialized driving skill. Maybe the person gleans what they are supposed to do at the wheel, and then again maybe driving that kind of a vehicle is ostensibly not in their realm of core competency.

Ergo you opt instead to hire a seasoned driver that has done hauling for a bunch of years and you assume that you can teach them about the sales process and the nature of the merchandise. Let's put our cards on the table and agree that not everyone is suited for being in sales. There would be an open question about how readily you can transform a seasoned driver that hauls trailers into becoming a stellar seller of fine goods (I'm not saying that this isn't feasible, only clarifying that these can be rather disparate trades).

Seems like quite a conundrum.

The store owner would prefer to hire one person rather than two. Finding someone that can do both tasks is difficult. Overall, the odds are that there would need to be two people required, one that drives the on-the-go store and the other that does the selling. This also means that once the trailer is parked at a locale for the time involved in having consumers do their shopping, the driver becomes idled and has nothing to do, thus incurring a cost that is not being put to productive use at that time.

Oh well, that's the way the ball bounces.

Maybe not.

Turns out that there is a solution is on its way.

The future of cars consists of self-driving cars. Self-driving cars are driven by an AI-based driving system and there is no need for a human driver. If a mobile store setup could somehow utilize an AI-based driving system, the need to hire a human driver would no longer be at play. This then allows for a focus entirely on hiring the salesperson and no need to try and find that needle-in-the-haystack that can do both the selling and the driving.

An intriguing question is this: *Will AI-based true self-driving cars be able to serve as drivers for mobile stores?*

Let's unpack the matter and see.

**Self-Driving Cars And Mobile Stores**

For Level 4 and Level 5 true self-driving vehicles, there won't be a human driver involved in the driving task.

All occupants will be passengers.

The AI is doing the driving.

One aspect to immediately discuss entails the fact that the AI involved in today's AI driving systems is not sentient. In other words, the AI is altogether a collective of computer-based programming and algorithms, and most assuredly not able to reason in the same manner that humans can.

Why this added emphasis about the AI not being sentient?

Because I want to underscore that when discussing the role of the AI driving system, I am not ascribing human qualities to the AI. Please be aware that there is an ongoing and dangerous tendency these days to anthropomorphize AI. In essence, people are assigning human-like sentience to today's AI, despite the undeniable and inarguable fact that no such AI exists as yet.

With that clarification, you can envision that the AI driving system doesn't natively somehow "know" how to cope with driving and nor the specially added dynamics of driving while towing something. This is a driving skill that needs to be programmed as part of the capabilities of the self-driving car.

Let's dive into the myriad of aspects that come to play on this topic.

First, by-and-large the automakers and self-driving car developers are concentrating on getting a car to drive from point A to point B. This does not involve towing things. The base assumption is that the car is on its own and does not entail using a tow hitch and hauling around a conjoined vehicle.

If you've ever towed a boat or a portable storage cart, you know that this can be a tricky form of driving. You need to be aware of the fact that the length of your vehicular conglomeration is much more than merely the length of the car. When you try to change lanes or make turns, you need to keep in mind the added length and how that changes the nature of the driving task.

Humans typically catch-on pretty readily to the chore of driving when towing something. You might tend to go a bit slower than you might otherwise proceed. Starting from a dead stop takes more effort and time because of the total weight involved. And, perhaps most importantly, coming to a stop is going to be less assured in terms of the stopping distance and allowed reaction time (you are not able to just jam on the brakes like you did when absent of a towed item).

Getting an AI driving system to properly and safely contend with the towing chore is somewhat arduous and decidedly not a quick-fix per se.

As mentioned, the AI is not sentient and cannot somehow reason what to do when in the act of towing. This needs to be programmed and possibly also gleaned via the use of Machine Learning (ML) and Deep Learning (DL). Those AI techniques of ML/DL involve computational pattern matching and can be undertaken to some extent by collecting data about towing and having the computer figure out what types of driving actions and adjustments might be needed.

Since doing towing is a tiny fraction of everyday driving, the earnest attention right now involves getting cars to drive by themselves and does not include the act of towing. The towing effort could be likened to an edge or corner case. This means that it is a matter on a priority list and sits further down on the listing. Only after other higher priority driving tasks have been appropriately devised, the towing aspect can then be considered and programmed accordingly.

On a related aspect, the ongoing efforts toward achieving self-driving trucks can be quite helpful in the quest toward expanding self-driving cars into the act of towing. Self-driving trucks entail having the AI driving system cope with lengthy and bulky vehicles. Also, trucks often undertake a towing effort. All in all, insights and AI-based driving capacities that are being developed towards self-driving trucks are useful for self-driving cars too.

There are numerous twists and turns involved in using a self-driving car to tow a mobile store.

For example, suppose that you were driving a mobile store and arrived at the home of someone that has requested the store to visit their location.

I ask you, where would you park the elaborate apparatus?

That's a tough question. If you decide to park in the middle of the street, this is bound to draw the ire of those that live on that block and indeed be frustrating to anyone driving up or down that particular avenue. Probably not going to be legally allowed anyway.

Hoping to find a parking spot at that location is rather optimistic. Keep in mind that the parking spot has to be long enough to accommodate the vehicle and the mobile store. Seems like parking is usually difficult for even a small-sized car, let alone an extremely lengthy rig.

You might be thinking that you could park in the driveway of whoever requested the store. I dare say that few people would have a driveway of that needed size. This would dramatically lessen the number of people that could request that the store visit.

The overarching point is that if a human driver would have a tough time figuring out where to park, this adds a challenge to using an AI driving system. Most AI driving systems are predominantly programmed to do driving. The parking aspects are often assumed to be relatively straightforward, such that an available spot to park the vehicle will be readily evident. With the mobile store aspects, that is assuredly not the case.

That makes clear another reason that using self-driving cars for the burgeoning use of mobile stores is going to have some twists and turns.

Don't worry, where there is a will, there is a way.

## Conclusion

You might be mulling over the mobile store and the use of self-driving cars and be wondering where the salesperson will be during a driving journey.

Usually, it would be the case that the salesperson would be riding inside the self-driving car. This is generally considered a safer placement than riding in the trailer or mobile store itself. Furthermore, some locales might have restrictions of riding inside a trailer or its equivalent. One concern too is that if the salesperson is riding inside the mobile store, there is a chance that the merchandise might jar loose and serve as a flying projectile that could harm them.

The expected scenario would be that the salesperson rides inside the self-driving car and might provide verbal guidance about where to park upon arriving at the destination. The salesperson would use the Natural Language Processing (NLP) capabilities of the AI driving system (akin to Alexa or Siri), telling where there might be suitable spots to park. After the parking task has been completed by the AI driving system, the salesperson would get out of the self-driving car and proceed to open up the mobile store.

Those wanting to do shopping would come into the mobile store and be aided by the salesperson. When the shopping effort was concluded, the salesperson would close-up the mobile store and get back into the self-driving car. The salesperson would then inform the AI driving system that it is time to head out and proceed to the next destination.

Voila, you have now been introduced to the future of at-home (or shall we say home-adjacent) shopping via the use of mobile stores that are towed around by self-driving cars.

One last twist, for now.

Why is the human salesperson needed at all in this scenario?

Perhaps they aren't needed.

Though this revelation might seem woeful for those in the sales realm, presumably the mobile store could be run entirely by an AI system that was devised for that purpose. The AI would open the mobile store by activating automatic doors. As people enter the mobile store, the AI could use facial recognition to figure out which shoppers have arrived. Via video cameras inside the mobile store, the AI could observe as the shoppers undertake their shopping activities. Etc.

You've likely seen in the news that there are brick-and-mortar stores that are being revamped to be run entirely by AI systems and there aren't any human attendants or other humans on-site. The same could be done with mobile stores.

Given that somewhat downbeat notion, I'd bet that the omission of human salespersons would not occur during the initial rollouts of mobile stores. That is, you can expect that the mobile stores will include at least one or more human salespersons. This seemingly brash prediction might provide some relief to those of you that relish those jobs and also for those shoppers that cherish interacting with human salespersons.

But if we do eventually have AI acting as both driver and as the salesperson, here's something else to keep on top of mind. Suppose the AI gets greedy and opts to keep some of those diamond necklaces for itself, potentially grabbing up a few of those fancy handbags too.

That's just the kind of thing that AI might opt to do, and we humans will need to make sure the goodies are well-accounted for and haven't been misappropriated by the egregiously shiftless form of AI.

# CHAPTER 16
# HITTING POLICE CARS AND SELF-DRIVING CARS

Code 3.

That's the usual parlance for indicating that a police car will activate its flashing lights and engage a blaring siren as the vehicle is driven at high speeds while rushing to a crime scene. The police car is apt to weave around normal traffic and ostensibly dodge other everyday cars during the heart-pounding effort.

If you've ever seen a police car go past you in such a fast-moving manner, the odds are that you were cognizant of the risks associated with that kind of driving. The officer driving the police car is hopeful that other nearby drivers will get out of the way and enable the rushing vehicle to proceed unimpeded.

The thing is, lots of ordinary drivers don't seem to take the kinds of avoidance actions that they ought to take and that they are typically required by law to perform.

Years ago, most drivers would readily pull over to the side of the road, doing so the moment they became aware of an upcoming police car that was fervently moving along. Nowadays, it seems like there are fewer and fewer conscientious drivers that do so. Perhaps some aren't sure of what to do, and thus they merely slow down and remain in their existing lane, figuring that the police car will route around them.

Others might not hear or see the police car and therefore fail to take any avoidance efforts. It could be that today's drivers are in their own bubble, as it were, ensconced in modern cars that can seemingly dampen noises from the outside and also boast impressive internal stereo systems that fill a car with earsplitting levels of musical sounds that you'd hear at a live rock concert.

Of course, there are also those drivers that are otherwise distracted and not entirely devoted to the driving task at hand. They might be watching those enchanting cat videos and ergo not paying attention exclusively to the roadway. Or they might be on their smartphone and chatting with someone at work or trying to respond to text messages while nonetheless still at the wheel of a multi-ton life-or-death in-motion vehicle.

Some assert that there is also a herd mentality that can overtake drivers. If a driver hears the siren or sees the flashing lights, the driver might first look around to see what other cars are doing. Upon noticing that few other cars are taking any avoidance actions, the driver shrugs their shoulders and figures they won't either. In fact, the driver might mentally calculate that if they opt to move over, it could create a worse situation, whereby other drivers that aren't doing so will get confused and possibly collide with the one car that is trying to abide by the lawful need to get out of the way.

The whole matter is quite a conundrum.

A potentially deadly conundrum.

A police car that is in a rush might end up coming to an intersection that presents a red light to the vehicle. Rather than coming to a stop, the officer is likely to proceed into the intersection and do so under the belief and hope that cars coming from the other sides will not intervene. This has got to be one of the most unnerving moments for an officer. A car that has the green light might proceed into the intersection and plow broadside into the speeding police car.

All told, you undoubtedly get the gist that when a police car is rapidly responding and underway, there are lots of outsized risks for the officers inside the police car, along with added risks to those driving perchance in the same path as the urgently proceeding emergency vehicle (as a side note, the same could be said for urgently responding ambulances, fire trucks, and the like, though usually, those tend to be larger vehicles and possibly proffer some added protection, though in any case still pose grave risks to all).

An added twist and a boatload of controversy entail a car chase situation. When a police car or a series of police cars are in avid pursuit of a car that is driving recklessly and at high speeds, there is a complex calculation that needs to be made. One aspect involves the risks to the general public during the course of the car chase. Another aspect includes the risks of allowing the car being chased to get away and thus potentially allow a criminal or presumed criminal to be on the streets. Different authorities and experts have various viewpoints on whether or when such pursuits should be undertaken and when those pursuits should be curtailed.

Let's do a quick overall recap.

There are instances whereby a police officer presses ahead with a designated Code 3 and undertakes what is usually depicted as a hot response. During that effort, the officer driving the speeding vehicle is tasked with getting around everyday traffic and also potentially taking outsized chances when crossing intersections. This means that there is a heightened chance that the police car might ram into a nearby car, and likewise a heightened chance that a nearby car might ram into the police car.

On top of this, intentions need to be weighed too.

By and large, when a police car and an ordinary car collide during a Code 3, this was unintentional. Neither the officer driving the police car and nor the everyday driver of the ordinary car was intending to run into each other. It happened as a result of the circumstances.

In contrast, during a hot police pursuit throughout a frenetic car chase, there is a chance of intentional rammings, such as a police car attempting to ram the fleeing car to end the chase, or the fleeing driver opting to ram a police car as part of their desperate escape efforts.

You can categorize these scenarios into two major facets entailing a police car that collides with an ordinary car versus an ordinary car that collides with a police car. Plus, we can add to this categorization the notion of intentionality versus unintentionality.

We then would have these four general classifications:

- A police car collides with an ordinary car, doing so unintentionally.
- An ordinary car collides with a police car, doing so unintentionally.
- A police car collides with an ordinary car, doing so intentionally.
- An ordinary car collides with a police car, doing so intentionally.

Most people probably don't know how dangerous Code 3 can be for police officers.

Per statistics reported by the CDC, the motor vehicle-related line-of-duty deaths for law enforcement officers are calculated as being on average approximately one officer per week being killed on our roadways. This analysis was based on reported incidents from 2010 to 2019. There was an indicated 53 law enforcement officer deaths per year, which included officers killed due to vehicle crashes (25% of the total) and in other circumstances such as getting struck by a vehicle while on foot.

Shifting gears, consider that the future of cars will encompass self-driving cars.

True self-driving cars are driven by an AI-based driving system, doing so without any need for human assistance during the driving task.

Assume for the sake of discussion that self-driving cars will gradually become viable and we'll see more and more of them on our roadways. Generally, the belief is that the emergence of self-driving cars will initially be quite gradual and it will take many years, if not decades, for self-driving cars to become a prevalent vehicle on our highways and byways.

Consider this intriguing question: *Will the advent of AI-based true self-driving cars suggest that we will no longer have any collisions with police cars?*

Let's unpack the matter and see.

**Self-Driving Cars And Police Cars On Code 3**

For Level 4 and Level 5 true self-driving vehicles, there won't be a human driver involved in the driving task.

All occupants will be passengers.

The AI is doing the driving.

One aspect to immediately discuss entails the fact that the AI involved in today's AI driving systems is not sentient. In other words, the AI is altogether a collective of computer-based programming and algorithms, and most assuredly not able to reason in the same manner that humans can.

Why this added emphasis about the AI not being sentient?

Because I want to underscore that when discussing the role of the AI driving system, I am not ascribing human qualities to the AI. Please be aware that there is an ongoing and dangerous tendency these days to anthropomorphize AI. In essence, people are assigning human-like sentience to today's AI, despite the undeniable and inarguable fact that no such AI exists as yet.

With that clarification, you can envision that the AI driving system doesn't natively somehow "know" about the act of driving. This is a capability that needs to be programmed as part of the hardware and software of the self-driving car.

Let's dive into the myriad of aspects that come to play on this topic.

First, assume that police cars will remain human-driven for quite some time to come.

In theory, we will ultimately have self-driving cars that are used as police cars, but this is a further out step in the emergence of self-driving cars. The current focus by most automakers and self-driving tech firms is to get an ordinary car to function on a self-driving basis. The somewhat extraordinary driving aspects that would be required for a police car are out-of-scope for the time being and sits on a so-called edge or corner case list for now (meaning that this is a low priority at this time).

Next, assume that we will have a mixture of human-driven cars and self-driving cars on our roadways.

Though some seem to think that a simple snap of the fingers will magically turn all conventional cars into self-driving cars, this is wild talk and not sensible. There are about 250 million conventional cars in the United States alone, and they aren't going to overnight be transformed into self-driving cars. The reality is that self-driving cars will gradually be made available and incrementally become more and more popular.

The proportion of self-driving cars to human-driven cars will initially be quite low. Over time, the proportion will shift. Whether we will ever completely do away with human driving is an ongoing debate, whereby some exhort that you will only take away their driving privileges when you pry their cold dead hands from their steering wheel.

Okay, we will have police cars being driven by human police officers, and we will have a smattering of self-driving cars and a swath of human-driven cars. That's the picture to keep in mind during this discussion.

A rushing police car will have to contend with both human-driven cars and self-driving cars.

There is also the oft chance of a rushing police car having to contend with another rushing police car, but let's put that less likely scenario as out of scope for this particular discussion since it is ostensibly a rarity and has its own specifics to be dealt with.

Your first thought might be that the self-driving car would indubitably do the right thing and abide by the speeding police car, namely that, unlike human drivers, the AI driving system would be programmed to consistently and persistently get over when a police car is zipping nearby.

Yes, that is likely to be true, but it also requires deeper digging to ferret out that there are potential gaps or loopholes, as it were.

Let's start with the key aspect that a self-driving car would need to realize that a speeding police car is nearby.

How will the AI driving system realize that a police car is on Code 3 and within the driving vicinity of the self-driving car?

Humans use their eyes and ears to try and ascertain that a police car is urgently underway and near to their location. You might see the flashing lights. You might hear the sound of the siren. Furthermore, you can likely determine how far away the police car is, such as by the distant sound of the siren or by how far away the flashing lights are on display.

Also, you might watch for movement associated with the flashing lights and the siren. All told you are trying to figure out whether the police car is getting closer to you or perhaps moving further away. Is the police car up ahead of you, or behind you someplace? And so on.

A self-driving car is outfitted with various sensors that are used to detect the driving scene. This includes streaming video cameras, radar, LIDAR, ultrasonic units, thermal imaging, and the like (this varies by automaker and self-driving tech maker). The AI driving system receives data from the sensors and has to try and combine the data to mathematically compute the driving environment. Part of this involves undertaking MSDF or Multi-Sensor Data Fusion, combining the myriad of sensory data into an attempted cohesive whole.

One sensor that has not been heretofore given much attention is the use of microphones or audio sensory input from the outside of the self-driving car. There are likely microphones inside the self-driving car, allowing for the AI to interact via Natural Language Processing with riders, but there has been less focus on microphones externally mounted on the vehicle.

I think you can guess why this sparsity of external microphones can be detrimental when it comes to the police car scenario. Without an externally focused audio pick-up, the odds of detecting a wailing siren are quite low. Sure, there is an oft chance that a microphone inside the vehicle might hear the siren, though this is probably unlikely and certainly not as reliable as would be an externally mounted microphone.

Currently, this means that self-driving cars would tend to rely more so on the detection of flashing lights and the kind of "facial recognition" of detecting a police car. By recognition, I am referring to the taken-for-granted notion that we can all instantly recognize a police car when we see one. As humans, we know that a police car usually is black and white, has markings that say it is a police car, has mounted light bars, and so on.

Realizing that an AI driving system does not inherently "know" this, the AI developers would need to train the AI on recognizing police cars. This is typically done via the use of Machine Learning (ML) and Deep Learning (DL), consisting of computational pattern matching. In brief, lots of pictures of police cars can be fed into the ML/DL and it will compute the features that seem to characterize police cars.

The point to this somewhat technical discussion is that it is not an assured aspect that an AI driving system will natively somehow be able to detect a police car. Furthermore, detection of the existence of a rapidly moving police car is just the start of the matter. The AI driving system would need to calculate where the police car is currently and where it is likely headed.

Generally, an AI driving system maintains an internal database that is a virtual model of the scene surrounding the self-driving car.

Upon potentially detecting a speeding police car, the virtual model would need to be marked that such a vehicle is at such-and-such likely position and that the police car is moving at such-and-such speed and potentially headed in a such-and-such direction.

The AI driving system typically contains a planning component that attempts to identify where the self-driving car should go. Based on detecting an urgently moving police car, the AI driving system would probably be programmed to try and move over, when the timing makes sense to do so, and enable the police car to proceed unabated. There are many complexities entailed in *simply moving over*, since there might be other cars nearby to the self-driving car or perhaps even pedestrians on the streets, etc.

None of this is surefire.

The self-driving car might not detect the police car. In which case, the AI driving system is going to proceed jauntily as though there is nothing else amiss. You might liken this to the human drivers that are unaware of the presence of a speeding police car and therefore take no avoidance actions accordingly.

When coming upon an intersection that is green to the self-driving car, the AI driving system is likely programmed to assume that the self-driving car can proceed through the intersection. Unless by chance the self-driving car detects the approaching police car, the AI driving system would proceed directly into the intersection and not be taking evasive action or coming to a stop.

All told, we know that there are risks associated with a police car that collides with a human-driven car. There are also risks associated with a police car colliding with a self-driving car. It can happen.

There are also risks associated with a human-driven car that collides with a police car. Likewise, there are risks associated with a self-driving car that might collide with a police car. It can happen.

If the AI driving system is unable to detect the presence of the police car, the only hope would be that at the last moment before a collision, there is a chance that the self-driving car would detect that another vehicle is about to collide with the self-driving car. This might or might not include detection that it is a police car, and merely be that another vehicle is moving at a fast rate of speed and mathematically is going to end up colliding with the self-driving car.

Whether there is sufficient reaction time to then avoid the collision will depend upon the situation at hand.

There is an interesting tangent associated with this matter. Human drivers have a mental model about the actions of other human drivers. We tend to rely upon our "theory of mind" about what other drivers are thinking and what they will do. This can be crucial in those split seconds before a collision and trying to decide what you should do versus what the other driver is going to do.

It is unlikely that many police officers have yet formulated a "theory of mind" about what a self-driving car is going to do. I want to emphasize that I am not suggesting the AI driving system has a "mind" and I earlier stated that it is unsavory to anthropomorphize AI.

What I am alluding to here is that a police officer might not be aware of how the AI driving system has been programmed, such that it is unclear as to what driving actions the AI driving system are going to take in such extreme circumstances.

**Conclusion**

One potential solution to this dire issue of rushing police cars and collisions with self-driving cars involves the use of V2V and V2I.

V2V refers to vehicle-to-vehicle electronic communications. A self-driving car outfitted with V2V could alert other nearby self-driving cars that a police car is rushing down the street on 5th avenue and headed northbound.

In addition, police cars can be outfitted with V2V and could beam out electronic messages to alert nearby self-driving cars as to where the police car is and where it is heading.

V2I refers to vehicle-to-infrastructure electronic communications. You might already be aware that traffic signals and other elements of the roadway infrastructure are gradually being computerized. A police car can emit an electronic signal that tells a traffic light to change to green for its passage and thus show red to other vehicles. Self-driving cars will also be set up to communicate electronically with the roadway infrastructure.

These and other kinds of electronic messaging solutions would dramatically lessen the risks of collisions between police cars and self-driving cars.

Indeed, there is a ready argument that conventional cars ought to also be equipped with similar devices, thus alerting human drivers too. One can somewhat confidently state that the AI driving systems will programmatically consistently tend to abide by such alerts, while human drivers are apt to drive with less uniformity (nonetheless, such devices for the human-driven car would still be vital and overall advantageous).

One nifty aspect about self-driving cars is that the chances of a self-driving car getting into a wild car chase are rather unlikely. In other words, you aren't going to likely see a criminal that is riding in a self-driving car taking the police on a high-speed chase (since the AI driving system is usually programmed to not allow such activity).

As a final thought, for now, imagine the world once there are AI driving systems for police cars. In that case, we'll have urgently driven police cars being piloted by AI, and they will be dealing potentially with human-driven cars and other self-driving cars on the roadways.

I think you can imagine how that type of AI is going to have its hands quite full trying to cope with traffic while attempting to safely fulfill a Code 3..

# CHAPTER 17
# BRAKE-CHECKING AND SELF-DRIVING CARS

We've all been brake-checked at one time or another.

Brake checking refers to the notion that a car ahead of you will pump on its brakes to try and send you a signal. Presumably, the signal primarily being conveyed is that you ought to slow down. In addition, the same signaling usually is trying to warn you to back off and keep a greater distance between your car and the car that is doing the brake checking.

Of course, one might argue that the brake checker is merely making sure that their brakes are functioning. Perhaps they are simply ensuring that when the time comes to be able to invoke the brakes, they are sufficiently capable of working. Sure, that kind of brake checking does happen, though the actual type of brake checking that most of us witness are not due to a driver that is innocently seeking to test their brakes as a precautionary measure.

Another somewhat innocuous form of brake checking entails the act of purposely slowing a car while on a steep downward sloping road. Many people do a series of short braking pumps while on an especially precarious downhill descent. This is in fact a usually recommended practice. Namely, rather than continuously riding on your brakes, it is typically advisable to intermittently utilize the brakes and bring about a staccato slowing action. The hope is that the brakes won't somehow otherwise burn out from overuse amid nonstop frictional forces being applied.

Setting aside those lesser alarming forms of brake checking, let's focus on the kind of brake checking that encompasses an intentional act of telling other cars that this driver is letting you know what's up.

Here's what oftentimes happens.

A driver looks in their rearview mirror and sees a car coming up quickly from behind. The driver doesn't like the driving antics of this upcoming miscreant. It could be that the car coming up fast is speeding and thereby flagrantly disobeying the law. Or perhaps the quickly approaching driver is weaving dangerously throughout traffic, an aspect that the brake checking driver finds distasteful and ought to be put to a stop.

All told, the brake checker decides that if there are no other means to get the other car to cease and desist its wrongful driving ways, the prudent and rightful course of action involves using the ubiquitous brake checking maneuver. Generally, this driving tactic consists of making sure to be directly in front of the offending car, and then tapping the brakes, doing so repeatedly. The brake lights will illuminate and are supposed to somewhat flash on and off, but not in too fast a repetition. The pace of the brake checking has to be just right, a kind of Goldilocks timing, not too fast and not too slow.

Not every brake checking aficionado does the action with the same aplomb. Some are feverish and pump those brakes as though they are pounding on a drumkit with all the energy they can muster. Others do the brake pumping at lengthy intervals, which then makes it difficult to discern whether the person is purposely pumping their brakes or maybe just lazily and by happenstance doing so.

That brings up an important aside. Some people just love their brakes. They use them all the time. By this, I mean that when there is not even any notable cause to apply the brakes, these drivers will do so anyway. For them, perhaps there is a sense of safety and warmth that comes from coddling the brakes and using them incessantly during a driving journey.

Such drivers might also do brake checking, though it can be hard to discern whether they are simply the brake riding types or they are suddenly shifting into a mode of being a bona fide brake-checking proponent.

You can usually readily figure out whether someone is purposely acting as a brake checking advocate by other additive telltale signs. For example, the brake checking driver might change lanes to position their car directly ahead of the oncoming car that is presumably being disrespectful or acting as a scofflaw.

Speaking of changing lanes, the upcoming car that spies a brake checking actor ahead of them is likely to change lanes, figuring it is easiest to simply go around the apparent self-selected traffic enforcer. So, in a cat and mouse gambit, the fast-moving driver will change lanes, and then if the brake checker also changes lanes, a series of the lane going ping pong will take place.

This is when things get extremely dicey.

It is already risky enough to be using the brake checking maneuver, let alone doing so by switching lanes repeatedly too. The chances of a collision are going to get heightened by this type of scary game. Keep in mind that the collision won't solely involve the two cars there are immersed in this vehicular battle, since the odds are that other cars nearby will inevitably get carried into the risky action taking place.

The person doing the brake checking is apt to believe that they are doing the right thing. Yes, they would admit, their brake checking driving efforts are adding risk, but this is worthwhile when you consider that they are going to presumably put to a stop the crazed driving of the other driver. In essence, one wrong can make a right, as it were. By aiming to get the wild driver to slow down and be more careful, the end result is that all nearby and ensuing traffic will be safer overall.

Some would say that this is both egotistical, meaning that the brake checking driver is over endowing their own driving acumen, and idealistic thinking too. The reason that there is idealism involved is that the other driver is apt to not react in the manner that the brake checking driver assumes they will.

A driver that comes upon a brake checking advocate is likely to resent being brake checked. That resentment is usually going to translate into a hardened belief that the brake checker is wrong, and either to be avoided or ought to be shown a lesson. This turns the already upcoming driver into having a now second passion. They want to proceed unfettered and simultaneously they want to showcase to the brake checking driver that the primitive and impotent effort to prevent traversal is not going to succeed.

In short, the whole matter can devolve into road rage.

Throughout this discussion, the implication has been that the brake checking driver was technically in the right per se, but that is unlikely to be the case. Suppose that the upcoming driver is not speeding and otherwise is perfectly law-abiding. There are certainly instances of a brake checking driver that decided to use the brake checking gambit even though there was no demonstrable cause to do so. You might say this is a type of misguided brake checking.

The other crucial facet to realize is that brake checking is normally considered unwise and altogether illegal in most states. For example, in California, the Department of Motor Vehicles (DMV) has a vehicle code numbered 22109 that is commonly referred to as the brake checking rule. Even if there isn't a specific rule or statute that makes brake checking a driving offense, there is usually a catchall rule that says you cannot impede traffic or driver in a manner that could be construed as improper.

A key point by most authorities is that intentionally doing brake checking is a bad thing to do (i.e., brake checking of the nature that is designed to try and instruct or obstruct other drivers). Though the driver doing the brake checking might believe in their own minds that they are helping the world at large, the chances are that instead, they are making a potentially bad situation into a worse one.

Despite that kind of admonishment, you can bet that those that believe in the brake checking method are going to continue to deploy the handy instrument. They would likely argue that it is a real-world practice and they are willing to take a chance on getting a ticket because they fervently believe that the brake checking on the-whole balances the world and makes for safer traffic conditions.

An example of this way of thinking entails circumstances wherein the upcoming driver does opt to slow down and does start to maintain a proper distance to other cars. Maybe that driver was in a muddled haze and the brake checking got their attention. The driver might have felt sheepish and embarrassed that they were mindlessly driving in a somewhat reckless manner. By being startled into a proper state of driving awareness, they are mentally restored into driving more safely.

All it takes is for a few of those instances to then reinforce to the brake checking driver that they are ostensibly correct in their brake checking ritual. You win some, you lose some, would seemingly be the mantra. There are going to be occasions when the brake checking accomplishes its goal, and then other situations wherein the brake checking flops.

To reemphasize, that kind of logic is not sound according to most authorities and is replete with problematic concerns.

Shifting gears, the future of cars entails the advent of self-driving cars.

True self-driving cars are vehicles that are driven entirely by an AI-based driving system (see my coverage at **this link here**). There isn't a human driver involved. We will gradually and inexorably have self-driving cars on our highways and byways, and we'll see them and be riding in them daily.

Here's an intriguing question: *Will the emergence of AI-based true self-driving cars cast away the infamous act of brake checking?*

Let's unpack the matter and see.

## Self-Driving Cars And Brake Checking

For Level 4 and Level 5 true self-driving vehicles, there won't be a human driver involved in the driving task.

All occupants will be passengers.

The AI is doing the driving.

One aspect to immediately discuss entails the fact that the AI involved in today's AI driving systems is not sentient. In other words, the AI is altogether a collective of computer-based programming and algorithms, and most assuredly not able to reason in the same manner that humans can.

Why this added emphasis about the AI not being sentient?

Because I want to underscore that when discussing the role of the AI driving system, I am not ascribing human qualities to the AI. Please be aware that there is an ongoing and dangerous tendency these days to anthropomorphize AI. In essence, people are assigning human-like sentience to today's AI, despite the undeniable and inarguable fact that no such AI exists as yet.

With that clarification, you can envision that the AI driving system doesn't natively somehow "know" about brake checking. This is an aspect that needs to be programmed as part of the hardware and software of the self-driving car.

Let's dive into the myriad of aspects that come to play on this topic.

First, we will set aside for the remainder of this discussion the *legitimate* uses of a brake checking maneuver such as invoked when going down a steep hill. Assume that self-driving cars will potentially be explicitly programmed with such a capability and are aiming to be used when the driving situation is aboveboard for the use of brake checking.

Thus, we will only consider the "illegitimate" uses of brake checking, which I encompass in quotes because there are some that would still argue that the use of brake checking to signify to other drivers that they are too slow down or maintain a proper distance is (in their view) entirely legitimate (I trust that I've already clarified that aspect earlier).

We might reasonably assume that AI-based true self-driving cars will not employ the illegitimate uses of brake checking.

Note though that this is predicated on being programmed to only use the brake checking technique in presumed legitimate circumstances. In other words, if self-driving cars do have a programmed capacity to do brake checking, in theory, this could be applied at any time in any situation. This means that the programming would also have to include the bounds upon which brake checking was to be used and that the AI driving system abided accordingly to these restricted bounds.

The point is that if the AI driving system is weakly programmed and does not encompass any particular bounds, this would imply that the AI driving system could use the brake checking technique whenever mathematically it was computed as something seemingly viable to employ.

We must also include the oddball chances of the AI driving system containing an error in logic or having some other malfunction or hack that led to the use of the brake checking, despite any other prior programmed boundaries or restrictions.

I think it is sufficient to suggest for now that the AI will be programmed with appropriate bounds and that the AI driving systems will usually and normally avoid using brake checking other than when a needed legitimate occasion arises.

Okay, so you don't have to worry as a human driver that a self-driving car is going to brake check you.

That seems reassuring.

There is though an unfortunate twist.

When human drivers encounter other human drivers, there is an assumed notion that brake checking could be used (encompassing the considered illegitimate instances). If human drivers realize that self-driving cars won't customarily use brake checking that human drivers do, will this be a kind of green light that self-driving cars are sheep and ought to be treated as such?

Most self-driving cars are being programmed to act as timid drivers. One concern that some have raised is that human drivers will rely upon that timidity and therefore drive in even worse and more brazen ways when they are nearby self-driving cars. Indeed, human drivers are already bullying self-driving cars (this is occurring in many ways, see my columns for numerous examples).

We don't need to worry that somehow the AI will get its feelings hurt (again, let's not anthropomorphize AI). The real problem is that human drivers already are apt to drive poorly, and when they begin to believe that self-driving cars can be bamboozled, it will be both fun (for some) and advantageous to leverage that aspect. This will likely lead to more car crashes as those human drivers become increasingly reckless at driving.

There is certainly a bit of irony that the advent of self-driving cars is anticipated to make driving safer, but at the same time, we need to include the role of human drivers that will still be driving conventional cars and might opt to drive worse than they do now.

There are about 250 million conventional cars in the United States alone, and they won't be transformed overnight into self-driving cars. The real world is going to be a mixture of conventional human-driven cars and those newly emerging self-driving cars, likely for many decades. We might always have human-driven cars if you take the absolute word of those that earnestly state they will never give up their driving until the day that you pry their cold dead hands from the steering wheel.

We've now covered that self-driving cars will presumably not do brake checking for any illegitimate reasons.

This regrettably bodes for some qualms in that human drivers will figure out that AI driving systems aren't going to brake check them and thus they can drive without any such blockage or concern. A potential saving grace could be that since self-driving cars are equipped with a suite of sensors, including video cameras, there is a possibility that the AI driving systems might detect foul driving by humans, and the sensory data sent to the police to then go after those so detected drivers (I'm sure my mentioning this possibility sent shivers up your spine since it has tremendous Big Brother-related implications).

What about human drivers that opt to brake check self-driving cars?

Sure, humans are going to do so.

In fact, I witnessed such an act the other day.

A self-driving car was next to me in traffic. The car ahead of the self-driving car was human-driven. I watched in rapt attention as the human-driven car proceeded to brake check the self-driving car.

Here's why it was seemingly odd.

The self-driving car and its AI driving system had appeared to have been programmed to keep a proper distance from other cars ahead while in traffic. Furthermore, the self-driving car was strictly obeying the speed limit. Unlike a human driver that might be violating one or both of those precepts, the self-driving car was being as lawful as one could envision.

Why was the human driver opting to brake check the self-driving car?

We weren't on a downhill slope. The self-driving car was keeping a good distance and driving cautiously. The human driver had started doing the brake checking at the same time that the self-driving car traversed into being behind the human-driven car, so it did not seem to be coincidental and instead appeared to be a purposeful act of brake checking.

Maybe the human driver was toying with the self-driving car. This could be done as a joke or out of curiosity (either way, don't do this!). Some human drivers try to justify playing tricks on self-driving cars by claiming they are helping to train the AI driving systems for coping with human-driven vehicles (no thanks, there are enough bad drivers for that already). Another possibility is that the human driver was unsure of what a self-driving car might do. To be on a defensive posture, the unsettled human driver might have opted to do brake checking in hopes of keeping the self-driving car at bay. That being said, the human driver could have switched lanes, or turned to take another street, if they were especially queasy about the self-driving car.

The thing is, human drivers are human drivers. We cannot necessarily discern what is going on in their noggins. In this case, the self-driving car maintained its distance. I am doubtful that the AI driving system had been programmed to detect brake checking per se, and likely was simply responding to the instances of the brakes being used, without noting an overall pattern.

Some believe strongly that AI driving systems ought to be able to analyze a driving setting and ascertain when brake checking is taking place. Of course, it is one thing to detect the physical act of brake checking, and an altogether different matter of trying to discern why someone is using brake checking. That's why AI driving systems need to include a "theory of mind" about how human drivers think, since human drivers are both fellow drivers on our public roadways and also, regrettably, adversaries in some ways too.

Digging into the human mind though is not necessarily the most pleasant of tasks. If AI is incrementally advanced and can someday aid in discerning the human mind, that's the kind of thing we might want to encourage, or if that seems untoward, possibly deploy some of that revered brake checking instead, stopping from not going too deeply into the inner sanctum of what makes humans tick).

# CHAPTER 18
# BIRD'S EYE VIEW AND SELF-DRIVING CARS

When driving a car, you could really benefit from having a bird's-eye view of the driving scene.

Let's explore why.

Imagine that you are driving in a crowded and altogether hectic downtown area.

There are humongous skyscraper buildings that are towering over you and ostensibly blocking any chance of seeing beyond an extremely narrow tunnel-vision perspective of the roadway. Among the visual obscurity, you cannot see anything on the streets that intersect with the road that you are currently driving on. Until you get directly into an intersection, you pretty much have no idea what is taking place on any of those perpendicular avenues that are to the left and right of you.

During your driving in this nightmarish of circumstances (a daily occurrence for many drivers), you opt to make a right turn onto an intersecting street.

So, you come up to the corner that is packed with pedestrians and signposts, once again blocking your view, and decide to engage a rapid and sharp right turn. Just as you poke forward into the turn, you'll have a very brief and minuscule chance to fleetingly glimpse whatever lies beyond. In that split second, you have to visually scan the entire driving scene and hope that you can mentally ascertain the considerations and contortions of whatever unknown menaces are looming ahead of you.

For example, as you make the right turn, you might suddenly

come upon a car that has opted to unlawfully park in the active lane and this irksome and quite inconsiderate driver doesn't seem to care that the roadway is now being blocked. You didn't see the halted car until engaging into making your turn. As such, you now are moving at a quick pace and could ram directly into the back of this reckless driver that has decided they own the roadway.

Your mind races feverishly as you frantically mull over your options.

You could hit the brakes, but this might get you violently rear-ended by a car that is closely following you during the turn. Another possibility would be to swing wide, going into the lane to the left of the illegally stopped car. The problem there is that other traffic is using that lane, and your attempt to dart into their path could be catastrophic. You will either sideswipe one of those innocent cars or possibly disrupt their steady flow and produce a series of automotive-screeching cascading collisions.

Sadly, none of the options are satisfactory.

This is the nature of driving. You are always on the edge of your seat because you are in the midst of continually making life-or-death decisions. Most people that sit down at the steering wheel are not actively thinking about the life-or-death matters involved in driving a car. Until they get themselves into a dicey driving situation, they take for granted the grim magnitude of the driving task.

All it takes is for you to make the wrong decision and you can end up striking other cars (or they could summarily ram into you). Besides the likely damage to the vehicles, there is a viable chance of you getting injured, plus your passengers getting injured. There is also the likely chance of injuring the driver of the other car and the passengers in that vehicle. Regrettably, there is also the real chance of producing fatalities. The startling statistics are that about 40,000 car crash-related fatalities occur in the United States annually, along with approximately 2.3 million related injuries.

Driving a car is dangerous and yet we generally tend to downplay the risks.

It sure would be handy if there were ways to reduce those risks. The example of making the right turn highlights especially the dismal conditions of driving when you are only able to see a small part of the overarching puzzle. Had you somehow been able to see or know that there was a car abruptly parked in the active turn lane, you would have been able to take proactive steps beforehand to avoid the pending crisis.

What could you have done differently if you had a better semblance of the roadway situation?

You might have come to a gradual stop before making the turn, which then presumably would have coaxed the car behind you to also slow down, thus reducing the risk of getting struck from behind. Alternatively, you might have chosen to *not* make the right turn at all, perhaps waiting to do so when you had driven down another block or two. In short, you would have had many more options available and been able to better make those life-or-death decisions if you had a macroscopic picture of the driving scene.

Voila, into this picture comes the proverbial bird's-eye view.

Suppose that you had some kind of extending periscope that was attached to your car. This oddball contraption could allow you to look down those intersecting streets, giving you a brief heads-up before reaching the point of potentially making a turn. That might work, but it doesn't seem particularly practical.

Imagine instead that you could somehow fly above the driving scene. There you are, sitting in your car at the steering wheel, and simultaneously you magically allow your spirit to soar into the sky. It is looking down upon the driving scene and able to inform you about what lies beyond your earthly-bound view. Now that's some kind of driving.

Rather than relying upon a farfetched notion, we can be much more down-to-earth and consider everyday options that are viable right now. Assume that we mounted a camera above the intersection that you were aiming to make that right turn at. The camera could be doing real-time streaming and send the video to your in-car display.

As such, you might glance at your in-car display and observe that a motionless car is sitting smack dab in the lane that you are expecting to use when you complete your right turn. Akin to the earlier emphasis about having crucial and timely beforehand options, you can make a wiser choice with this added vantage point.

The idea of having a camera that overlooks an intersection is altogether practical and doable today. No magic is required. We might further increase the sensing capability by including other kinds of sensory devices. For example, we could include radar, LIDAR, thermal imagining, and so on. This array of sensors would allow for detecting the driving scene in a wide variety of conditions, such as even when it is foggy, raining, snowing, etc.

That certainly seems tempting and a valuable way to give drivers an enhanced perspective about the driving scene.

There are some potential downsides.

A human driver has various limitations on how much input they can absorb at one point in time. Furthermore, their eyes can only usually be looking at one aspect at any given point in time. Thus, if you are looking down at an in-car display to see what is beyond the upcoming corner, the odds are that you've now taken your eyes off the road directly ahead of you. At that moment, you might not notice that a pedestrian has suddenly stepped into the street and you are about to run them over.

The question arises as to how a human driver can readily assimilate the expanded scope of perceiving a driving scene. This would have to be arranged in a fashion that would somehow keep your attention still riveted to the straight-ahead driving, and meanwhile allow for glimpsing what is beyond your ordinary viewpoint.

Even if this could be arranged (perhaps via some kind of HUD or heads-up display), there is also the open issue of making sense of this additional perspective. When you glance at the in-car display, you need to mentally analyze the added perspective and combine it with whatever you already have in your noggin about the driving scene.

The odds are that people would have difficulty doing this, certainly at first try. Unless you had some specialized training or a lot of experience using this kind of perspective-augmenting facility, you would undoubtedly struggle to use it. You might entirely ignore the secondary perspective. You might fail to spot the key elements in the secondary perspective that apply to your existing driving efforts. And so on.

Some people would readily take to the feature, others might never make use of it (they could presumably disengage the feature and choose explicitly to avoid using it).

You can imagine how this would play out in societal terms. A person gets into a car crash and if they had used the augmented perspective, they perhaps would have been able to avoid the collision. They are then held culpable for not having used the capability. Likewise, somebody using the augmented perspective gets into a car crash, and the claim is made that the additional info was confusing or led the driver to somehow make a worse choice than if they had not been using the secondary perspective.

Human drivers are subject to human foibles.

That's just the way the world works.

Shifting gears, the future of cars consists of self-driving cars. Self-driving cars are going to be using AI-based driving systems and there won't be a human driver at the wheel.

Here is an intriguing question: *Could AI-based true self-driving cars successfully leverage a bird's-eye view perspective of the driving scene?*

Let's unpack the matter and see.

## Self-Driving Cars And Bird's Eye View

For Level 4 and Level 5 true self-driving vehicles, there won't be a human driver involved in the driving task.

All occupants will be passengers.

The AI is doing the driving.

One aspect to immediately discuss entails the fact that the AI involved in today's AI driving systems is not sentient. In other words, the AI is altogether a collective of computer-based programming and algorithms, and most assuredly not able to reason in the same manner that humans can.

Why this added emphasis about the AI not being sentient?

Because I want to underscore that when discussing the role of the AI driving system, I am not ascribing human qualities to the AI. Please be aware that there is an ongoing and dangerous tendency these days to anthropomorphize AI. In essence, people are assigning human-like sentience to today's AI, despite the undeniable and inarguable fact that no such AI exists as yet.

With that clarification, you can envision that the AI driving system won't natively somehow "know" about how to leverage a bird's-eye view perspective of the driving scene. This is an aspect that needs to be programmed as part of the hardware and software of the self-driving car (I've referred to this as part of the "computational omnipresence" that self-driving cars can potentially attain, see my **columns for coverage**).

Let's dive into the myriad of aspects that come to play on this topic.

First, the AI driving system would have to contain some device or equipment that would receive the being beamed out secondary perspective. As mentioned earlier, the bird's-eye view electronics might contain a multitude of sensory devices. In addition, there would need to be an electronic communications capability to transmit the data being collected. In turn, any vehicle wishing to make use of the transmission would need to be equipped with an appropriate receiving device.

The point is that the self-driving car would have to contain some form of hardware and software to receive the bird's-eye view data. This might be undertaken by communications devices already on-board the vehicle, or there might need to be an added component installed into the self-driving car. Some might argue that this potentially adds an additional cost to the self-driving car. In that case, there would need to be an appropriate ROI (Return on Investment) calculated to ascertain whether the added cost is worth the benefits that would accrue.

Via a back-of-the-envelope kind of hunch, the odds are quite high that this ROI would be worthwhile since if the capability is well-implemented, it could boost the AI driving system safety and reduce the chances of self-driving cars getting into calamitous issues.

Okay, so let's assume that a self-driving car is equipped to receive the data streaming from the bird's-eye view.

We next need to consider the timeliness of the data.

Here's what I mean.

Suppose the data is time-delayed in being sent. As such, as the vehicle comes up to make a right turn, and yet the data is provided to the AI driving system is let's suppose several seconds behind real-time. In that case, the somewhat outdated data is problematic. The driving scene might have already changed, and the AI driving system is trying to use stale data.

That's bound to create difficulties.

In that sense, the data coming from the bird's-eye view has to be timely to considered especially valued. The latency is a factor. That being said, let's clarify that a timing delay of a split-second might not fully undermine the value of the data, and likewise even a delay of several seconds would not necessarily obviate the value. The point is that though the timing is vital, at least if it is time-stamped, the AI driving system would presumably be programmed to take into account the recency of the data and give weight accordingly to what is being received. Some are suggesting that the use of 5G will be significant to this timing aspect (**see my column** for discussions about edge computing and 5G networking).

The next aspect for the AI driving system consists of programmatically intertwining the bird's-eye view with the existent sensory data from the in-car onboard sensory suite. In essence, the self-driving car already has its own set of sensory devices. There is a computational analysis that takes place and is commonly referred to as Multi-Sensor Data Fusion (MSDF). You can consider the bird's-eye view to be an added set of sensors that are now being applied to the otherwise customary MSDF computational effort of the AI driving system.

Here's something else to ponder.

Suppose the bird's-eye view provides the entirety of the raw data being collected.

This could amount to extraordinarily voluminous transmissions, taking precious time to do so. Also, the self-driving car has to have sufficient computational processing capabilities to crunch through the data, once it has been received. All told, within the self-driving car, there has to be a lot of added or presumably available computing resources for undertaking this calculation-intensive effort. Plus, it will take time for that kind of data-related interpretation and processing to occur.

You might be thinking, well, in that case, just transmit a shorthand version. Perhaps the bird's eye system ought to have its own computing capabilities and pre-crunch the data. Instead of sending the streaming video of that car parked in the active lane, the bird's-eye capability might just send a text message stating that a car is going to be blocking that upcoming turn.

This seems readily usable, but it turns out that there are thorny consequential issues that arise.

For example, is the car completely blocking the lane or only partially intruding into the lane? Is the car truly at a complete standstill or perhaps rolling forward slowly? A zillion questions can readily be divined. Without the raw data, the AI driving system will be getting an incomplete semblance of what issues might be awaiting the self-driving car. There is a challenging tradeoff of whether to only transmit a shorthand notation versus the full set of data.

I'll throw you another curveball.

Should the AI driving system entirely trust the data coming from the bird's-eye view?

On the one hand, this bird's-eye view could be a tremendous added asset. At the same time, suppose the data is delayed and no longer viably accurate about the driving scene. Worse, suppose that the data coming from the sensors is corrupted or perhaps been hacked. The key is that the AI driving system is considered "responsible" for the driving of the vehicle. As such, whatever the bird's-eye view provides is not as vital as the aspects of what the AI driving system is going to do when undertaking the driving task.

Without seeking to create an anthropomorphic analogy, recall that earlier I mentioned that human drivers might struggle to combine the bird's-eye view with their own recognition of the driving scene. You could suggest that the AI driving system is in the same boat.

That being said, the beauty of the AI driving system is that, unlike a human that seemingly can only provide their riveted attention to one thing at a time (i.e., looking at the roadway versus looking at an in-car display), the AI system can be doing those types of actions simultaneously. Assuming that there is sufficient processing speed available and that the software is well-written, the AI driving system ought to be able to analyze the totality of the perspectives that are available via the amalgamated data from the widened sensory indications.

We can add more icing to that cake.

It is expected that self-driving cars will be equipped with V2V (vehicle-to-vehicle) electronic communications. This allows a self-driving car to send electronic messages to other nearby self-driving cars. For example, a self-driving car that perhaps made the right turn at the corner could send out a V2V cautioning that a car is parked just beyond that turn. Other nearby self-driving cars could receive the message, and the AI driving systems would accordingly (hopefully) be programmed to consider that added info.

There is also going to be V2I (vehicle-to-infrastructure). For example, traffic signals will be beaming out electronic messages. Thus, rather than having to rely solely on a visual indication of whether a traffic signal is green-yellow-red, this can be transmitted electronically.

All told, a self-driving car is apt to have a plethora of outside info that will be flowing into the AI driving system. This data needs to be computationally examined. There needs to be a fusing of the data to try and determine what the driving scene consists of. Plus, the AI driving system cannot necessarily assume that all the data is valid or truthful. Some of the data will be, while perhaps other parts of the data might be noisy, corrupted, or otherwise have misleading indications.

Various experimental or pilot uses of birds-eye view capabilities are taking place today.

For example, Ford has devised a bird's-eye view sensory set up in Miami Beach, doing so as part of the joint effort of Ford and Argo AI's self-driving vehicles. Specifically, a busy intersection in South Beach that is known for especially being hectic has been selected for the tryout (the corner of Lincoln Road and Lenox Avenue). This selection makes indubitable sense since it will provide a plentiful opportunity to test the bird's-eye capability (versus if a quiet and otherwise seldom-used intersection was chosen).

The expectation is that a bustling and ongoing flow of bicyclists, pedestrians, and human-driven cars will be readily encountered at that intersection (this expectation is notably likely since the intersection is near to an outdoor mall and lots of popular stores and eateries). As with any of these efforts, it is prudent to do so in conjunction with roadway and related authorities. This effort includes the Florida Department of Transportation, the City of Miami Beach, and Miami-Dade County.

Per an indication by Scott Griffith, CEO of Ford Autonomous Vehicles and Mobility Businesses, this effort brings together the added pieces of the puzzle that underlay the emergence of self-driving cars, including the use of state-of-the-art infrastructure capabilities (see his LinkedIn coverage): "Bringing together the future of self-driving requires us to think about every piece of the puzzle. One part of this is researching emerging technologies, like smart infrastructure, to explore how we can provide our self-driving vehicles with as much information as possible to navigate complex urban areas."

Bryan Salesky, CEO of Argo AI, and as I've previously covered in my columns, is well-known for his focused mission of seeking to develop and deploy self-driving cars for the betterment of making getting around cities safer, easier, and more thoroughly enjoyable experience for all. By Argo AI actively participating in these kinds of birds-eye view efforts, the synergistic impact of leveraging such capabilities is undoubtedly an incremental step in that commendable path.

**Conclusion**

Overall, the bird's-eye view provides a handy add-on for the advent of self-driving cars.

I mention that this should be considered an *add-on* since the philosophical bent must be that an AI-based true self-driving car will still operate effectively without having a bird's-eye view available. This is important due to the obvious aspect that many locales won't have a birds-eye setup in place. In addition, there is always the chance that any such equipment might suddenly be disrupted or experience troubles, in which case the AI driving system has to be programmed to work as though the birds-eye view is no longer functional.

There are other twists and turns to be considered.

For example, assume that the bird's-eye view is being operated 24x7, naturally so since cars can be coming through an intersection at any time of the day. The concern by some is that this is essentially a spying type of capability, one that can record the coming and going of people in whatever locale has the bird's-eye view established. Yes, this is ostensibly the case, though keep in mind that we already have lots and lots of video cameras set up in many areas and the trend toward doing so continues to expand (partially due to the low-cost nature of today's surveillance-style technologies).

The key here is that the aspect of having a bird's-eye view for car traffic is presumably not markedly different than if there were conventional video cameras put in place. The same kind of debate and qualms would ensue. You might try to argue that the added array of sensors makes the bird's-eye capability somewhat different, such as including perhaps radar, LIDAR, and the like, though this seems not demonstratively indistinguishable for the overarching qualms involved per se.

One last quick point for the moment on this topic.

There are other means to gain a bird's-eye view.

For example, I've covered the use of autonomous drones that would work in concert with self-driving cars. A self-driving car might have a launchpad that can place into the air a drone, which then would fly around at the command of the AI driving system and provide sensory data from a birds-eye perspective. This could be done via the self-driving car capabilities, or there might be drones that are provided by others, such as a local roadway authority that has autonomous drones.

All of the same issues earlier stated are likely to be encompassed by a drone-based bird's-eye view. Will the AI driving system be programmed to make use of the drone-added perspective? Will the AI be programmed to deal with any faulty data coming from a drone (which could happen)? Etc.

The privacy aspects also come to play, which can be worsened or lessened via the use of a drone. On the one hand, a drone is likely to be only temporarily in the skies, while a fixed-in-place bird's-eye view mounted sensory equipment is likely to be somewhat permanently put in place. At the same time, realize that the drone could wander around and glean a likely wider swath of data. On and on this matter goes.

The other futuristic consideration involves how many of these bird's-eye views will we end up having?

Suppose that an intersection has several different bird's-eye views that have been put in place. You could argue that this is fine since the more the merrier, on the other hand, the counterbalancing argument is that things are getting out-of-hand and too much can be overbearing and overwhelming.

Similarly, when you consider the use of drones for a bird's-eye view, just imagine if all the cars in a given area opted to launch their respective drones, you would seemingly have a sky utterly cluttered with a massive flock of such mechanical beasts. Anyway, we can certainly aim to start someplace, seeking to crawl before we walk, walk before we run, and run before we fly, so to speak.

Speaking of birds and flying, when I was a youngster, I had a canary as a beloved pet. I used to dream about what the canary could see when it took flight (we would let it out of the cage in our house and allow the bird to cheerfully fly throughout).

Maybe I could get another canary now and train it to carry around some sensory devices, proffering yet another means of getting a bird's-eye view for self-driving cars. Besides toting around the sensors, perhaps it would sing those delightful warbling bird songs. And the costs to keep the canary on duty would be appealingly low, only requiring everyday birdseed.

You could cheekily assert that the canary could forewarn about impending car collisions, serving as a veritable canary in a coal mine.

# CHAPTER 19
# CROSSOVER TECH AND SELF-DRIVING CARS

There's an old proverb that dates back to at least the year 1670 and declares that sauce for the goose is also sauce for the gander.

Say what?

A more modern and altogether familiar version is the assertion that what is good for the goose is good for the gander. That's a saying that we all know well. In today's world, this ostensibly suggests that something applicable in one instance is likely applicable in another (consult your favored online dictionary for further elaboration).

Here's how that adage can be applied in a context that you might find somewhat surprising.

As per my coverage about autonomous vehicles and especially self-driving cars, I oftentimes highlight cutting-edge new technology that bolsters the advent of AI-based true self-driving cars. Describing the latest state-of-the-art AI driving systems is handy to showcase what is being deployed into existent tryouts of self-driving cars. Furthermore, this highlights much of the foundational R&D work taking place in research labs that are focused on creating autonomous vehicles. Those lab projects are typically vetted and then progressed into field-based pilots.

The thing is, a lot of the autonomous tech will also end up being added to human-driven cars too. This might seem surprising or at least catch you somewhat off-guard. Many assume or are otherwise under the presumption that the tech devised to aid AI-based autonomous driving would solely be used by autonomous driving vehicles. That just seems like a rather plain-faced two-plus-two kind of proposition.

Turns out that there are numerous handy ways in which the tech derived for self-driving cars can be leveraged for human-driven vehicles too.

That being said, there are tricky aspects involved too, which I'll be explaining to you in a moment. This brings up the important insight that not every piece of tech that goes into a self-driving car is necessarily going to find its way into a human-driven vehicle. Some contraptions will, some will not.

In addition, the nature or use of the tech that gets crossed over into a human-driven car is bound to have other aspects included, recasting the tech and making it more readily accessible or usable by humans versus when the target "user" being an AI driving system (note that I've put the word "user" into quotes since I don't want to suggest or imply that today's AI is somehow human-like).

Capabilities that are being crafted to attain self-driving cars can sensibly be reused for human drivers in human-driven automobiles, though this crisscrossing might necessitate some recrafting or reimagining of what the tech proffers. All told, one could persuasively make the case that what is good for the goose is good for the gander, namely that the new tech for self-driving cars can be applied to human-driven cars, though hopefully done with aplomb and not just by cramming in of something for the sake of reuse.

The overarching question is this: *Can the advanced tech devised for self-driving cars be leveraged for use in human-driven cars on a crossover or crisscrossing basis?*

Well, I've already tipped my hand and propounded my answer, which is a resounding yes, albeit the seemingly outsized affirmation is tempered with the strident precaution to mindfully undertake any such crossovers.

Before we get deeper into the matter, let's make sure we are on the same page about what constitutes a self-driving car.

**Self-Driving Cars And Tech Crossovers**

For Level 4 and Level 5 true self-driving vehicles, there won't be a human driver involved in the driving task.

All occupants will be passengers.

The AI is doing the driving.

One aspect to immediately discuss entails the fact that the AI involved in today's AI driving systems is not sentient. In other words, the AI is altogether a collective of computer-based programming and algorithms, and most assuredly not able to reason in the same manner that humans can.

Why this added emphasis about the AI not being sentient?

Because I want to underscore that when discussing the role of the AI driving system, I am not ascribing human qualities to the AI. Please be aware that there is an ongoing and dangerous tendency these days to anthropomorphize AI. In essence, people are assigning human-like sentience to today's AI, despite the undeniable and inarguable fact that no such AI exists as yet.

Now that we've laid the stage appropriately, time to dive into the myriad of aspects that come to play on this topic about tech crossovers.

Let's start with the most obvious crossover candidates.

The sensors.

On a self-driving car, there are a bunch of specialized sensors that are used to detect the driving scene. The kinds of sensory apparatus utilized will tend to include video cameras, radar, LIDAR, ultrasonic devices, thermal imagining units, and the like (these differ by automaker and self-driving tech approaches and system packages).

Generally, the sensors are used to gather data about the world surrounding the vehicle. Visual images are streamed into the onboard systems via the video cameras. Computer processors inside the car make use of image processing software and attempt to ferret out what kinds of objects and blobs are discoverable in the visual imagery. The same can be said of the radar. Radar returns are examined computationally to try and find patterns and identify objects outside of the vehicle. Etc.

Computational analysis of the sensory data is only just the start of the AI-based driving process. Once the data has been mathematically explored, the AI driving system is usually set up to make use of an internal virtual world model that acts as a type of internal database about the driving scene. For example, the driving scene might currently consist of a car ahead of the self-driving car, a car to the right in an adjacent lane, and some pedestrians that are attempting to cross the street.

The virtual world model would be marked to indicate where each of those objects seems to be, along with their anticipated pace and predicted future path. Based on the status of the virtual world model, the AI driving system attempts to ascertain what the self-driving car should next do. Perhaps the self-driving car should come to a stop and wait for the pedestrians to proceed. In that case, the AI driving system would issue electronic commands to the vehicular controls to indicate that a halt or stopping action is to take place.

Without those sensors, the self-driving car would be unable to properly undertake those calculations about what to do, since the external world or nearby driving scene would be completely unknown. You can somewhat liken this to human drivers in the semblance of how human drivers look outside the car to try and identify what the driving scene consists of. People turn their heads back and forth, they strain to see distant objects, and otherwise primarily use their vision to figure out what is around them.

Okay, so we have human drivers that use their eyes as their cornerstone sensory element, while self-driving cars make use of video cameras, along with likely other sensory equipment such as radar,

LIDAR, and the rest.

Would it be useful to consider putting video cameras onto a human-driven car, presumably for purposes of aiding the driving task (and not simply to do a GoPro-like recording for posterity's sake, which of course is somewhat commonly done)?

Your first thought might be that it would not seem prudent to have video cameras to aid human drivers during the driving chore. The reason for this concern would be the question of how the human driver would watch the video and do so without being distracted from the roadway. We already are all worried about distracted drivers that watch cat videos while they are supposed to be driving a car. It seems that even though a video camera aimed at the road ahead would certainly be more relevant than a cat video, it nonetheless is a potential distractor.

On top of that notable point, the video camera would seem duplicative and therefore unnecessary.

A person using their eyeballs does not seem to need to have a video camera at their fingertips. They can see the world with their own eyes. The idea of taking your gaze away from the actual roadway to glance at a video screen showcasing the imagery being captured by a video camera is a seemingly loony idea. Just keep your eyes on the darned road and don't look elsewhere, that would be a prudent mantra, many would contend.

Yes, those are worthwhile points.

What this does not though include is the potential for the video camera to be able to "see" in ways that a human cannot normally naturally see things.

For example, you are driving on a wide-open highway. You notice that way up ahead there is something in your lane. The distance is rather far away and your eyes cannot discern what the object is. You aren't sure either whether the object is stationary or possibly moving around. All that you can detect for the moment is that there is definitely something out there, and it will inevitably potentially be in your path.

We've all had those moments.

You could switch lanes and hope that the object stays in the prior lane. Perhaps you might begin to slow down, figuring that whatever the object is, if you are going at a slower speed you will have more time to decide what to do when your car gets closer to the unknown object. Your mind is filled with ideas about what the object might be.

Suppose the object turns out to be a tumbleweed. In that case, it is bound to float and flit around on the highway. You might not be able to readily avoid it. That could be okay since most of the time a tumbleweed will harmlessly bounce off your car. On the other hand, maybe this is a piece of furniture that dropped off the back of a truck. Hitting a sturdy piece of furniture is not a good idea. You could damage your car, and possibly lose control of your vehicle in the process of striking the solid object.

You hopefully get the notion that if you could somehow better determine what that object is, you would have more options available and be able to sooner decide what to do. This in turn would increase your safety and the safety of other nearby cars. I point this out because if you opt to suddenly swerve at the last moment to avoid the object, any cars around you could get caught off-guard and a cascading series of catastrophic crashes could ensue.

A video camera might provide the visual imagery that your eyes cannot provide. Assume that the video camera has long-range scanning optics and can much more clearly present the object to you.

Wouldn't you want that capability?

I dare say, most of us probably would.

Taking a look at the video, you would be able to figure out what the object is, along with mentally considering what to do about the object. And due to the optics of the video camera, you are able to do all of this far in advance of when your human eyes alone could have discerned concerning the details of the object.

This seems to demonstratively illustrate the value of using a video camera for a human-driven vehicle, though we still need to explore how the human driving and the video camera imagery can be dovetailed together.

Recall that one serious and quite realistic concern is that the human might look down at a video screen to try and see what the object is, and meanwhile lose sight of the active roadway. In that split second, imagine that another car has cut in front of the driver, looking down when they should have been intently observing the existing traffic.

One possibility would be to make the video available as part of a HUD or heads-up display. The driver looks through the windshield and simultaneously is presented with the video imagery as showcased on the windshield. This can work, somewhat, though it has downsides too.

Another approach involves wearing special glasses used for driving purposes. Even if you don't need glasses, nonetheless, when you get into a specially equipped car, you put on glasses that then will display the video onto the glasses themselves. This is a kind of augmented reality (AR) approach, somewhat similar to the famous Pokémon Go AR experience or the infamous Google Glasses.

But some insist that the driver ought to not be looking at any video, no matter has pertinent to the driving task at hand. It is just much too risky.

Ergo, another approach involves using the same kind of AI driving system capabilities that do the visual image processing for self-driving cars. The computer system onboard a vehicle would do a computational analysis of the streaming video, doing this in real-time. Upon detecting an object in the roadway, the system might emit a tone or bell or alter that an object is up ahead.

Going further, the system could describe vocally the object, telling the human driver what the object seems to be. Perhaps the computer would via Natural Language Processing (NLP) akin to Alexa or Siri indicate to you that there is an object up ahead and the object is in your lane. Furthermore, if the NLP was more extensive, the driver could interact with the system.

For example, while still keeping your eyes riveted to the roadway, you might ask the NLP whether the object is stationary or moving. You might ask the NLP to provide a guess of what the object is. And so on, entering into a dialogue with the NLP (a stilted dialogue, mind you, given the NLP available to date).

In the use case of a human-driven car, this illustrates how a type of tech used in a self-driving car, and for which a self-driving car could be said to require such capabilities, can be reused in the human driving circumstance.

For a self-driving car, the AI driving system doesn't need to verbally discuss the imagery analysis with the image processing capability. There are electronic messages sent back and forth, but that's different than verbalizing the matter. The reason I point this out is that it highlights that the tech used in a self-driving car might need to be adjusted or tailored for use by humans.

The example of the video camera would indicate that merely slapping video cameras onto human-driven cars is not a good idea. The same goes for merely tossing the image processing software and hardware into a human-driven car (not a particularly useful notion by itself). No, the wholescale tit-for-tat of using something from a self-driving car for a human-driven car is rife with problems and ought to be done with some sensibility involved. Having covered the video camera as a type of self-driving car sensory device, we can reapply the same logic to the other sensory devices too. It could be handy to have radar units on a human-driven car, providing additional detection about the driving scene. Whatever the radar though captures would need to be analyzed computationally and then seamlessly relayed or made available to the human driver, doing so without distracting the driver. Repeat this same aspect for the LIDAR, ultrasonic units, and the like.

**Conclusion**

There's a lot more potential crossover where that came from.

You can dissect all of the components of a self-driving car and its AI driving systems and find a realistic means to suggest fruitfully that some aspect of the tech can be reasonably and usefully reused for human-driven cars. I wish to emphatically stress that anyone that does this and yet takes the inane perspective of doing so without considering the human-driving ramifications is playing with fire.

Poorly integrated tech from self-driving cars could actually undercut human driving and produce a human driving calamity of the likes that none of us would want. There is a tendency to find grand excitement and outstretched attention by jamming new tech into human-driven cars. Without taking into account the human factors of driving, and driver behaviors, the tech might be wasted and never used, or worse still, utilized and lend itself to stoking more car crashes than otherwise might have occurred.

When it comes to dealing with human foibles of driving, the cure should not be worse than the disease, as they say.

Another realm that provides a handy possibility for crossover includes V2X (vehicle-to-everything) electronic communications. For example, V2V is vehicle-to-vehicle electronic messaging that allows a self-driving car to send messages to another self-driving car, such as warning that a piece of debris is sitting in the roadway up ahead. The expectation is that self-driving cars are going to be outfitted with V2V. In addition, you can anticipate V2I too. V2I is vehicle-to-infrastructure and consists of roadway devices that would transmit aspects such as the traffic signal is green, the bridge up ahead is passable, and so on.

Many construe these capabilities as solely being done for the benefit of AI-based driving systems and self-driving cars and similar autonomous vehicles. Once again, you can relook at these capabilities and upon doing so would readily realize they are *potentially* advantageous to human drivers too.

A human driver would certainly find it useful getting V2V communications, when applicable. For example, on that open highway that we discussed earlier, assume that a car ahead of your car is coming upon the object that has been sitting in your lane. That vehicle might transmit a message indicating that the object is a tumbleweed.

We return to the earlier indication that we would need to find a useful and prudent means of you receiving that message. If you have to look down at a screen or your smartphone, this would be a lousy and obviously dangerous distraction from the roadway. Similar to the discussion about the sensory data being relayed to you in some more efficacious way, the same goes for any of the V2X transmissions.

One last comment for now. Some wonder whether human drivers can cope with the potentially massive amount of additional capabilities that could be arranged for their use while driving a car. Talking with an NLP about the roadway is still a form of distraction. Getting V2X transmissions, even if spoken to you, would be a form of distraction. Each additional piece of information has to be weighed as to the value it provides to safely driving a car versus the potential for undermining the driving of the car.

That's a tough balancing act, for sure. This is precisely why some vehemently say that we need to arrive at true self-driving cars.

Rather than putting more and more tech into human-driven cars, let's get the human driver out of the equation altogether, they implore. If you give a human driver more tech, you are misleadingly making them believe that they can be a better driver. The best possible driver is not a human one, some would assert, and instead, we need to have AI-based driving systems. To that degree, there is a somber worry that if there is any significant crisscrossing and crossover of tech from self-driving cars into human-driven cars, this is only sustaining something that ought to be excised anyway. Don't allow human driving to be extended and thus prolong the agonies associated with the act of human driving (others counterclaim that the tech might improve human driving and lessen the foibles and adverse impacts arising from unaided human driving).

# CHAPTER 20
# XAI AND SELF-DRIVING CARS

Our lives are filled with explanations.

You go to see your primary physician due to a rather sore shoulder. The doctor tells you to rest your arm and avoid any heavy lifting. In addition, a prescription is given. You immediately wonder why you would need to take medication and also are undoubtedly interested in knowing what the medical diagnosis and overall prognosis are.

So, you ask for an explanation.

In a sense, you have just opened a bit of Pandora's box, at least with regards to the nature of the explanation that you might get. For example, the medical doctor could rattle a lengthy and jargon-filled indication of shoulder anatomy and dive deeply into the chemical properties of the medication that has been prescribed. That's probably not the explanation you were seeking.

It used to be that physicians did not expect patients to ask for explanations. Whatever was said by the doctor was considered somewhat sacrosanct. The very nerve of asking for an explanation was tantamount to questioning the veracity of a revered medical opinion. Some doctors would gruffly tell you to simply do as they have instructed (no questions permitted) or might utter something rather insipid like your shoulder needs help and this is the best course of action. Period, end of story.

Nowadays, medical doctors are aware of the need for viable explanations. There is specialized "bedside" training that takes place in medical schools. Hospitals have their own in-house courses. Upcoming medical doctors are graded on how they interact with patients. And so on.

Though that certainly has opened the door toward improved interaction with patients, it does not necessarily completely solve the explanations issue.

Knowing how to best provide an explanation is both art and science. You need to consider that there is the explainer that will be providing the explanation, and there is a person that will be the recipient of the explanation.

Explanations come in all shapes and sizes.

A person seeking an explanation might have in mind that they want a fully elaborated explanation, containing all available bells and whistles. The person giving the explanation might in their mind be thinking that the appropriate explanation is short and sweet. There you have it, an explanation mismatch brewing right before our eyes.

The explainer might do a crisp explanation and be happily satisfied with their explanation. Meanwhile, the person receiving the explanation is entirely dissatisfied. At this point, the person that received the explanation could potentially grit their teeth and just figure that this is all they are going to get. They might silently walk away and be darned upset, opting to not try and fight city hall, as it were, and merely accede to the minimal explanation proffered.

Perhaps the person receiving the explanation decides they would like to get a more elaborated version. They might stand their ground and ask for a more in-depth explanation. Now we need to consider what the explainer is going to do. The explainer might believe that the explanation was more than sufficient, and see no need to provide any additional articulation.

The explainer might be confused about why the initial explanation was not acceptable. Maybe the person receiving the explanation wasn't listening or had failed to grasp the meaning of the words spoken. At this juncture, the explainer might therefore decide to repeat the same explanation that was just given and do so to ensure that the person receiving the original explanation really understood what was said.

You can likely anticipate that this is about to spiral out of control.

The person that is receiving this "elaborated" explanation is bound to ascertain that it is merely the same explanation and has been repeated, nearly verbatim. That's insulting! The person receiving the explanation now believes they are being belittled by the explainer. Either this person will hold their own tongue and give up trying to get an explanation, or try hurtling insults about how absurd an explanation the explanation was.

It can devolve into a messy affair, that's for sure.

The overarching point is that there is a delicate dance between the explainer and the providing of an explanation, along with the receiver and the desired nature of an explanation.

We usually take for granted these aspects. In other words, you rarely see an explainer ask what kind of explanation someone wants to have. Instead, the explainer launches into whatever semblance of an explanation that they assume the person would find useful. Rushing into providing an explanation can have its benefits, though it can also start an unsightly verbal avalanche that is going to take down both the explainer and the person receiving the explanation.

Some suggest that the explainer ought to start by inquiring about the type of explanation that the other person is seeking. This might include asking what kind of background the other person has, such as in the case of a medical diagnosis whether the other person is familiar with medical terminology and the field of medicine. There might also be a gentle inquiry as to whether the explanation should be done in one large fell swoop or possibly divided into bite-sized pieces. Etc.

The difficulty with that kind of pre-game formation is that sometimes the receiver doesn't want to go through that gauntlet. They just want an explanation (or so they say). Trying to do a preamble is likely to irritate that receiver and they will feel as though the explanation is being purposely delayed. This could even smack of hiding of the facts or some other nefarious basis for delaying the explanation.

All told, we usually expect to get an explanation when we ask for one, and not have to go through a vast checklist beforehand.

Another twist to all of this entails the interactive dialogue that can occur during explanations.

The manner of explanations is not necessarily done in a one-breath fashion from start to end. Instead, it is more likely that during the explanation, the receiver will interrupt and ask for clarification or have questions that arise. This is certainly a sensible aspect. If the explanation is going awry, why have it go on and on, wherein instead the receiver can hopefully tailor or reshape the direction and style of the explanation.

For example, suppose that you are a medical professional and have gone to see a medical doctor about your sore shoulder. Imagine that the doctor doing the diagnosis does not realize that the patient is a fellow medical specialist. In that case, the explanation offered is likely to be aimed at a presumed non-medical knowledge base and proceed in potentially simplistic ways (with respect to medical advice). The person receiving the explanation would undoubtedly interrupt and clarify that they know about medicine and the explanation should rightfully be readjusted accordingly.

You might be tempted to believe that explanations can be rated as being either good or bad. Though you could take such a perspective, the general notion is that explanations and their beauty are in the eye of the beholder. One person's favored explanation might be a disastrous or terrible one for someone else. That being said, there is still a modicum of a basis for assessing explanations and comparing them to each other.

We can add a twist on that twist.

Suppose you receive an explanation and believe it to be a good one.

Later on, you learn something else regarding the matter and realize that the explanation was perhaps incomplete. Worse still, it could be that the explanation was intentionally warped to give you a false impression of a given situation. In short, an explanation can be used to purposely create falsehoods.

That's why getting an explanation is replete with problems. We oftentimes assume that if we ask for an explanation, and if it seems plausible, this attests that the matter is well-settled and above board. The thing is, an explanation can be distorted, either by design or by happenstance and lead us into a false sense of veracity or truthfulness at hand.

Another angle to explanations deals with asking for an explanation versus being given an explanation when it has not been requested. An explainer might give you an explanation outright because they assume you want one, whereas maybe you possibly don't want and nor care for getting an explanation and are satisfied to just continue on. At that point, if you disrupt the explanation, the explainer might be taken aback.

More twisting turns can arise.

Why all this talk about explanations?

Because of AI.

The increasing use of Artificial Intelligence (AI) in everyday computer systems is taking us down a path whereby the computer makes choices and we the humans have to live with those decisions. If you apply for a home loan, and an AI-based algorithm turns you down, the odds are that all you'll know is that you did not get the loan. You won't have any idea about why you were denied the loan.

Presumably, had you consulted with a human that was doing the loan granting, you might have been able to ask them to explain why you got turned down.

Note that this is not always the case, and it could be that the human would not be willing or able to explain the matter. The loan granting person might shrug their shoulders and say they have no idea why you were turned down, or they might tell you that company policy precludes them from giving you an explanation.

Ergo, I am not suggesting that just because a human is in the loop you will necessarily get an explanation. Plus, as repeatedly emphasized earlier, the explanation might be rather feeble and altogether useless. For example, the loan granting person might tell you that you were denied because you were turned down for the loan.

Say what?

Yes, that is a non-explanation explanation under the wink-wink fakery cloak of being an explanation.

In any case, there is a big hullabaloo these days that AI systems ought to be programmed to provide explanations for whatever they are undertaking.

This is known as Explainable AI (XAI).

XAI is growing quickly as an area of keen interest. People using AI systems are going to likely expect and somewhat demand that they get an explanation provided to them. Since the number of AI systems is rapidly growing, there is going to be a huge appetite for having a machine-produced explanation about what the AI has done or is doing.

The rub is that oftentimes the AI is arcane and not readily amenable to generating an explanation.

Take as an example the use of Machine Learning (ML) and Deep Learning (DL). These are computational pattern matching algorithms that examine data and try to ferret out mathematical patterns. Sometimes the inner computational aspects are complex and do not lend themselves to being explained in any everyday human-comprehensible and logic-based way.

This means that the inherent design of the AI is by its structure not intrinsically set up for providing explanations. In that case, there are usually attempts to add on an XAI component. This XAI either probes into the AI and tries to ferret out what took place, or it sits aside from the AI and has been preprogrammed to provide explanations based on what is assumed has occurred within the mathematically enigmatic mechanisms.

Some assert that you ought to build the XAI into the core of whatever AI is being devised. Thus, rather than bolting onto the AI some afterthought about producing explanations, the design of the AI from the ground-up should encompass a proclivity to produce explanations.

Amidst all of that technological pondering, there are the other aspects of what constitutes an explanation. If you revisit my earlier comments about how explanations tend to work, and the variability depending upon the explainer and the person receiving the explanation, you can readily see how difficult it might be to programmatically produce explanations.

The cheapest way to go involves merely having pre-canned explanations. A loan granting system might have been set up with five explanations for why a loan was denied. Upon your getting turned down for the loan, you get shown one of those five explanations. There is no interaction. There is no particular semblance that the explanation is fitting or suitable to you in particular.

Those are the pittance explanations.

A more robust and respectable XAI capability would consist of generating explanations on the fly, in real-time, and do so based on the particular situation at hand. In addition, the XAI would try to ascertain what flavor or style of explanation would be suitable for the person receiving the explanation.

And this explainer feature ought to allow for fluent interaction with the person getting the explanation. The receiver should be able to interrupt the explanation, getting the explainer or XAI to shift to other aspects or reshape the explanation based on what the person indicates.

Of course, those are the same types of considerations that human explainers should also take into account. This brings up the fact that doing really good XAI is harder than it might seem. In a manner of speaking, you are likely to need to use AI within the XAI in order to be able to simulate or mimic what a human explainer is supposed to be able to do (though, as we know, not all humans are adept at giving explanations).

Shifting gears, you might be wondering what areas or applications could especially make use of XAI.

One such field of endeavor entails Autonomous Vehicles (AVs). We are gradually going to have autonomous forms of mobility, striving toward a mobility-for-all mantra. There will be self-driving cars, self-driving trucks, self-driving motorcycles (yes, that's the case, see my coverage at **this link here**), self-driving submersibles, self-driving drones, self-driving planes, and the rest.

You might at first thought be puzzled as to why AVs might need XAI. We can use self-driving cars to showcase how XAI is going to be a vital element for AVs.

The question is this: *In what way will Explainable AI (XAI) be important to the advent of AVs and as showcased via the emergence of self-driving cars?*

Let's clarify what I mean by self-driving cars, and then we can jump further into the XAI AV discussion.

**Self-Driving Cars And XAI**

For Level 4 and Level 5 true self-driving vehicles, there won't be a human driver involved in the driving task.

All occupants will be passengers.

The AI is doing the driving.

One aspect to immediately discuss entails the fact that the AI involved in today's AI driving systems is not sentient. In other words, the AI is altogether a collective of computer-based programming and algorithms, and most assuredly not able to reason in the same manner that humans can.

Why this added emphasis about the AI not being sentient?

Because I want to underscore that when discussing the role of the AI driving system, I am not ascribing human qualities to the AI. Please be aware that there is an ongoing and dangerous tendency these days to anthropomorphize AI. In essence, people are assigning human-like sentience to today's AI, despite the undeniable and inarguable fact that no such AI exists as yet.

Now that we've laid the stage appropriately, time to dive into the myriad of aspects that come to play on this topic about XAI.

I promised that we would use self-driving cars as our showcase for XAI.

First, be aware that many of the existing self-driving car tryouts have very little if any semblance of XAI in them. The initial belief was that people would get into a self-driving car, provide their destination, and be silently whisked to that locale. There would be no need for interaction with the AI driving system. There would ergo be no need for an explanation or XAI capability.

We can revisit that assumption by considering what happens when you use ridesharing and have a human driver at the wheel.

There are certainly instances wherein you get into an Uber or Lyft vehicle and there is stony silence for the entirety of the trip. You've likely already provided the destination via the ride-request app. The person driving is intently doing the driving and ostensibly going to that destination. No need to chat. You can play video games on your smartphone and act as though there isn't another human in the vehicle.

That's perfectly fine.

Imagine though that during the driving journey, all of a sudden, the driver decides to go a route that you find unexpected or unusual. You might ask the driver why there is a change in the otherwise normal path to the destination. They would hopefully prompt an explanation from the human driver.

There you go, I just said it, the notion of an explanation has come up in the context of driving a car.

Indeed, there are lots of situations in which a passenger is likely to seek an explanation from a driver.

We'll cover a few of those in a moment.

Now, in this ridesharing example, it could be that the human driver gives you no explanation or provides a flimsy explanation. Humans do that. In theory, a properly done XAI will provide an on-target explanation, though this can be challenging to do. Maybe the human driver tells you that there is construction taking place on the main highway, and to avoid a lengthy delay, an alternative course is being undertaken.

You might be satisfied with that explanation. On the other hand, perhaps you live in the area and are curious about the nature of the construction taking place. Thus, you ask the driver for further details about the construction. In a sense, you are interacting with an explainer and seeking additional nuances or facets about the explanation that was being provided.

Okay, put on your self-driving car thinking-cap and consider what a passenger might want from an XAI.

A self-driving car is taking you to your home.

The normal path that would be used is unexpectedly diverted from the AI driving system. You are likely to want to ask the AI why the driving journey is altering from your expected traversal. Many of the existing tryouts of self-driving cars would not have any direct means of having the AI explain this matter, and instead, you would need to connect with a remote agent of the fleet operator that oversees the self-driving cars.

In essence, rather than building the XAI, the matter is shunted over to a remote human to explain what is going on. This is something that won't be especially scalable. In other words, once there are hundreds of thousands of self-driving cars on our roadways, the idea of having the riders always needing to contact a remote agent for the simplest of questions is going to be a huge labor cost and a logistics nightmare.

There ought to be a frontline XAI that exists with the AI driving system.

Assume that a Natural Language Processing (NLP) interface is coupled with the AI driving system, akin to the likes of Alexa or Siri. The passenger interacts with the NLP and can discuss common actions such as asking to change the destination midstream, or ask to swing through a fast-food eatery drive-thru, and so on.

In addition, the passenger can ask for explanations.

Suppose the AI driving system has to suddenly hit the brakes. The rider in the self-driving car might have been watching an especially fascinating cat video and not be aware of the roadway circumstances. After getting bounced around due to the harsh braking action, the passenger might stridently and anxiously ask why the AI driving system made such a sudden and abrasive driving action.

You would want the AI to immediately provide such an explanation. If the only possible way to get an explanation involved seeking a remote agent, envision what that might be like. There you are, inside the self-driving car, and it has just taken radical action, but you have no idea why it did so. You have to press a button or somehow activate a call to a remote agent. This might take a few moments to engage.

Once the remote agent is available (assuming that one is readily available), they might begin the dialogue with a usual canned speech, such as welcome to the greatest of all self-driving cars. You, meanwhile, have been sitting inside this self-driving car, which is still merrily driving along, and yet you have no clue why it out-of-the-blue hit the brakes.

The point here is that by the time you engage in a discussion with the human remote operator, a lot of time and driving aspects could have occurred. During that delay, you are puzzled, concerned, and worried about what the AI driving system might crazily do next.

If there was an XAI, perhaps you would have been able to ask the XAI what just happened. The XAI might instantly explain that there was a dog on the sidewalk that was running toward the self-driving car and appeared to be getting within striking distance.

The AI driving system opted to do a fast braking action. The dog got the idea and safely scampered away.

A timely explanation, and one that then gives the passenger solace and relief, allowing them to settle back into their seat and watch more of those videos about frisky kittens and adorable puppies.

**Conclusion**

There are lots and lots of situations that can arise when riding in a car and for which you might desire an explanation. The car is suddenly brought to a halt. The car takes a curve rather strongly. The car veers into an adjacent lane without a comfortable margin of error. The car takes a road that you weren't expecting to be on. Seemingly endless possibilities exist.

In that case, if indeed XAI is notably handy for self-driving cars, you might be wondering why it isn't especially in place already.

Well, admittedly, for those AI developers under intense pressures to devise AI that can drive a car from point A to point B, doing so safely, the aspect of providing machine-generated explanations is pretty low on their priority list.

They would fervently argue that it is a so-called edge or corner case. It can be gotten to when the sunshine of having achieved sufficiently self-driving cars has been achieved.

Humans that are riding in AVs of all kinds are going to want to have explanations. A cost-effective and immediately available means of providing explanations entails the embodiment of XAI into the AI systems that are doing the autonomous piloting.

One supposes that if you are inside a self-driving car and it is urgently doing some acrobatic driving maneuver, you might be hesitant to ask what is going on, in the same manner, that you might worry that you would be distracting a human driver that was doing something wild at the wheel.

Presumably, a well-devised XAI won't be taxing on the AI driving system and thus you are free to engage in a lengthy dialogue with the XAI. In fact, the likeliest question that self-driving cars are going to get is how does the AI driving system function. The XAI ought to be readied to cope with that kind of question.

The one thing we probably should not expect XAI to handle will be those questions that are afield of the driving chore. For example, asking the XAI to explain the meaning of life is something that could be argued as out-of-bounds and above the paygrade of the AI.

At least until the day that AI does become sentient, then you can certainly ask away.

# CHAPTER 21
# SKATEBOARDERS AND SELF-DRIVING CARS

The skateboarder was eyeing a self-driving car and decided that it might be quite rad to try and hitch a ride.

The overall act of skateboard hitching has lots of slang names such as skitching, skate-hitching, bumper hitching, bizzing, bumper shining, and so on. One thing for sure is that it can be assuredly labeled as ultra-dangerous and an altogether bad idea.

You might be tempted to think that a skateboarder that rides up along a moving car and grabs onto the vehicle is perhaps demonstrating tremendous prowess as a skater or boarder. There are plenty of online videos and amateur social media postings that seem to highlight this crazy act. The person riding the skateboard is usually waving recklessly at the camera and acting like they are having the time of their life.

Oftentimes, these brazen efforts are done without a so-called *brain bucket* (that's lingo for wearing a helmet).

Acrid critics are quick to point out that those trying to do these inappropriate stunts are probably brainless to start with, thus the omission of a helmet is (smarmily) suggested as befitting the circumstance. Anyway, without getting into endless name-calling, some also point out that you don't see the number of times that the skateboarders took a fall, including suffering an injurious abject face plant into the unforgiving street and experiencing a total and calamitous wipeout.

Many people though do customarily think fondly of this skate-hitching activity overall, perhaps as a result of having seen Michael J. Fox adroitly do so in the famous *Back To The Future* movie series. You might hazily recall that there is a scene in the movie (spoiler alert!) that entails his fictional character, Marty McFly, riding on a skateboard and grabbing onto the bumper of a car for a bit of a relatively short joyride. The funny joke underlying the brash act is that it is repeated in the present, the past, and the future. It is a quite memorable gag and a clever way to weave into the plot those seemingly everyday activities of life that tie together the passage of time.

The thing is, some might construe that wanton action as perfectly fine and merely shrug off the underlying perils that it entails. A plethora of video games portray bumper hitching in various heroic fashions, as do lots of shows on TV and cable.

Not wanting to sound like a fuddy-duddy, but you've got to admit that this is a hazardous and ill-advised skateboarding ploy.

What can go wrong?

Lots.

The skateboarder can fall and get injured. This can be magnified immensely due to the speeds involved.

If you fall from a skateboard while going at an ordinary walking speed of a few miles per hour, you might not especially get broken apart. Possibly scrapes and bruises, maybe some broken bones. It isn't pretty. Grasping to a car that is increasing speed and could end up reaching twenty or thirty miles per hour is not simply going to be an injurious fall, it could be a death sentence kind of fall.

Take a look online and you'll see reported deaths when the skateboarder was hitching onto cars going somewhere between even a seemingly piddling five and ten miles per hour. This doesn't seem to be fast-moving, but a human that takes a tumble is going to, unfortunately, discover that the human body is not made for those types of smacking blows at those speeds.

The obvious danger is landing on the harsh asphalt at a high rate of impact. There is also the consequent rolling and tumbling that can be hazardous to your health too. You could uncontrollably tumble into a parked car. The parked car will win that type of collision, and you will lose.

Another scary aspect is that you might roll under the very car that is towing you. In that case, the wheels and undercarriage can scrape and drag you along. This is bound to do irreparable damage to you. The driver of the car might suddenly realize what is taking place and try to hit the brakes, but the odds are that you'll have nonetheless gotten death-inducing flopping despite the car coming to a screeching halt.

There is also the chance of your falling into the path of another nearby in-motion car.

The driver of that vehicle might not see you on the ground or simply assume that you rolled on past. Alas, they might not realize that you've gotten actively entangled under *their* vehicle. I realize that it seems veritably impossible for a driver to not know when they have a person being dragged along under their car, yet this does happen. No sense in trying to roll the dice on whether other drivers will be paying attention to the roadway and not driving distracted when watching an enchanting cat video while at the wheel.

We probably can presume that a skateboarder knows what they are doing when they attempt one of these risky bumper hitching maneuvers. Some skateboarders are likely to underestimate the risks, especially for teenagers that tend to consider themselves invincible and have a carefree attitude. Having seen it done by skateboarding celebrities and stars, the trickery seems doable, and the excitement or thrill of the ride is extraordinarily alluring.

What about the driver?

The driver is assumed to be a licensed driver and therefore a full-fledged adult or at least a young adult that has been granted the government-divined privilege to drive on our public roadways. You could assert that the driver is equally at fault in this gambit of doing bumper hitching. Maybe more so, since a licensed driver is supposed to know about the dangers of driving and how people can get hurt.

Well, sometimes the driver is unaware of the bumper hitching rider.

The driver was driving along, minding their own business. Suddenly, out of nowhere, a skateboarder swiftly gets their board underway and catches up with the rear of the vehicle, thereupon grabbing the bumper and perhaps stooping or crouching down to not be seen.

If you are shocked to believe that a driver would not know that someone is hanging off the back of their car, you might want to ponder that aspect for a moment. I dare say this could happen to any of us. Your attention as a driver is primarily about the road ahead. You earnestly stare at the upcoming traffic. Sure, you look to the sides of your vehicle too, and you glance in your rearview mirror, though your principal focus is straight ahead.

I submit though that if someone wanted to be sneaky and came up behind your car, they could potentially hitch a ride. Unless you were intentionally on the look for such actions, it could readily occur, and you would not know at first that it was happening.

You might be of the resolute opinion that the extra weight and dragging of the grasping skateboarder would undoubtedly be felt while you are at the wheel of the car. This seems doubtful. The skateboard is wheeled. The amount of combined weight and counter forces of the skateboarder are negligible to the power of the car. They are like a flea on a camel's back.

There is something that you might notice.

The sound of the skateboard as it is clicking and clacking along the street surface would be potentially heard by the driver. Of course, modern cars are purposely engineered to provide a noise-free interior. Plus, most people have their car radio going or employ a full-on entertainment system blaring as they drive along. Hearing that bumper hitcher is not necessarily a sure thing.

Then again, if the skateboarder is whooping and hollering at the top of their lungs, and if pedestrians are staring, pointing, and yelling that a person is hanging onto your car, perhaps that would be a clue for even the most clueless of drivers.

Imagine what you might do if the outside world suddenly brought to your attention that a bumper hitching act was taking place on your very car.

It is hard to say how drivers would react.

Some drivers might calmly slow down and come to a gradual halt. Other drivers might jam on the brakes. Some drivers keep going and figure that the bumper hitcher is getting a free ride and can merely opt to drop off the vehicle whenever they wish to do so. One supposes too that there are devilish drivers that might think to hit the gas, accelerating, doing so to scare the dickens out of the errant skateboarder and get them to unleash their grasp (or, worse still, forcefully fling them from the car).

The unpredictability of what an unaware driver will do is yet another of the many adverse risks entailing the bumper hitching scheme (note that this doesn't imply that a driver *knowing* what is taking place will somehow be any safer).

We've focused on the notion of bumper hitching as taking place solely via accessing the bumper of a car. That doesn't have to be the case. The phrase still applies when a skateboarder opts to grab onto the trunk, or onto a side-view mirror, or onto a door handle, or pretty much grasp any part of the car that they can get a hold of.

The other variation to keep in mind is that the rider doesn't necessarily need to be using a skateboard. Sometimes a hitched ride is done by a person wearing skates. It can be done by people riding on a bicycle, or on a scooter, and so on. Anyone that has some form of wheeled contraption is a potential bumper hitching rider.

Is it illegal to do these kinds of bumper hitching acts?

First, to clarify, whether or not it perchance is illegal, it is not an act that should be performed. Let's make that abundantly clear.

Unless you are on a special closed track, and have trained professionals, and are stunt experts, only then should bumper hitching be even a morsel of an idea. The professionals that do take special precautions and are well-aware of the risks, and yet some complain that they are nonetheless tending to glorify the act and making it seem insider cool.

Yes, they often alert others to not try this at home, but that is still going to inspire the at-home bumper hitching efforts, some lament (the counterargument is that people are going to do these antics anyway, regardless of seeing professionals do so, and therefore it is a helpful outlet to have professionals perform such stunts as an alternative to people trying to do so at home).

The legality of doing a bumper hitching is somewhat murky, here's why.

Some states indicate in their vehicle code that you cannot do a bumper hitching while making use of a bicycle, nor when roller skating, and yet do not specifically mention skateboards. In that case, some skateboarders try to argue that because it isn't specifically cited as a particular form of transport in the list of banned possibilities, it ergo must be assumed as legally permissible.

Best to have a serious talk with a lawyer about that.

Some states do explicitly mention skateboards as a mode of transport that cannot be used for undertaking bumper hitching. Thus, it is a relatively straightforward conclusion that doing such an act is bound to be seen as illegal in that state. In addition, many localities have various ordinances that declare any skateboard bumper hitching is considered illegal.

Plenty of other twists and turns exist.

For example, sometimes the law indicates that skateboards cannot be used in the street, and only used on sidewalks. Think about that. If you use a skateboard to bumper hitch, and presumably you would need to be in the street to do so, you are violating the provision of not riding a skateboard while in the street. It kind of shunts to the side that you were bumper hitching and instead catches the rider with the crafty caveat that you aren't supposed to be skateboarding in the street, to begin with.

Without seeming to be overly repetitive, we ought to not be trying to figure out these minuscule head-of-a-pin kinds of twists, and instead lucidly agree that no one should ordinarily be doing any kind of bumper hitching.

Shifting gears for a moment, the future of cars will entail the advent of self-driving cars. Self-driving cars are going to be using AI-based driving systems and there won't be a human driver at the wheel (see my extensive coverage of self-driving cars at **this link here**).

Here is an intriguing question: *Could AI-based true self-driving cars become fodder for those skateboarders that wish to do the act of bumper hitching?*

Let's unpack the matter and see.

**Self-Driving Cars And Bumper Hitching**

For Level 4 and Level 5 true self-driving vehicles, there won't be a human driver involved in the driving task.

All occupants will be passengers.

The AI is doing the driving.

One aspect to immediately discuss entails the fact that the AI involved in today's AI driving systems is not sentient. In other words, the AI is altogether a collective of computer-based programming and algorithms, and most assuredly not able to reason in the same manner that humans can.

Why this added emphasis about the AI not being sentient?

Because I want to underscore that when discussing the role of the AI driving system, I am not ascribing human qualities to the AI. Please be aware that there is an ongoing and dangerous tendency these days to anthropomorphize AI. In essence, people are assigning human-like sentience to today's AI, despite the undeniable and inarguable fact that no such AI exists as yet.

With that clarification, you can envision that the AI driving system won't natively somehow "know" about bumper hitching. This is an aspect that needs to be programmed as part of the hardware and software of the self-driving car.

Let's dive into the myriad of aspects that come to play on this topic.

We'll begin by dividing the matter into two separate conditions.

There is the condition of having an automaker or self-driving tech maker purposely devising a capability within the AI driving system for the overt detection of a bumper hitching instance. The other condition consists of an "everyday" self-driving car that has not been intentionally programmed per se for the detection of a bumper hitching instance.

The first listed condition is the easiest to discuss.

Developers of the AI driving system could make use of the existing sensor suite to try and detect that a bumper hitching act is underway. This could include using the onboard image processing capability to try and identify that someone is attempting to hitch a ride on the self-driving car. Generally, the video cameras that are streaming images into the AI driving system would be used to look for a person or persons that are approaching the vehicle and appear to be trying to grab hold of the self-driving car.

Don't falsely assume that this is an easy task for the object recognition image processing subcomponent. A person outside the vehicle might be very sneaky, perhaps hiding behind a parked car and suddenly dart into the street. There might be little advance notification of the bumper hitcher getting into action.

Once the bumper hitcher grabs onto the vehicle, it might be hard to see them via the cameras. The cameras are usually aimed rather outward, wanting to capture a wide scene and be able to collect data about where other cars are, where the sidewalk is, and so on. It is rarer that a camera would be angled down toward the bumper.

There is also the problem of potentially generating false alerts. If a pedestrian perchance came into the street and stood near the self-driving car, this could inadvertently be construed as a bumper hitching activity that is about to get underway. A human driver would realize that the pedestrian is not holding a skateboard and nor standing on one, which is something that the image processing software would need to be programmed to look for.

Other sensors could come to play, assuming that the self-driving car is equipped with them. For example, the radar and LIDAR could potentially detect the presence of the bumper hitcher. This though is also bound to be tough to do when once the skateboarder is in a crouched position and hugging to the side of the car. The odds are that neither the radar and nor the LIDAR would readily pick up that an object is that close to the vehicle.

Another possibility involves ultrasonic sensory devices. These are usually used for aiding the AI driving system when the vehicle is being parked. The units can detect nearby objects, such as when doing parallel parking or if the vehicle is attempting to park and an object such as a shopping cart might be in the way. Depending though on the speed of the car and where it is in traffic, trying to use the ultrasonic units for detecting a moving skateboarder that has grabbed onto the vehicle could be somewhat problematic.

Given the rarity of someone doing a bumper hitching ride, the argument could be made that it makes little sense to try and program the AI driving system to cope with this outlier possibility. Most of the developers and engineers have their hands full with simply trying to get self-driving cars to safely go from point A to point B. This kind of edge or corner case would likely be listed as a low priority that eventually might come up for being worked on.

You can bet though that if someone does do a bumper hitching with a self-driving car and gets injured, there will be a huge outcry from regulators and the public about how this could have been allowed to happen. In that sense, the seemingly low priority of detecting and responding to a bumper hitching activity will become a vocally outsized must-be-handled issue, causing the automakers and self-driving tech firms to scramble to make up for the lost time.

Imagine that a bumper hitching detection capability did exist and was reliable enough to be utilized on an ongoing basis. A vexing question arises as to what to about the wayward skateboarder. What would we want the AI driving system to do?

I'm sure you might suggest that the answer is obvious, namely the AI driving system should stop the car. Sure, that generally makes sense, but the devil is in the details. How quickly should the vehicle be brought to a stop? Suppose the skateboarder falls while the stopping action is underway, then what? Should the AI somehow try to warn the skateboarder that the AI driving system has detected their presence and is going to stop? Etc.

This brings up another interesting and somewhat beguiling topic. Assume that in some instances there might be passengers inside the self-driving car. This complicates matters. If the AI driving system suddenly slams on the brakes, this could harm the passengers.

I'll add another wrinkle for you to contemplate. Suppose a passenger notices the skateboarder and does so before or in lieu of the AI driving system making such a detection. If the passenger tries to tell the AI driving system that a person is grabbing onto the vehicle, will the AI driving system be able to make use of that exhortation?

Most of the existing self-driving cars have very rudimentary

Natural Language Processing (NLP) capabilities, akin to the likes of Alexa and Siri. Those NLP are not likely at this time to be capable of hearing a human exclaim that a skateboarder is hugging the car and then turn that into something usable as a part of the AI driving system activities. Right now, any kind of utterances beyond the desired destination are routed to a remote agent of the fleet operator, which in the case of the bumper hitching could be too little, too late, in terms of the AI driving system getting directed about what to do.

**Conclusion**

I mentioned that there were two major conditions to be considered. One was that the AI driving system was purposely augmented or devised to detect and cope with a bumper hitching vagabond. We've taken a close look at the ups and downs of that programming.

The other condition entails an "everyday" self-driving car that has no special provision for this particular use case. What would the de facto self-driving car that has no specific programming for this situation be able to potentially do?

An apparent aspect is that without devoted programming, the odds are lessened that the AI driving system is going to "natively" (as generically crafted) be able to do much about being able to detect the bumper hitching nomad. There is a slim chance of doing so, and perhaps the AI driving system would enter into its standard programming for any such exigency, such as gradually bringing the car to a halt, along with notifying the passengers that the vehicle is being stopped and sending an electronic alert to the fleet operator.

The trouble for the skateboarder is that they might be able to get away with the bumper hitching, just as it might be possible to do so with a human driver at the wheel, but the skateboarder is taking a huge risk in doing so. Envision that the self-driving car opts to increase speed since it is entering into a major highway, and all of sudden the skateboarder is faced with having to decide whether to let go or not. If they summarily let go, their heightened speed puts them at an intensified risk.

The skateboarder might try to feverishly bang on the trunk or the sides of the car, clamoring frantically to have someone or something slow down the vehicle. A human driver might or might not hear this, and might or might not accede to the request. Similarly, the AI driving system might or might not detect this (generally, currently unlikely to do so), and the skateboarder has now led themselves into a worsening and perilous catastrophe. The hitching rider has somewhat dug their own grave, as it were.

Be resolved: Just don't do any bumper hitching and ergo avoid getting into dire straights altogether.

Recall that I began this discussion by mentioning that a skateboarder was eyeing a self-driving car and appeared to be mulling over an attempt at undertaking a bumper hitching ride. Upon observing this, I was thankfully relieved to witness that the self-driving car was moving at such a speed that the bumper hitcher was unable to reach the vehicle. You could suggest that the AI driving system was scooting away to avoid the skateboarder, but that is an unlikely explanation in this particular instance.

On this occasion, the self-driving car was most likely merely proceeding on its driving journey.

To that degree, the skateboarder was quite lucky. Whether it was fate or blind luck, their high-risk ill-advised attempt was rebuffed or at least not able to be completed. This was a case wherein the fish that got away was better off for all and averted what could have been a gut-wrenching and atrocious outcome.

I am hoping that the teenaged skateboarder will live a long life and maybe, just maybe, will one day be involved in the development of AI-based true self-driving cars, possibly getting assigned to figuring out how to try and ensure that AI driving systems can cope with those misbehaving rad-seeking skateboarders (which, he would certainly know a lot about).

Score one for humanity and AI.

# CHAPTER 22
# WALKING MILES AND SELF-DRIVING CARS

A smooth ride.

Your grandparents probably had a lot to say about what life was like when they were growing up.

They had to walk five miles to get to school.

Uphill, both ways.

In the snow.

That's the classic tale told by many grandparents when regaling their children and grandchildren about how tough things were in *their* day. You've undoubtedly heard such stories, plenty of times.

There is no question that those prior days were likely harsh and entailed all sorts of ordeals. Nobody can reasonably dispute that type of claim.

That being said, there could be a bit of teensy-weensy embellishment going on. Just a tad. If you've gone online to look for stories about having to arduously walk to school as a child, you've also assuredly noticed the zillions of memes and parodies that have been placed onto the vast and a rather smarmy internet. I'm sure that those satirical markings and artistic elaborations are all in good jest and intended as a lighthearted piece of folly.

We can assume that in some cases the original travails did indeed match precisely to the engaging verbal versions told by those doting and erstwhile grandparents. Of course, there is also the demonstrative chance that the tale grew an inch at a time, getting bigger and bolder with each telling.

Eventually, these heartwarming anecdotes become the equivalent of the tall tales often told about having caught a colossal fish. The reality might be that it was actually a tiny minnow, and upon the recounting and retelling, the watery creature captured has morphed into the heroic snagging of a gargantuan swordfish.

For the parents of today, some are unsure of what to tell their children about their own trials and tribulations as a youngster going to school.

Though there was certainly walking involved, the odds are that a car was involved too. Many children of that era were given a lift to school by their parents. The kids got into the car in the mornings and were lugged to campus, being dropped off in front of the main building or perhaps at the edge of the school ground.

You cannot readily complain about marching in the snow for five miles when the reality was that you were taken in a car and adroitly deposited within a few dozen yards of where you had to be. This seems to take the air out of the proverbial "how rough things were" balloon.

But where there's a will, there's always a way.

Yes, there are viable and nearly believable "transformational conversions" used to make that fish become a mighty prized catch.

How so?

Well, some parents tell their children that being driven to school was altogether tortuous and nerve-wracking. Numerous exhortations are proffered as evidence to the court in an effort to prove to today's young listeners that this is all rather heavy stuff and showcases a solemn life of extraordinary burdens.

For example, you had to get your parents to wake up and then pressure them to proceed on a timely basis to get out of the house and into the car. If your parents overslept or maybe forgot that they had promised to give you a lift that day, you become momentarily the adult in the house and had to boss them around to do the things they said they would do.

It was maddening!

You knew that arriving at school late was going to be a penalty you would endure and not one that particularly impacted your parents. The odds were that you would have to report to the attendance office and provide a sheepish explanation about why, once again, you've arrived at school on a tardy basis. At those moments, you really wished you did have to walk five miles in the snow since it would be better than having to indicate that your parents delayed getting underway and you were essentially helpless to do anything about their lethargy.

Another eye-rolling example of how bad things were involved the intrepid search for the lost keys.

It went something like this.

Your driving parent managed to get into the driver's seat and then suddenly realized they did not have the car keys with them. Those darned keys were somewhere inside the deep bowels of the house. Everyone leaped out of the car and would run feverishly back into the revered domicile. A panicky search would take place that encompassed tossing over every sofa cushion and looking frantically in every nook and corner. Upon finally discovering the hidden keys, a huge rush out to the car took place and one could only hope and pray that the delay could be made up by driving fast.

And, this takes us to the next harrowing part of the gut-wrenching story about how bad it was to be driven to school.

Your parents would drive like maniacs.

They acted as though racecar driving had been approved for your neighborhood streets. Friends and other parents that were walking to the school knew what your car looked like. As such, when your parent, as the driver, managed to veer dangerously toward pedestrians and drove in an entirely maniacal way, you would get lambasted about the craziness after having arrived at school.

Yet, you knew that you were powerless to get your parents to slow down and drive carefully. They told you in stern terms that you were much too young and immature to understand. The world is dog-eat-dog, they would adamantly assure you. You need to take what is yours. This included being the type of take-no-prisoners driver that owns the road. Don't let other drivers treat you like sheep. You are the wolf and accordingly, grow up to drive as wolves do.

The pièce de resistance had to be the car-based dogfight that would occur in front of the school. All the parents in the area were trying to drop off their young offspring at the same place at the same moment in time, each morning. This was not merely a venue for overwhelming congestion. It also became a hotspot for road rage and trying to see which parent was willing to be more domineering and aggressive to get their child to the closest drop-off point possible.

No child of theirs was going to be let loose a block away or even a handful of car distances from the main drop-off locale. Darwin must be observed and the survival of the fittest had to be demonstrated to your own children and to the other kids and parents that were also in line for the drop-off.

You would tell your parents, actually implore them, that you could readily and happily get out of the car early on and walk the rest of the way.

No sir, that was not about to happen.

To add insult to injury, as it were, when you got older and entered into your teens, this drop-off aspect became even more humiliating. Not necessarily due to the jockeying for position, which everyone eventually got used to seeing and took merely in stride. The problem was that *your parents* were dropping you off, and you weren't of an age to be able to drive yourself as yet. That was painful.

Okay, so this provides a quick and vivid depiction of how the now outdated walking-to-school story can become the modernized version encompassing the act of being driven to school, amidst the wild adventures of your out-of-control and abysmally embarrassing parents.

Alas, what will your children be able to tell their children about?

We can make some reasoned speculation.

Here's the deal. The cars that we use today are going to eventually give way to the advent of self-driving cars. Those self-driving cars are going to be driven by an AI-based driving system and no human driver is at the wheel.

Consider this interesting question: *How will self-driving cars end up changing the stories and tall tales about the chores and escapades of being driven to school?*

Let's unpack the matter and see.

**Self-Driving Cars And Going To School**

For Level 4 and Level 5 true self-driving vehicles, there won't be a human driver involved in the driving task.

All occupants will be passengers.

The AI is doing the driving.

One aspect to immediately discuss entails the fact that the AI involved in today's AI driving systems is not sentient. In other words, the AI is altogether a collective of computer-based programming and algorithms, and most assuredly not able to reason in the same manner that humans can.

Why this added emphasis about the AI not being sentient?

Because I want to underscore that when discussing the role of the

AI driving system, I am not ascribing human qualities to the AI. Please be aware that there is an ongoing and dangerous tendency these days to anthropomorphize AI. In essence, people are assigning human-like sentience to today's AI, despite the undeniable and inarguable fact that no such AI exists as yet.

With that clarification, you can envision that the AI driving system won't natively somehow "know" about driving kids to school. This is an aspect that needs to be programmed as part of the hardware and software of the self-driving car.

Let's dive into the myriad of aspects that come to play on this topic.

We'll begin with a controversial element that not many are yet contemplating.

Presumably, children can ride in a self-driving car and do so without any adult presence at all. This is simply and obviously a consequence of removing the human driver from the vehicle. In a sense, you usually have a twofer, namely, an adult driver is needed to make a car go, and ergo the driver becomes the watchful adult to oversee any children inside the vehicle.

Not so, anymore.

I've discussed at length that this will be an emerging and acrimonious dilemma. Nobody is discussing this just yet because there are so few self-driving cars on our roadways. Once the advent of self-driving cars becomes more predominant, you can bet your bottom dollar that people are going to be tempted to send their kids on errands via the use of self-driving cars. The parent will be busy and won't go along or maybe believes that it is perfectly fine for their kids to be taken around town via a self-driving car.

If you are shocked at the idea of children riding in self-driving cars absent of any onboard adult, you had better get used to the idea. I assure you that many parents will do so willingly and possibly even gleefully. They can point out that self-driving cars are likely to get into fewer car crashes and will be driving carefully at all times. On top of that point, they would argue that anyone letting their kids go in a "strangers car" such as via human-driven ridesharing is taking more risks than having the kids by themselves inside a self-driving car (these are argumentative points, so please refer to my coverage for more insights).

Anyway, the essential notion in this particular use case of being driven to school is that your children and their children can inevitably be driven to school by a self-driving car.

This undercuts the fundamental theme about how rough things were when parents had to drive their kids to school. Parents won't need to do so. Kids won't have any stories to tell about how crazily their parents drove.

Here's how things will likely occur.

A self-driving car is arranged to arrive at your house each morning at a designated time. It shows up precisely on time. Unlike the prior era of searching for car keys or getting a parent to be timely, you can set aside that narrative in the future.

A child exits from their home and gets into the waiting self-driving car. The youngster might be entirely alone or they might have a buddy from a nearby house that opts to go along to school together. Furthermore, the self-driving car might be scheduled to pick up other kids throughout the neighborhood, acting as a type of local school bus of sorts.

As an aside, in case you are wondering, there will eventually be self-driving buses too.

The self-driving car will make its way to the school. This will be done on a driving basis that is generally slow-moving and exceedingly cautious. All driving laws and rules will be strictly obeyed by the AI driving system.

What will the kids inside the self-driving car be doing?

The kids might be sitting quietly and trying to get themselves ready for the school day ahead. Some might be making last-minute changes to their homework or putting the final touches on their school project due that day. The interior of self-driving cars is anticipated to eventually have swivel seats and small tables, allowing for riders to do various kinds of work while on a roadway journey.

Wait for a second, you think to yourself, maybe those rambunctious and unsupervised kids are whooping it up, hollering and partying like it is 1999. That doesn't seem like a good way to go to school. By the time they arrive at the campus, they will be out of their gourds and unfit to seriously do their schoolwork.

No worries.

The AI driving system can potentially be monitoring their activity while inside the self-driving car. Via the use of inward-facing cameras, the AI can be detecting what the kids are doing. Any outlandish behavior can spur the AI system to tell the kids to knock it off. Furthermore, the AI can send an electronic alert to you, the parent, and indicate that little George or Samantha is acting up again and will soon get banned from using self-driving cars henceforth.

We'll add more twists into that in-car activity.

Via the use of the inward-facing cameras, the kids can be doing Zoom-like remote efforts. For example, the teachers at the school might provide early morning pre-class sessions. Thus, while your child is inside the self-driving car and on a perhaps lengthy commute to school, they can be interacting remotely with their teacher and getting already underway with their educational instruction.

Another use of that inward-facing camera is that it can allow you to chat with your child while they are riding to school.

You see, one aspect that might be missed is the bonding of a parent and a child that can sometimes arise simply due to the daily commute together since the parent doesn't need to drive their offspring to school. The potential solution is that via your smartphone or smartwatch, you simply connect to the in-motion self-driving car and engage your child in a parent-child discussion that will be just as heartwarming as when you were driving the car (well, not everyone agrees with that notion that remote chatting is the same as in-person, but you get the general gist).

The coup de gras is that upon arriving at the school, the self-driving car won't need to undertake the same wild driving efforts of jockeying for position that parents once did. Instead, the self-driving car will make use of V2V (vehicle-to-vehicle) electronic communications and coordinate with the other arriving self-driving cars. They will each message the other, indicating their upcoming arrival. Traffic will run smoothly and the self-driving cars will seamlessly slip into line and disembark their young passengers, doing so at the stipulated drop-off point.

No madness, no maniacs, no undue stress. Those kids will listen to your stories about the travails of being driven to school and look at you with a quizzical expression.

Why did a human drive you to school? That seems unnecessary and old-fashioned.

Kids will shake their head in mild disdain that you endured having a parent drive you to school. Sorry to hear about that, they will sympathetically say. It will be up to you whether you decide to further play up the angst and agony of it. Walking to school in the snow and entirely uphill has got to be inspirational toward bolstering the parent-driving tales into some pretty amazing and nearly unbelievable yarns.

**Conclusion**

Lest you think that those modern-day kids are going to have a life of grandness due to being driven to school by self-driving cars, I feel compelled to inform you that even they will have their dramatic stories to tell too. It might go something like this (imagine the future, whereby a child of today is now a mature adult, conveying what happened when they were a youngster and used to go to school in a self-driving car).

The elder stands up and relates the following saga. I remember when self-driving cars were first getting underway, and we used to go to school in them. You won't believe me when I tell you what occurred, so just go with me and allow me a moment to try and explain. They were pretty stupid. The AI system could not carry on any kind of intelligible conversation. Natural Language Processing (NLP) was nascent and not at all fluent. About the only thing you could do was give one-word and simplistic commands or instructions to the AI driving systems, otherwise they had no inkling of what you were saying.

I remember on one occasion, a self-driving car that I was in came to a sudden halt. We didn't know why. Turns out that the vehicle had a mechanical breakdown. A remote agent spoke to us via the onboard screen and told us to wait inside the car for help to arrive. When I called my parents, they freaked out. For the next several months, my parents insisted on driving me to school and no longer were willing to have me take a self-driving car. They eventually went back to having me ride in a self-driving car There was a funny occasion when the self-driving car that I was in had allowed all of my friends and their friends to pile into the car. Those were the days when AI driving systems weren't in real-time keeping track of each passenger and would let us get away with some quite outlandish pranks, let me tell you.

We rolled down the windows and were sticking our heads and bodies outside of the car, yelling, screaming, waving, and altogether having a good time. When we arrived at the school, the administrators were very upset, and we all were put into detention for the day.

Probably the weirdest thing of all was that self-driving cars didn't fly at that time. They went only on the ground. This seems unimaginable now, but that's the way it used to be. All those ridiculous contraptions could do was roll along on the ground. It was slow. It took forever to get places. By the way, those self-driving cars, they drove me in the snow, while going uphill, and it was something like probably 500 miles to drive from home to school (I'm a bit hazy about the details). Honestly, I wouldn't make that kind of thing up.

End of the tale.

# CHAPTER 23
# STANDARD UPDATED AND SELF-DRIVING CARS

The new phonebook is here, the new phonebook is here!

That's a famous line that people use to exclaim when the latest iteration of the local phonebook came out and was available for use. It was exciting since the venerated document contained the latest info about how to get ahold of someone. For those of you that perchance remember the antics of Steve Martin in the movie *The Jerk*, I'm sure you are already chuckling at the mention of a new phonebook and the accompanying delight that oftentimes arose due to the latest release of a thick tome that merely contained updated phone numbers and names.

It might seem like an oddball reaction nowadays, yet there was some validity to the keen interest in seeing the revisions and updates that arose in the latest incarnation of your local phonebook.

Shifting gears, there is some effervescent excitement going on for those that are deeply versed in the realm of self-driving cars and it has to do with a kind-of newly iterated phonebook of sorts. Actually, in this case, the document is a cornerstone standard that many consider the Rosetta Stone for delineating the nature of self-driving capabilities, known as the SAE International standard and stuffily entitled as (here's a mouthful, get ready): "Taxonomy and Definitions for Terms Related to Driving Automation Systems for On-Road Motor Vehicles."

Those that are in the know refer to the standard by its official designation, namely J3016.

Within the high-tech field of self-driving cars, there is of course a breathless heralding of any brand-new updated release of this altogether famous (or some bitterly say infamous) J3016 defining standard for ground-based autonomous vehicles.

Having been just posted a few days ago, those within the self-driving car realm are undoubtedly pouring through the document, seeking to discern what types of changes and revisions have been enacted.

I'll be happy to bring you up-to-speed on what the latest release proffers.

Before any of you start to pull out your hair that perhaps there is an entirely new definition or taxonomy for self-driving cars, the bottom line is that this is a relatively tame and altogether tepid set of revisions. Let me clarify, it is good nonetheless to see the rendering of various useful and erstwhile revisions having been made. The result is certainly a tidier and more approachable version of the revered standard.

No doubt about that.

On the other hand, in case you don't already know, the reason that I earlier referred to the document as the "famous or infamous" standard is that there are some within the self-driving car industry that think the whole thing ought to be redone. Yes, start from scratch, they fervently say. There are a plethora of arguments about the number of levels of autonomy and how to best define the nature of self-driving or driverless technology.

You can easily engage in a heated debate on the J3016 that will cause your ears to wear out and your eyes to glaze over. Some insist it is a valuable keystone and thank goodness it was established and put into the world for all to use. Others decry it as either misguided or plainly out of touch.

Anyway, for those that are wanting a complete overhaul of J3016, you need to prepare yourself for the stony fact that this is not at all a do-over and instead of a subtle refinement of what was already in place. I know that some pundits will lament that it is akin to merely moving around the chairs on the deck of the Titanic, but anyway, it is what it is.

Save those bellicose arguments for another day.

Meanwhile, I'll provide a smattering of highlights about the revisions made. I won't go through all the revisions and urge interested readers to peruse the new standard as they might so desire.

Before I get into the various changes, it would be useful to make sure we are all on the same page about what the self-driving car's standard generally conveys. There are six levels identified that range from zero to five. Many of you have undoubtedly heard that some levels are considered true self-driving, and some levels that are not.

Allow me a moment to briefly indicate what that portends.

**Self-Driving Cars And The Updated Standard**

For Level 4 and Level 5 true self-driving vehicles, there won't be a human driver involved in the driving task.

All occupants will be passengers.

The AI is doing the driving.

One aspect to immediately discuss entails the fact that the AI involved in today's AI driving systems is not sentient. In other words, the AI is altogether a collective of computer-based programming and algorithms, and most assuredly not able to reason in the same manner that humans can.

Why this added emphasis about the AI not being sentient?

Because I want to underscore that when discussing the role of the AI driving system, I am not ascribing human qualities to the AI. Please be aware that there is an ongoing and dangerous tendency these days to anthropomorphize AI. In essence, people are assigning human-like sentience to today's AI, despite the undeniable and inarguable fact that no such AI exists as yet.

Now that we've laid the stage appropriately, time to dive into the myriad of aspects that come to play regarding the latest revisions of the lionized J3016.

To make sure we are all aligned, this discussion entails the officially labeled *J3016 APR2021* revision, released at the tail-end of April 2021, and will be forever known as the *J3016 2021-04*.

For those of you that perchance have a well-worn copy of the prior latest version, which came out in June 2018, you can toss that into the trash. There is a new king in town. If you don't believe me, then maybe this quote from the J3016 2021-04 will convince you: "This edition cancels and supersedes the SAE J3016_201806."

Clunk, that's the sound of those old copies being placed into the recycling bin.

Moving on, the stated rationale for the standard has gotten a bit of an update. The key being that the opening rationale now provides pointed insights about why this April 2021 version exists and the prior June 2018 version is considered outdated.

Indeed, we can let the standard speak for itself in that it begins with this explanation about the overarching semblance of this revision: "This revision of SAE J3016 was undertaken in close cooperation between the SAE On-Road Automated Driving (ORAD) Committee and ISO TC204/WG14 through a Joint Working Group formed in 2018. This collaboration brought to bear the knowledge and expertise of global experts in driving automation technology and safety. Several new terms and definitions have been added and multiple corrections and clarifications have been made to address frequently misunderstood concepts and improve the utility of the document, especially for non-native English speakers."

There is a bit of potential argumentation even for that presumably helpful introduction, but I won't get into the weeds on that herein. Ask me after I've had a few beers.

There are plenty of backstories for just about every change that exists.

Here's a newly added pronouncement at the start of the document that might seem entirely innocuous to the untrained eye: "Attention is drawn to the possibility that some of the elements of this document may be the subject of patent rights. ISO and SAE International shall not be held responsible for identifying any or all such patent rights."

Okay, no big deal, they added a cautionary notation about the nature of patents. You probably would have skipped right past that paragraph.

I'll give you a glimpse into the cavalcade of backstories that are hidden behind the scenes and only insiders would be aware of.

As an expert witness in Intellectual Property (IP) rights cases involving autonomous vehicles and various AI technologies, I can tell you that there is a slew of patent fights that will inevitably engulf the entirety of the self-driving cars field.

It will be an IP lawyer's billable hour bonanza, for sure.

The skinny is that there is a boatload of patents that have been granted in this tech space. Many of the hardworking heads-down self-driving tech developers and engineers are (at this time) blissfully unaware of those patents. As such, there are tons of development and engineering efforts that are likely infringing on those patents, for which the firms making the self-driving cars are not yet cognizant.

Eventually, once self-driving cars start to be rolled out and become prevalent, they will become huge moneymakers. When they are making money, it will become worthwhile for the patent holders to dredge up their related patents and take those infringers to court (some refer to this disparagingly as being patent trolls). The odds are that much of this will be dealt with via out-of-court settlements, encompassing eyebrow-raising topnotch dollars being handed over, though occurring only once the specter of big court wins looms over the self-driving car makers and their fleet operators.

Given that context, the potential basis for the J3016 stating that it has nothing to do with those patents is to try and stay out of the morass of IP lawsuits and entanglements that will someday be a tidal wave. There are already some that believe the standard somehow entails or overlaps onto their patents, rightfully or wrongly, and thus the matter has already inched its way into view. The added narrative about the patents is presumably a get out of jail free card, put in place now and will be cited in the future by either side of those bruising patent battles to arise.

The main point here is that the subtlest of revisions and additions are more than what perhaps meets the eye. Entire and extensive complexities and intricacies are at the underpinnings of most of the changes.

The standard is akin to an iceberg whereby the only thing the naked eye is bound to see is the teensy-weensy tip of the iceberg. Be assured, there is a heap of fractious ice underneath.

Let's take a quick look at another artful addition: "SAE Executive Standards Committee Rules provide that: This document is published to advance the state of technical and engineering sciences. The use of this document is entirely voluntary, and its applicability and suitability for any particular use, including any patent infringement arising therefrom, is the sole responsibility of the user."

There is at least a twofer in that portion.

You can readily detect the patent topic. The other aspect is the notion of the standard being of a voluntary arrangement and that people can take it or leave it.

Due to space constraints, I can't go into the entirety of the alluded to conflagration, but the gist is that some assert that the standard has been overplayed by some in industry and somehow become a type of "requirement" rather than something mere of an informative and industry helpful manner, i.e., being voluntary.

Enough said on that for now.

See if you can guess what this addition is about: "Any trade name used in this document is information given for the convenience of users and does not constitute an endorsement."

Did you make your guess?

As you might have surmised, the concern about any type of promulgated and independent standard is that if it includes references to existing products or companies there is a chance that this might imply an endorsement for those so named. This would be a potential windfall for the named parties. It would also be a quite disconcerting slap in the face to other products or firms that believe they should be getting an equal footing.

Thus, it is best to excise such references as much as possible, averting the conundrum, or at least provide an escape clause that states any such references are not to be construed as an endorsement.

So far, none of those modest changes have much to do with the actual acts of self-driving. I'll shift into that mode and give you a taste of the more technical nuances of the embodied revisions. One technical term that you'll need to know is that DDT refers to the Dynamic Driving Task, which for herein simplicities sake you can blankly consider to be the act or task of driving a car.

See if you get the behind-the-scenes nature of this added line in the passage about what is considered inside of scope and outside of scope for the standard: "In addition, systems that inform, alert, or warn the driver about hazards in the driving environment are also outside the scope of this driving automation taxonomy, as they neither automate part or all of the DDT, nor change the driver's role in performance of the DDT (see 8.13)."

It might be helpful if I give you the passage that just precedes this added line: "Active safety systems, such as electronic stability control (ESC) and automatic emergency braking (AEB), and certain types of driver assistance systems, such as lane-keeping assistance (LKA), are excluded from the scope of this driving automation taxonomy because they do not perform part or all of the DDT on a sustained basis, but rather provide momentary intervention during potentially hazardous situations. Due to the momentary nature of the actions of active safety systems, their intervention does not change or eliminate the role of the driver in performing part or all of the DDT, and thus are not considered to be driving automation, even though they perform automated functions."

I realize that if you aren't steeped in the nature of self-driving cars, those mentioned passages might seem like a strange foreign language, maybe a variant of Klingon.

In brief, there is an open question as to the boundaries associated with the automated and autonomous operation of a car. Imagine a person sitting at the steering wheel. They are responsible for the driving act. All of a sudden, someone outside of the car yells out that there is a dog loose in the roadway. Hopefully, the driver hears the exhortation, mindfully considers it, and then steers the car to successfully avoid the beloved pooch.

I ask you, did the warning by the person outside the vehicle cause the vehicle to veer away from the canine?

Most would reasonably agree that the yelling didn't change the actions of the car, and instead it was the driver that changed the actions of the car. The helpful shouting was useful to the *driver*, but in the end, it was the driver that was doing the driving. In that way of consideration, we could assert that the screaming was out-of-scope of the driving task. The driving task was still in the hands of the driver and the outside stimulus was nothing more than if the driver had seen the dog with their own eyes.

Just to let you know, not everyone would concur that the outside stimulus belongs outside of scope, and there is a rather complicated philosophical discussion that can ensue. In any case, for purposes of

J3016, the revision now clearly states that any "systems that inform, alert, or warn the driver about hazards in the driving environment" are outside the scope.

I'm sure that you are entranced to now know that.

Let's next consider an example of how there has been some significant technical rewording that has taken place.

The rewording in this example involves the definition of a commonly used phrase within the self-driving specialty, referring to the notion of achieving a Minimal Risk Condition (MRC).

Here is the prior definition of MRC: "A condition to which a user or an ADS may bring a vehicle after performing the DDT fallback in order to reduce the risk of a crash when a given trip cannot or should not be completed" (from the old section 3.17).

Here is the new definition of MRC: "A stable, stopped condition to which a user or an ADS may bring a vehicle after performing the DDT fallback in order to reduce the risk of a crash when a given trip cannot or should not be continued" (from the new section 3.16).

Though this might seem like a nonchalant or perhaps trivial difference, it actually is quite notable and proffers a substantive change that either can be interpreted in the context of the subsection as merely clarifying what was originally the overall intent about MRC or has perhaps given MRC a new meaning.

Studious self-driving devotees (or, some might prefer the cherished title of *self-driving nerds*), will be going toe-to-toe on that seemingly innocuous change.

Speaking of nerds or techies (again, meant in a most honored way), those of you that are staunchly familiar with the J3016 June 2018 standard will be somewhat taken aback at the aspect that the sections and subsections have been essentially renumbered (somewhat), thus the numbering that you memorized over these last several years will no longer do. For example, the portion on the MRC is an indication of that kind of change in numbering, previously being labeled as 3.17 and now it is 3.16.

But, hey, the good news is that this new version of the standard has finally earned itself a veritable table of contents, something sorely needed and well appreciated having been added.

Diehard fans of the June 2018 version will notice that the *ADS-Dedicated Vehicle* section 3.3 and the *Conventional Vehicle* 3.5 are now no longer in place. Meanwhile, you'll want to check out an interesting new section 3.1.3 on *Fleet Operations*. And section 3.9 on *Driving Automation System Feature Or Application* has gotten a decidedly notable oil change and engine overhaul, as it were. Within the new incarnation of 3.9, now known as 3.7, there are these added subsections: 3.7.1 *Maneuver-Based Feature*, 3.7.2 *Sub-Trip Feature*, and 3.7.3 *Full-Trip Feature*. Make sure to give those depictions some close attention and focused reading.

I could go on and on, but I believe this gives you a taste of what the revised standard consists of.

**Conclusion**

If you are someone that is deeply dedicated to the advent of self-driving cars, you'll want to get the J3016 2021-04 standard and have your red marker handy. It is well worth your time to pour through the revised standard and make sure that you know the ins and outs of what is currently the reigning king.

This will also require reorienting your prior predisposition of being able to quote verbatim from the June 2018 version. You don't want to get caught by your colleagues or smarmy others that will stop you mid-statement and rightly point out that you are no longer with it. That you have fallen behind. That you are living in the past.

By and large, most everyone other than those that are nose deep into the details about self-driving cars will not especially know and nor particularly care about these revisions. It will be as though as Jedi master has told those neophytes to walk on past, nothing to see here.

# CHAPTER 24
# WINDSHIELD SMASH AND SELF-DRIVING CARS

Florida is certainly well-known for its gators and crocodiles. The handy rule of thumb is don't mess with those cranky carnivores.

In addition to those semiaquatic reptiles, there is also an abundance of sea turtles. Florida is said to be the home of the densest population of nesting Loggerhead Sea Turtles in the entire Western Hemisphere. I dare say that most of us have a rather positive viewpoint about turtles and generally consider them to be relatively harmless and (shall I suggest?) cute or endearing (they are portrayed that way in movies and TV shows).

But even sea turtles can get down and dirty. If you approach a sea turtle and appear threatening, please know that they can bite you quite fiercely. The strong jaws of sea turtles are legendary and not to be trifled with.

The good news is that you can usually readily outrun a turtle.

About the only way to get bitten by a turtle involves your persistence in poking at them. Rarely would a sea turtle slink up behind you and catch you entirely off-guard. That's the type of ploy that is usually reserved for those sneaky alligators and dastardly crocs.

Okay, so we probably can all agree that getting harmed by a turtle is a low odds proposition. Normally, you would need to go out of your way, quite a bit, in order to antagonize a turtle and prod it into a seething and overt attack toward you.

Leave them be, and you'll be scot-free of inherent danger.

Of course, if a turtle smashes through your car windshield at high speeds and strikes you within the confines of your car, all bets are off. In that case, you likely are going to get banged up.

Say what?

Yes, a recent news report out of Florida indicates that a turtle burst through the front windshield of a car that was cruising along on the popular Floridian highway known as Interstate 95. The turtle struck a female passenger in the head. This was the 71-year-old mother of the driver. You can imagine the shock and horror of the driver upon witnessing a turtle suddenly and unavoidably puncturing through the windshield and plowing into your mom.

Turns out that the driver summarily jammed on the brakes and brought the vehicle to a quick stop, frantically calling 911 for assistance. The arriving first responders took her mother to a nearby hospital and thankfully the cut she got above the eye did not do any demonstrative damage. She will be okay.

Firefighters that had responded to the emergency were able to determine that the turtle was still alive and pretty much unhurt. They gingerly removed the turtle from the car and released it into the woods. One supposes that the turtle has quite a story to tell, being able to explain to all the other turtles about the day that it perchance landed inside a moving car and lived to tell the tale.

I'll give you a moment to ponder the wonderment of the news story.

You might also be thinking about how the turtle got into such a predicament, to begin with. This was not a flying turtle, though it did manage to get airborne. Did the turtle want to undertake this highly hazardous act? Maybe it is the revered daredevil amongst all the other turtles in the vicinity.

The guess by local authorities is that the turtle was crawling along on the active highway and got picked up by a passing semi-truck that then launched it from the massive wheels and into the air. We can logically assume that the two women in the car were somewhere behind the semi-truck and had the bad luck of being in the wrong place at the wrong time.

In case you are questioning whether a turtle could actually penetrate through a car windshield, this is a strong possibility and it indeed happened in this particular case. The hardness of the shell and the weight of the turtle, along with its shape, and being propelled into the air, would all be factors in being able to strike the windshield with tremendous force and effecting a puncturing aptitude. Keep in mind too that the car was traveling along at a high rate of speed.

The point is that we can reasonably conclude that the story is true and that in fact, a turtle can crash through a car windshield. There are numerous reported cases. Sometimes the turtle comes all the way into the vehicle, while on other occasions it becomes lodged in the windshield. At times, the turtle survives the calamity, and sadly there are instances whereby the turtle succumbs to the effort and perishes.

For this latest incident, we can count this as a happy story since the woman struck by the turtle is going to be okay and the turtle was fine and returned to its natural habitat. You can't always expect a happy ending in real life, but this was such an occasion.

Should you constantly be on the alert as a driver that a turtle might appear out of nowhere and shatter your windshield while driving along and minding your own business?

I don't think so.

Unless you live in an area that is massively populated with turtles, you aren't obligated as a driver to be continually scanning the horizon for turtles that might be errantly on the highways and byways that you traverse. Airborne turtles that strike cars are the stuff of fanciful (yet real) stories and not a matter that needs to preoccupy your mind while at the steering wheel of a moving car.

That being said, the overall concept of roadway debris that can fly up at your car, well, that's something you indeed should be constantly scanning for. Rather than a turtle, maybe the object might be a discarded piece of junk, or perhaps a hood ornament that fell off the front of a fancy car, etc. Those semi-trucks and large vehicles can easily grab up the most innocuous of debris and toss it into the air, becoming an unguided missile that can ruin your day.

Shifting gears, consider that the future of cars entails the advent of self-driving cars. Self-driving cars are going to be using AI-based driving systems and there won't be a human driver at the wheel (see my extensive coverage of self-driving cars at **this link here**).

Here is an intriguing question: *How would AI-based true self-driving cars cope with a hurtling turtle that smashed through the windshield while underway at high speeds on an open highway?*

Let's unpack the matter and see.

**Self-Driving Cars And Flying Turtles**

For Level 4 and Level 5 true self-driving vehicles, there won't be a human driver involved in the driving task.

All occupants will be passengers.

The AI is doing the driving.

One aspect to immediately discuss entails the fact that the AI involved in today's AI driving systems is not sentient. In other words, the AI is altogether a collective of computer-based programming and algorithms, and most assuredly not able to reason in the same manner that humans can.

Why this added emphasis about the AI not being sentient?

Because I want to underscore that when discussing the role of the AI driving system, I am not ascribing human qualities to the AI. Please be aware that there is an ongoing and dangerous tendency these days to anthropomorphize AI. In essence, people are assigning human-like sentience to today's AI, despite the undeniable and inarguable fact that no such AI exists as yet.

With that clarification, you can envision that the AI driving system won't natively somehow "know" about those airborne turtles. This is an aspect that needs to be programmed as part of the hardware and software of the self-driving car.

Let's dive into the myriad of aspects that come to play on this topic.

First, we can consider the matter of whether it is vital to detect that the threatening object is a turtle.

Allow me to explain.

The sensors of the self-driving car are intended to examine the environment surrounding the vehicle and provide data about whatever is able to be detected. There are video cameras that are streaming live videos of the driving scene. There are usually radar devices, LIDAR units, ultrasonic detectors, and so on, all of which are attempting to sense the nearby scenery.

This torrent of data is then examined by the AI-based driving system. For example, there is image processing software that is running on the onboard computer processors. The software is oftentimes based on today's Machine Learning (ML) and Deep Learning (DL) algorithms. In brief, these are computational pattern matching techniques that try to identify what an object is.

Programmers and engineers have usually pre-trained the ML/DL. They might have used thousands of pictures of cars and trucks to train the ML/DL on what such vehicles look like. Thus, when the video images come pouring into the system, the pattern matching can identify that a car is up ahead and a truck is further ahead of the car.

The pattern matching is done for pretty much all discoverable objects in the driving scene (well, not necessarily, since this could be computationally expensive and exhaustive). Anyway, the idea is that the AI driving system will need to identify where other cars are, where pedestrians are, and the like. This requires mathematically examining the sensory data and trying to ferret out which objects are present.

In addition, the detection should also be trying to figure out the movement of the objects that are being identified. A lamppost at the side of the rode is likely stationary and fixed in place. A parked car at the edge of the roadway is perhaps stationary at this moment in time but could get underway suddenly. A crucial element of the self-driving car and the AI driving system entails being able to find objects, categorize them, and predict what those objects are doing and what they might do next.

All right, with that important preamble, we can return to the matter at hand.

Should the AI driving system try to ascertain whether a turtle is a turtle, assuming that a turtle is findable within the driving scene?

One argument is that of course, the AI driving system ought to be programmed to identify turtles.

Suppose that a turtle is crawling along the roadway and a self-driving car is approaching the beloved creature. We don't want the self-driving car to simply drive over the top of the sweet turtle. If the AI has simply categorized the turtle as say a boxy-shaped object of no known configuration, this implies that the AI would not be able to factor into the equation that this is a possible living animal.

That might be a significant factor when making a driving decision.

A human driver might opt to roll over a fragment of broken furniture that is laying on the street. You might do so because trying to swerve away could be dicey and get you into a worse car accident. Sometimes the easiest approach involves driving over a roadway piece of debris. At the same time, a human driver might take some desperate attempts to avoid striking a breathing animal, and thus knowing whether an object is a turtle versus a piece of scattered furniture is a notable aspect.

Please be aware that there are more twists and turns involved.

As a driver, if an object is flying straight toward your windshield, does it matter whether you are able to figure out what exactly the object is?

In one sense, it is obviously important to try and ascertain the size, weight, shape, and trajectory of the object. This can be done without necessarily being able to identify the specific nature of the object. All you need to know at that moment is that it is either big or small, going to be bouncing off your windshield or smashing into it, and could land inside the vehicle.

I recall that one day I was driving past a golf course and an errant golf ball came over the top netting and smacked into my windshield while I was going at about 45 miles per hour. It happened very fast. I did not see the golf ball while it was in the air. All I managed to see was something that at the last moment struck my windshield. I then watched as the white-colored and ball-like object bounced off the now cracked windshield and landed onto the highway, bouncing merrily along.

In a somewhat after-the-fact Sherlock Holmes deductive logic, I reasoned that it was a golf ball. Perhaps it could have been some other similar object, though the preponderance of anecdotal evidence suggests it was likely an everyday golf ball. Luckily, other than the shocking impact, the windshield remained intact, I could still see the road, and I kept driving. Later on, I had to replace the severely cracked windshield and was cursing those idiot golfers that couldn't keep their game on the golf course (I don't like to use foul words, so I won't refer to the golfer as a duffer).

Returning to the flying turtle, in the case of a turtle that was hurled into the air and is stridently heading toward the windshield of a self-driving car, it would seem arguable whether or not the AI should necessarily need to be programmed to identify this darting object as a turtle (i.e., this ostensibly is a nice to have capability versus an ironclad required function). You could readily assert that as long as the AI driving system is able to assess the size, shape, and other factors, the act of not discerning that it is a turtle could be considered adequate in this particular scenario.

I bring this up for several reasons.

One reason involves the so-called edge or corner case problem that confronts the advent of self-driving cars.

An acrimonious issue being hotly debated consists of the zillions of edge or corner cases that can arise when driving a car. Some believe that self-driving cars ought to not even be on our public roadways until all possible scenarios have been tested via a simulation or via a closed track testing facility.

Others point out that it would likely never be the case that self-driving cars would ever get onto our roadways if you first had to figure out every conceivable scenario. There are always additional variants that can be dreamed up and thus the number of possible permutations would seemingly be endless.

As a result, most of the automakers and self-driving car tech firms are concentrating on the more likely scenarios and leaving the edge or corner cases for being dealt with later on. This would seem like a prudent and realistic way to get underway with self-driving cars, especially if you believe that a prevalence of self-driving cars will ultimately reduce the number of car crashes and consequently reduce the number of human injuries and fatalities associated with driving.

For those that accept the notion of proceeding and then, later on, coping with edge cases, there is another problem at hand, namely, what constitutes a reasonable definition for an edge case? Suppose a self-driving car tech firm decides that jaywalking pedestrians is an edge case, and it can be dealt with later on. I doubt that any reasonable person would decidedly go along with that scenario as an edge case and instead would insist it needs to be a core or cornerstone capability of the AI driving system.

Time for a brief sidenote. That was notably a somewhat outrageous or outlandish exemplar and so don't be dinging me about the idea that anyone in their right mind would claim that jaywalking pedestrians is an edge case. I was trying to use some provocative hyperbole to help make a point. Please go with the flow.

The totality of all of this back-and-forth is that the use case of the hurtled turtle could be "reasonably" handled as any generic kind of debris that is coming at the windshield of the self-driving car. Having to figure out in real-time that it is a turtle is not quite as vital as is ascertaining the profile of the object and what it might do.

**Conclusion**

The saga of how a self-driving car would deal with a flying turtle has only just begun.

There is a lot more to be considered, though due to space constraints I can't cover the whole shebang.

In the case of the Florida driver, the driver likely had little if any recognition of the turtle before it struck the windshield. By this, I mean that the driver probably not only did not realize it was a turtle, but the driver might also not have consciously been aware of the object at all (similar to how I was taken by surprise by the alleged golf ball).

Ergo, a human driver can get caught unawares.

For an AI driving system, there is a chance of that kind of being caught unawares, though only likely in the sense that the object might be moving so fast that there was insufficient time for the computer processors to do the needed image analyses and electronically calculate what to do.

To clarify, it would seem generally likely that the sensory devices captured imagery or other data that would record the aspect of a flying object like this (assuming that it was visible and otherwise not obscured or hidden). The problem would next consist of how fast the hardware and software could undertake the needed analysis.

Even if the computational processing was done within sufficient time, the next question is what should the AI driving system do about the emerging predicament. Should the self-driving car swerve? Should the self-driving car go faster and try to get under the object, maybe having the object hit the roof of the car instead of the windshield? Should the self-driving car try to hit the brakes? And so on.

These are all very hard questions and bring to the foreground the famous (or some say infamous) Trolley Problem (see my coverage **in my columns**).

Suppose the turtle hits the windshield, enters violently into the vehicle, and strikes a passenger. This could absolutely befall a self-driving car. The question then arises as to whether the AI driving system will have detected this infiltration and be able to ascertain what driving action is next most suitable to perform. Hitting the brakes might not be a proper action, since doing so could cause cars behind the struck car to get hit from behind.

All told, this turtle story provides a plethora of handy points about what self-driving cars need to be programmed to deal with.

Fortunately, the humans were okay, and the turtle did not lose its life while garnering this opportunity to glean some lessons learned. One hopes that the turtle though reads this article and realizes that meandering into the highway is a risky gambit, including even once self-driving cars are abundantly on our highways and byways.

Stay safe, courageous turtle.

# CHAPTER 25
# BUG SWARMS AND SELF-DRIVING CARS

They are hiding underground and have been growing and maturing, getting ready for their grand unveiling that takes place just for a few weeks, doing so every 17 years. You might say they are akin to eager teenagers waiting to get their moment in the sun and party until they drop.

And there are trillions of them.

Yes, the incredible swarmageddon entailing possibly trillions of cicada bugs are soon to be emerging and do so with a great deal of fervor and fanfare. These young adults don't have much time once they burrow out of the dirt. They are pressed by nature to do their mating rituals and meanwhile get ready for their demise. In a near blink of an eye lifecycle, these red-eyed buggy creatures will seek to produce their offspring in just a couple of weeks, die off, and their progeny or brood will fall to the ground and in term mature, while buried, earnestly arising in yet another 17 years passage of time.

Where is this going to happen?

You can count around fifteen states in the northeastern part of the country as subject to the burst of cicada activity, including Indiana, Georgia, New York, Tennessee, Virginia, Ohio, Michigan, North Carolina, and similarly situated locales.

The official name given to all of this is the Brood X generation (wherein this is the roman numeral standing for ten) or ostensibly referred to as *The Great Eastern Brood.*

Whether you feel lucky and fortunate to live in a place that will witness the Brood X is entirely up to individual preferences. There are many that loath the emergence of the cicada and would just as soon that things were Brood 0 (that's a big fat zero).

The good news is that the cicada is relatively harmless and is primarily an annoyance rather than something to be dreaded as a dire pest. They don't sting. They don't bite. They don't scratch. They don't emit poison. All told, they might seem creepy (that's for darned sure) and you are bound to react with abject dismay at their presence, though you won't be especially harmed.

There is though the noise.

They make quite a racket, especially when there are millions nearby you and they are desperately and blaringly producing their mating calls. At around 105 decibels, they can collectively sound like an approaching train. Some liken the noise to the sounds you'd encounter while being in a crowded nightclub or bar, which is kind of a handy comparison but also seems a bit off base since at least you are having a good time and drinking while in your local tavern (not something you are advised to try while amidst a swarm of the cicada).

Most of the time, the cicada do not want to be near humans anyway. They want to be in the trees. By being in the trees, they are able to perform the mating ritual and attract their perfect mates. Thus, usually what happens is the cicada comes out of the ground, climb up nearby trees, and remains pretty much in the trees.

This would seem relatively fine if those clever creatures weren't also able to fly. Because they can somewhat fly, they are able to get from tree to tree. This in turn means that it is feasible for them to swarm. I think we can all agree that there is nothing more sinister and frightening to humans than seeing large clouds of bugs that are flitting and flying back and forth. It is assuredly a common theme in movies and TV shows that try to scare the heck out of us all.

These aren't though the same as flying locusts. The cicada really just wants to find a tree and have some fun. They aren't especially interested in flying great distances or otherwise doing things that a swarm might do when it is tasked with special deeds to be performed. Romance in the trees is their true mantra and anything else is undertaken for that enthusiastic purpose.

This is all done as a race against death. They will nearly all be deceased by around the end of June, depending upon when they came out of the ground (it's about a three to four weeks lifetime).

Speaking of death, the cicada face quite a gauntlet of ways to die. Possums are filled to the brim when they get a chance like this to dine wantonly on these crunchy bugs. Raccoons are also eagerly at the dinner table to consume the delicious cicada. I must tell you that cats will eat cicada too, which if you have a beloved pet feline would maybe seem disgusting to see, so keep that potential ghastly spectacle in mind if you let your cat roam outside during this upcoming Brood X season.

Theories abound about the cicada and one viewpoint is that part of the reason there are so many of them that will emerge, and doing so at roughly the same time, sparks a semblance of survivability. By having gobs and gobs of them darting all about, the odds are that their predators won't be able to eat them all. The probability is that enough or certainly some of the bugs will last long enough to complete the mating aspects and generate the next generation.

You see, there does seem to be credence to the old saying that there is safety in numbers.

Speaking of safety, you might be wondering what would happen if you perchance were in your car and came upon a sizable portion of the Brood X.

In the past, people have complained that the cicada comes into their cars via the open windows of their cars. Not wanting to seem overly critical, but it does seem patently obvious that flying cicada might inadvertently end up in your car if you allow this to happen. Realize that the cicada doesn't particularly want to be inside your car. They likely would just as soon get out of your car.

In any case, people inside a car are apt to freak out when they find themselves bunking with a cicada. The freaking out is mainly done by the passengers, but drivers can readily go into freak-out mode too.

I mention this aspect due to the twofold concern about what could happen if cicada got inside your moving vehicle. First and foremost, the driver might go nuts and become inattentive to the roadway, including potentially swerving the car while trying to swat the bugs. That's bad. Second, passengers in the vehicle might also go nuts, possibly alarming the driver. That's bad, once again. The most sedate of drivers might not care about the bugs, but if they have human passengers that are going berserk, it could very well disrupt the driver and lead to an unfortunate car accident that didn't have to happen.

The point is that if you do somehow drive to wherever the Brood X might be, and if some of them perchance get into your vehicle (because you had the windows rolled down, and not because they somehow could sneak their way in), the onus is on you, the humans, to be cool. Remember that these bugs aren't going to hurt you. Stay relaxed and find a means to help shoo them out of the car. I know this seems like a sensible way to approach the matter, meanwhile in the heat of the moment it is hard to remain calm and collected.

Dare I suggest that if some cicada does get into your car, it might be prudent to find a safe spot to pull over, try to herd out the ones that got in, and give yourself a chance to catch your breath before continuing your driving journey. Oh, and please roll up the windows.

Can the cicada impact your car in other ways?

Yes, they can, primarily due to the volume of them and that they can fly.

You could end up driving into a swarm and they will splatter all over your windshield.

Yuk!

The thing is, if you get enough of them becoming bug guts and bug juice on your windshield, it might be very hard to see the roadway. It makes sense to check beforehand that your windshield wiper blades are in good shape and that you have plenty of windshield wiper fluid ready to be used. Nonetheless, the stickiness and glue-like substance of their smashed innards still might not get completely erased by wiper blades alone and you'll need to by hand do something to clean off the glass.

There is also a chance that the bugs can clog your radiator grill. Besides looking unsightly, the bigger danger is that your car might not get the engine ventilation needed to keep your car running properly. An overheated and damaged engine that was caused by the mass demise of cicada is not the type of writeup you want when filing a car insurance claim.

The primary concern is of course that the cicada could disturb your ability to drive a car due to clouding up the windshield or obscuring what is up ahead on the roadway past the swarm that you are encountering. Those are all key safety issues and deal with the act of driving.

One supposes you can also be concerned about other matters such as the paint job on your car. These bugs are especially acidic, and they can do some harm to your paint, though mainly if their deceased carcasses and leftover bits and pieces are not soon washed off from the exterior of your car. You are unlikely to get immediate paint damage and it is more likely that if the bug guts remain for any lengthy time, then the paint will suffer accordingly.

Do not though be thinking about the paint on your car when you should be thinking about the traffic on the roadway whilst immersed in a swarm of the cicada. Staying alive at the wheel is paramount in comparison to any fancy paint job.

All told, human drivers need to keep their wits about them when coming upon the Brood X.

Make sure to keep your windshield highly visible and pay close attention to the road. Do not be watching that fascinating cloud of cicada and inadvertently veer into another lane and crash into another car. Keep the rapt cicada watching for when you are no longer behind the wheel and can resolutely and safely relish watching these bugs.

Furthermore, be on the watch for other drivers that do get distracted by the Brood X. Those other drivers are a by far larger danger for you than are the bugs themselves. People do stupid things in these kinds of circumstances. Some dolt might decide to try and ram the cicada or take driving actions to avoid running into them, doing so at the peril of other nearby drivers and pedestrians.

You would think that since the Brood X will only be around for a few weeks that therefore those human drivers and passengers could ready themselves and be perfectly relaxed and prepared for the buggy onslaught.

I sincerely hope so.

Shifting gears, consider that the future of cars entails the advent of self-driving cars. Self-driving cars are going to be using AI-based driving systems and there won't be a human driver at the wheel.

Here is an intriguing question: *How would AI-based true self-driving cars cope with the emergence of the cicada and this so-called swamageddon?*

Let's unpack the matter and see.

**Self-Driving Cars And Brood X**

For Level 4 and Level 5 true self-driving vehicles, there won't be a human driver involved in the driving task.

All occupants will be passengers.

The AI is doing the driving.

One aspect to immediately discuss entails the fact that the AI involved in today's AI driving systems is not sentient. In other words, the AI is altogether a collective of computer-based programming and algorithms, and most assuredly not able to reason in the same manner that humans can.

Why this added emphasis about the AI not being sentient?

Because I want to underscore that when discussing the role of the AI driving system, I am not ascribing human qualities to the AI. Please be aware that there is an ongoing and dangerous tendency these days to anthropomorphize AI. In essence, people are assigning human-like sentience to today's AI, despite the undeniable and inarguable fact that no such AI exists as yet.

With that clarification, you can envision that the AI driving system won't natively somehow "know" about those swarming cicada. This is an aspect that needs to be programmed as part of the hardware and software of the self-driving car.

Let's dive into the myriad of aspects that come to play on this topic.

We'll start with the aspect that the AI driving system will not freak out akin to how human drivers might go a bit nutty in this swarmageddon encounter. The AI is not going to go into some kind of emotional roller coaster about the massing bugs or otherwise get excited or upset about the swarms. This is somewhat reassuring that we can excise out of the equation any qualms that we might have about human drivers that lose their minds due to the Brood X, for which the AI won't suffer.

One thing though to keep in mind is that self-driving cars are likely to be driving nearby human-driven cars, something that will be happening for many decades to come. Some pundits have a crazy Utopian idea that overnight there will be a sudden switchover to all and only self-driving cars, but that's just plainly not going to happen. You can expect that there will be a mixture of human-driven cars and self-driving cars on our roadways.

That's a fact.

I bring this up because self-driving cars are going to still need to deal with the foibles of human drivers that are in traffic nearby to the self-driving cars. If a self-driving car enters into a swarm of cicada, and meanwhile a human-driven car is doing the same thing at the same place and time, the AI driving system needs to cope with the potential antics of the human driver that might readily and unexpectedly veer errantly or do something stupid in reaction to the swarm.

Of course, we would expect a well-devised AI driving system to always be on alert for the antics of nearby human-driven cars. This seems like the standard table stakes to be proffering an autonomous vehicle and avidly playing in the self-driving game, as it were.

At the same time, it makes sense to have the AI driving system be especially on high alert when the situational factors make the probability of human-driven antics heightened. There is the normal everyday check-and-balance about what human drivers will do. There should also be a provision for the acts of human drivers in settings that we can all reasonably anticipate that a human driver will potentially go haywire and make brash or unbridled driving moves.

Okay, so we might agree that the AI driving system does not necessarily need to be programmed to cope with the swarms, though it ought to be detecting the swarms and be computationally ready for the potential of nearby human drivers to do bad driving.

There are plenty of additional facets for the AI driving system and the self-driving car that are vital in these matters.

For example, I had earlier mentioned that the windshields of cars could become blotted and obscured by the bug guts, which would be highly dangerous for human drivers because they would no longer adequately see the roadway. In the case of the AI driving system, we don't especially need to be worried about the windshield.

What we do need to be worried about are the numerous sensors and sensory devices that are on the self-driving car. There are likely video cameras, radar, LIDAR, ultrasonic units, thermal imagining, and other elements of the sensory suite. Those need to be unobstructed.

They are the proverbial eyes and ears of the AI driving system.

Thus, in the same complication of bugs splattering on the windshield being bad for human drivers, the bugs splattering on the numerous sensors are bad for the AI driving system. The sensors might be unable to properly detect the driving scene. The data being collected is either confounded or noisy. When the AI attempts to mathematically analyze the data, there will be difficulties in finding what objects exist outside the car. In addition, it might be difficult to figure out where those objects are, their speeds, their direction of travel, etc.

In brief, the sensors could get mired in the muck and therefore the AI driving system is now blind about what the driving scene consists of.

This is not a problem that is solely unique to the Brood X. Any kind of swarming bugs could produce the same result. Even everyday grime and the occasional bug hitting could create problems for the sensors in terms of clarity about detection. I've written previously about the multitude of proposed and being tried out solutions to the sensor cleaning aspects. There are tiny wiper blades, there are jets that spray out special liquids, and so on.

Anyway, the point is that a self-driving car can find itself caught in the morass of a bug swarm and end up with sensors that are no longer able to sufficiently detect the road. Presumably, the AI software would ascertain that the sensors aren't performing properly and that the vehicle should be safely brought to a halt.

That seems like the prudent thing to do.

On the other hand, imagine passengers inside the self-driving car that are fearful about the cicada (I'm not saying they are justified in their fear, only that they are indeed afraid). You can imagine the angst and frustration of the passengers when the AI driving system summarily declares that it is pulling over and coming to a stop. In the minds of the passengers, this might seem like the worst of choices. Rather than driving through the swarm and popping out of it, the self-driving car is going to sit right in the middle of the swarm.

I'm sure that the passengers would invoke an in-car capability of calling up a remote agent of the fleet operator and proffer a word or two about their dissatisfaction. They might entirely be in the wrong and the AI driving system is in the right, it is just that the passengers might not think so.

Furthermore, they might claim or insist that if a human driver was at the wheel, perhaps the driving would continue (rightly or wrongly so).

**Conclusion**

You can bet that some people are going to intentionally take a drive to go see the cicada. They want to see the spectacle. Perhaps some will bring their youngsters and emphasize that the next time they'll see the Brood X will be when the next generation appears will be seventeen years hence.

That would be the year 2038.

Where will we with the advent of self-driving cars when the year 2038 rolls around?

Many believe that we will by then have widely adopted self-driving cars. They will be pervasive. If that is so, just envision that your children of today opt to go see the cicada, telling the AI driving system to take them there. While on that journey, those now adults will tell any youngsters on board about the time that they took a human-driven car to go see the prior brood.

Those kids will shake their heads in disbelief. What a silly way to travel when you can just let the AI do the driving. Maybe even the cicada that arises out of the ground in 2038 will look around and notice that there is a slew of self-driving cars in their midst.

I'd bet the cicada will be thinking, well, by gosh, it's about time.

# CHAPTER 26
# LAMPPOSTS AND SELF-DRIVING CARS

Are you giving due credit and appreciation to the numerous lampposts wherever you live, work, and play?

Probably not.

Most of us tend to not notice lampposts. Well, actually, you probably notice when they aren't working and especially at night time when there is darkness rather than a helpful plume of light. That is decidedly an occasion whereby we become aware of a lamppost, ostensibly when they are most needed.

Some estimates suggest that there are over thirty million lampposts in the United States and around 320 million worldwide. Counting of lampposts is not necessarily a pastime or a requirement, thus the number of lampposts is principally an approximation rather than a fully verified figure. It does seem intuitive that there are a lot of them and that they are nearly ubiquitous.

Seems like there is always a need for even more lampposts. You might be driving your car down a road and realize that your headlights alone are not sufficient to adequately light the way ahead. At that moment, your mind fleetingly thinks about the lamppost topic. Why isn't there a lamppost here? Do people not realize that a lamppost would be worthwhile and boost safety for drivers and pedestrians?

All told, you could reasonably predict that we are inevitably going to have more and more lampposts. Lampposts rarely get removed from a locale. Once they are put in place, taking them away is bound to get flak. Adding more is not usually associated with getting criticism. There are though the qualms about the light pollution of cities and that aspect that you cannot see the beauty of the nighttime skies. That is a consideration, of course.

The lighting of roadways is a longtime tradition. History indicates that the Greeks and the Romans used lanterns and that this was a vital spurring element of their civilizations. There were people specially trained and hired to light the oil lanterns, doing so in an occupational role that we today might refer to as a lamplighter. Perhaps you've seen lamplighters in books or movies that showcase candle lighting.

The lampposts of modern times are usually powered by electricity. If you look at the top of a lamppost, you might see the electrical wires that connect the post to an electric grid or network. A lot of the lampposts have been converted over to using underground electrical wiring, which makes the lamppost almost seem magical that it can somehow seemingly function without any direct evidence of receiving power.

To try and reduce the electrical consumption of lampposts, there has been an ongoing effort of adding solar panels to the lamppost. The idea is that perhaps some or possibly all of the power consumed by the use of the lamppost can be gleaned from sunshine. This might not work out particularly well in all locales, especially in places that have very little sunshine. Usually, the solar panel is considered a secondary source of power, and the lamppost is still connected to the electrical grid, thus the lamppost will still function even if there is insufficient power coming from the solar panel or any batteries being used.

You might be under the impression that lampposts are solely used to provide lighting.

Alas, you'd be mistaken in that presumption.

When you think about the nature of a lamppost, the value of having posts that are scattered all about can provide a number of other handy uses. You can hang all kinds of other devices and mechanisms onto that otherwise lowly lamppost.

What might a lamppost be used for other than as a source of

lighting?

Tons of things.

You could mount a WiFi electronic communications router onto a lamppost. This would provide anybody nearby with potentially being able to have a clear and perhaps free WiFi connection. That's pretty handy these days.

Another possibility is to include a 5G transmitter, which can aid in speeding up electronic communications.

Digital signs can be mounted onto a lamppost. This is in addition to potentially having a good old-fashioned printed sign too. The nice thing about the digital sign is that it can be changed up in terms of messages shown. Whoever controls the digital sign can send messages to it and have those displayed for any passersby.

Some are aiming to have lampposts become a charger station for Electrical Vehicles (EVs). Yes, that is right, you would park your EV next to the lamppost and plug into the lamppost (using whatever power source it has). Seems kind of oddball or quirky to some, but it makes potential sense as we see more and more EVs on the roadway. There are though some complications that arise as to whether parking in front of the lamppost is sensible in a given circumstance, and other matters make this a bit challenging.

Yet another possibility consists of putting environmental sensors on a lamppost. If you want to track how foul the air is or whether there is an overwhelming amount of noise pollution, you could potentially do so via sprinkling environmental sensors on lampposts in a given area. You can add to this aspect the idea of using conventional weather detecting sensors too, such that they could measure the rainfall, temperatures, and the like.

Some places have put loudspeakers onto their lampposts. This can be handy to blare out a horn when an emergency occurs, such as during an earthquake or a tsunami. The speakers could be used for everyday activities too. Perhaps a speaker might be used to play music and soothe the souls of those that perchance walk past the lamppost.

I realize you might be wearing out in terms of the vast array of ways to use lampposts.

Let's at least cover one more and something that is at times quite controversial, namely the use of video cameras on lampposts.

Here's the deal.

Some locales are placing video cameras onto their lampposts. The idea is that this can be handy for security purposes. If someone tries to commit a crime, presumably the video camera will see all. This can then be used to find the suspect and arrest them, or potentially be used as evidence in a criminal trial. There is also the aspect that the video camera can be a deterrent, causing potential crooks to think twice about committing a crime because they know that they are being observed.

There is also the potential for real-time use of such a video camera. Suppose the video camera is being monitored by a security firm or the police. If the video camera is showcasing someone that seems to be on the verge of a criminal act, the appropriate security could be sent to the location.

The reason that this imbues controversy is that the video camera can also be considered an intrusion of privacy. Perhaps the video camera on lampposts will take us down the Big Brother route. All-day long we will all be under constant surveillance. That is worrisome. A counterargument usually given is that if you are in a public place, you are already ostensibly agreeing to be seen. In that logic, the addition of a video camera does not presumably change the circumstances materially.

Anyway, it is going to be an ongoing discussion and debate, that's for sure.

There is an umbrella rubric often used to refer to these expanded uses of lampposts, typically coined as the possibility of intelligent street lighting or sometimes referred to as smart lampposts. The overarching notion is that a lamppost is more than just a pole and a light. You can turn a lamppost into something much more impressive and altogether beneficial.

Along those lines, I'd like to add an additional and rather an innovative way in which the mighty lamppost can be utilized.

This has to do with traveling cars and traffic aspects. Turns out that a lamppost again is handy, since they tend to be next to roads and streets. Of course, cars proceed along on roads and streets. Ergo, making use of lampposts regarding the traversal of cars and other vehicles is a quite sensible strategy.

These traffic aiding devices could be useful for anybody that perchance is driving nearby. An added twist is that the traffic-related electronic wares could also be used to help in advancing the emergence of self-driving cars. The future of cars entails the advent of self-driving cars.

Self-driving cars are going to be using AI-based driving systems and there won't be a human driver at the wheel.

Here is an intriguing question: *How might lampposts that are augmented with electronic-based traffic-related devices aid the advent of AI-based true self-driving cars?*

Let's unpack the matter and see.

**Self-Driving Cars And Lampposts**

For Level 4 and Level 5 true self driving vehicles, there won't be a human driver involved in the driving task.

All occupants will be passengers.

The AI is doing the driving.

One aspect to immediately discuss entails the fact that the AI involved in today's AI driving systems is not sentient. In other words, the AI is altogether a collective of computer-based programming and algorithms, and most assuredly not able to reason in the same manner that humans can.

Why this added emphasis about the AI not being sentient?

Because I want to underscore that when discussing the role of the AI driving system, I am not ascribing human qualities to the AI. Please be aware that there is an ongoing and dangerous tendency these days to anthropomorphize AI. In essence, people are assigning human-like sentience to today's AI, despite the undeniable and inarguable fact that no such AI exists as yet.

With that clarification, you can envision that the AI driving system won't natively somehow "know" about the use of traffic-related devices. This is an aspect that needs to be programmed as part of the hardware and software of the self-driving car.

Let's dive into the myriad of aspects that come to play on this topic.

Lampposts are handy because they usually exist in a stationary position and will remain relatively fixed in place for a lengthy period of time. I'm not suggesting that lampposts are somehow cast in stone and can never be moved, and merely emphasizing that they are generally reliable and won't suddenly walk down the street on their own.

Furthermore, a lamppost is also useful due to being a post or pole, meaning that it extends upward from the ground level and rises several feet high. You can hang things onto a lamppost and those items will then tend to be above the fray, as it were. This can be useful too since it tends to lessen the chances that people will muck around with the devices. That is definitely a consideration about placing any kind of device into the public sphere, namely that somebody might either fuss with it, attempt to break it, or outright steal it.

Okay, so we have these lampposts that are reliably in specific spots and can retain devices that will have a heightened vantage point and potentially be somewhat safe from tampering (of course, a determined miscreant can still likely do untoward acts if desirous of doing so). And these poles are readily connected to electrical power and are typically next to roadways.

Perfect!

These are rife for use with the latest in edge computing.

Self-driving cars are going to be leveraging edge computing to the advantage of us all.

There will be edge devices that are used for V2I (vehicle-to-infrastructure) electronic communication. Imagine a traffic signal that uses V2I and can beam out electronic signals to indicate whether the upcoming intersection is green, yellow, or red. A self-driving car can receive the signal and accordingly prepare to brake or continue on the gas and proceed unabated through the intersection.

V2I is going to be everywhere. Bridges will be outfitted with V2I that electronically conveys the status of the bridge. If a recent flood has damaged a bridge and it is considered no longer passable for now, the V2I can broadcast a signal warning any vehicles to stay away. On a freeway or highway, if there is debris that is blocking traffic, a V2I nearby could be cautioning cars and trucks to slow down and be prepared for delays.

The V2I is brought about by an electronic device. One question to ponder is where in the heck will all of these V2I devices be placed. Some suggest that V2I devices could be placed onto buildings or other major structures. That might make sense in many cases.

A really convenient place to put these V2I devices would be on lampposts.

Unlike just strapping a V2I to the side of a wall or a girder, the lamppost is going to have electrical power available. This is a crucial aspect for the V2I, else it would either have batteries that run out and need someone to come and replace or charge the batteries (that's an extra labor cost) or might have solar panels but not necessarily ensure a consistent and all-the-time ready charge.

Self-driving cars that are outfitted with V2I capabilities would be able to easily receive the transmissions. Envision that as a self-driving car makes its way throughout a city, there are numerous V2I devices that the vehicle can communicate with. V2I devices could be placed on one lamppost at every certain distance and provide essentially a continual stream of broadcasting info.

I won't go into the technological details about V2I herein, other than to point out that of course the V2I has to be digitally secure and data trustworthy.

If a hacker can overtake a V2I, this could be disastrous as the V2I might be misinforming self-driving cars about things that are dangerously untrue or confounding. Some worry that if the V2I devices are placed onto lampposts, this is not yet high enough to prevent or at least discourage hackers from trying to physically access the device. The notion is that maybe the V2I devices should be mounted at the top of telephone poles if the lampposts being considered are not sufficiently high enough.

Some critics say a lamppost can be run over by an errant car, presumably a human-driven car, and knock down the pole, along with also destroying the V2I device. Sure, that is a possibility, but it is quite a rarity and not something so abundant that it would undermine the value of using a lamppost for these purposes.

We can ramp up the use of the lampposts for the advent of self-driving cars by also reconsidering the video cameras that might be included onto those revered poles (recall, earlier I mentioned that lampposts sometimes are outfitted with video cameras).

Here's what I mean.

A self-driving car is going to make a turn at a tight corner up ahead. There is no viable way to see around the corner, at least not until having committed to making the turn. It would be assuredly handy if there was a means to see around that corner, doing so before starting the turn. Voila, if a video camera was mounted on a lamppost that was near that corner, the camera could be beaming in real-time whatever it sees.

A self-driving car could receive that video and use the video to try and ascertain whether making the turn is safe to do or not. I've referred to this capability as a type of *computational omnipresence*, wherein a self-driving car can glean a bird's eye view of the surroundings by tapping into video cameras and other sensory devices that are aimed at the streets and roadways being traversed.

**Conclusion**

A cynic might say that we are ultimately going to have everything imaginable hanging on those lampposts. Don't be surprised, they exhort if perchance one day you astonishingly see a kitchen sink dangling from your local lampposts.

There is a kernel of truth to this type of diatribe in that we have to be measured about what lampposts are going to be used for. We probably don't want them to look like an unsightly collective of strange-looking doodads and contraptions. Some also wring their hands at the massive electrical bill that might arise for a municipality that lets so many electricity guzzling devices be used. There is also concern about the maintenance and repairs aspects.

And so on.

I won't necessarily try to defend all of the accessories and augmented uses that are being dreamed up for lampposts, but it is relevant here to briefly talk about the vehicular realm and how safety can be demonstrably enhanced.

It is also important to emphasize that the V2I and related edge computing for aiding self-driving cars will be advantageous to conventional cars too. You can fully expect that human-driven cars will be including V2I receivers and showcase the messages to humans at the wheel of a vehicle. Plus, anything that makes driving safer, regardless of human-driven or via self-driving capability, will save lives and also likely reduce pedestrian injuries and fatalities too.

The light provided by a lamppost gets little praise and rarely receives the glory that it deserves.

The first street lights in the United States that were electrified have been attributed to occurring around 1879 (before that date, street lights were usually gas lamps). Some would say it is about time that lampposts become "intelligent" or "smart" and increase their worth to society.

Lampposts did get some acclaim when Gene Kelly opted to do his famous *Singin' In The Rain*, for which he danced and swirled by using a lamppost during the enchanting treat. The lowly lamppost can still reach for the skies, even today, and stand tall to be a vital contributor toward the advent of self-driving cars.

That deserves yet another delightful song.

# CHAPTER 27
# CARE PACKAGES AND SELF-DRIVING CARS

Sending a care package is a kind-hearted gesture and something we all have likely done or possibly been the recipient of.

A frequently cited example of sending a care package entails the now-classic summer camp gift-giving gambit. It goes something like this. A parent has let their youngster go off to summer camp and frets that all is going well. Is the food at the summer camp edible? Does the youngster have enough clothing for the duration of the summer camp experience?

And so on.

In an era prior to smartphones, there was no ready means to directly communicate with your child while they were ensconced in faraway forests and other hideaways. Parents would therefore opt to send a care package containing various additional provisions and get a twofer by doing so. One winning aspect was to ensure that their child had needed items on hand. The other was that the care package itself was a form of communication and basically said that the parent was thinking of their camp-going offspring.

Most kids would be delighted to receive such a care package, especially if it was packed with youngster-approved useful items. A parent that sent a spare toothbrush would probably be looked upon as being overly protective and the youngster might rebuff the gift. On the other hand, gobs of chocolate and delicious cookies were bound to go over successfully, and the child would thence have the upper hand in negotiations with other camp goers for the trading of provisions.

Few people realize that the notion of a care package ostensibly began as the official CARE package, wherein the acronym denoted by those four capital letters stood for the Cooperative for American Remittances to Europe. Turns out that seventy-five years ago, the first official CARE packages arrived in France on May 11, 1946. A multitude of charities had banded together to form the CARE non-profit organization and sought to deliver food relief to people in Europe that were starving or otherwise nearly so as a result of World War II.

What was included in those initial CARE packages, you might be wondering.

Items included beef in broth, steak and kidneys, liver loaf, corned beef, luncheon loaf, bacon, margarine, lard, fruit preserves, honey, raisins, sugar, powdered eggs, whole-milk powder, coffee, and chocolate.

Note that chocolate has always been a wise inclusion into any kind of CARE or care package.

The CARE entity changed the meaning of the CARE letters to Cooperative for American Remittances to Everywhere as the effort expanded, and eventually landed on the Cooperative for Assistance and Relief Everywhere. CARE still exists today and continues to provide assistance, having done so extensively during the existing pandemic. Besides providing food, today's CARE also includes essential supplies, monetary assistance, and other forms of humanitarian support.

Celebrations are taking place this week to honor the CARE effort on its seventy-fifth anniversary.

Following the end of WWII, the aspect of sending someone a CARE package morphed into also becoming known as sending someone a care package. People leveraged the concept and the name, though many today do not realize that the origins consisted of the CARE acronym. In any case, the semblance of sending somebody something because you care about them is a heartfelt act and one that takes place routinely and often quietly.

If you think about care packages, you also need to encompass the notion of actually sending the gift items. In other words, you nearly always say in one breath that you are *sending* a care package. I point this out because a large difficulty with care packages is that the sending aspects can complicate or confound the desire to provide someone with the items being sent.

Simply stated, getting the care package from point A to point B can be quite an arduous logistical chore.

Not only is physical transportation a difficulty, but there is also the cost associated with the shipping effort. Believe it or not, the cost of transporting a care package could readily exceed the cost of the items contained within the care package.

We often do not consider the cost element of shipping, and it is a somewhat hidden factor that can make or break the desire to send out a care package. The items in the care package seem to us as evidently having some form of cost. Bundling those items together and getting them to wherever they need to go is another cost and one that has to be given due consideration.

If you could somehow reduce the transportation cost, this suggests that you could potentially send out more care packages (by using the "savings" to cover the cost of additional care packages that otherwise would have consumed monies solely for the transportation aspects). Anyone that wants to send out as many care packages as feasible will undoubtedly be agonizing over the shipping costs. Ways to minimize the cost of transportation will be eagerly sought.

Putting on our thinking caps, we can postulate how care packages might be delivered as we begin to enter into an era of Autonomous Vehicles (AVs).

AVs consist of any kind of self-driving vehicles such as self-driving cars, self-driving delivery vans, self-driving rolling bots, self-driving trucks, self-driving drones, self-driving airplanes, self-driving submersibles, self-driving boats, and the like. They all use Artificial Intelligence (AI) to bring about the act of driving, sailing, flying, or in whatever manner of transit, doing so without the need for a human driver or pilot at the wheel.

We are gradually and inexorably entering into an era of AI-based true self-driving.

We aren't there yet. I mention this perhaps "shocking" revelation that we are not yet in a self-driving era because much of the media regrettably seems to be touting that we already have achieved true self-driving. That's a misleading distortion and can spark a lot of problems and ultimately spur a backlash on the entirety of self-driving and AVs altogether.

I'll explain further in a moment.

Meanwhile, about those care packages, we can consider how useful AVs will be to aid in transporting CARE or care packages. The hope overall is that self-driving vehicles will bring down tremendously the costs of transportation. If that can occur, there is the splendorous idea that we could finally end up with mobility-for-all. This mobility-for-all is a handy catchphrase that proffers the desire to ensure that mobility is entirely affordable and accessible to everyone and that the barriers of trying to enact mobility are demonstrably reduced.

We can focus on self-driving cars and other related self-driving vehicles to get a glimpse of where things are heading, using the delivery of care packages as a foil or construct to explore the latest on this emerging innovation.

Let's then address this question: *What will be important to know about the advent of self-driving vehicles as they relate to the delivery of care packages?*

Time to unpack the matter and see.

**Self-Driving Cars And Care Package Delivery**

For Level 4 and Level 5 true self-driving vehicles, there won't be a human driver involved in the driving task.

All occupants will be passengers.

The AI is doing the driving.

One aspect to immediately discuss entails the fact that the AI involved in today's AI driving systems is not sentient. In other words, the AI is altogether a collective of computer-based programming and algorithms, and most assuredly not able to reason in the same manner that humans can.

Why this added emphasis about the AI not being sentient?

Because I want to underscore that when discussing the role of the AI driving system, I am not ascribing human qualities to the AI. Please be aware that there is an ongoing and dangerous tendency these days to anthropomorphize AI. In essence, people are assigning human-like sentience to today's AI, despite the undeniable and inarguable fact that no such AI exists as yet.

With that clarification, you can envision that the AI driving system won't natively somehow "know" about delivering care packages. This is an aspect that needs to be programmed as part of the hardware and software of the self-driving car.

Let's dive into the myriad of aspects that come to play on this topic.

First, it seems straightforward that you would merely load your care package into a self-driving vehicle and then command the AI driving system to proceed on a delivery journey.

End of story.

Well, not quite.

Turns out there are a lot of twists and turns that underlie this seemingly easy task.

One aspect entails the nature of the care package and whether the self-driving vehicle is well-prepared to properly store and keep safe the care package until it reaches the designated destination.

For example, if you placed a care package into the backseat of a self-driving car and told the AI driving system to start driving, suppose that the trip originated in Los Angeles and the delivery destination was New York City. That's quite a long traversal. A care package that contained perishable goods might not make the journey unscathed. Imagine that the self-driving car goes through hot desert regions as it makes its way out of California and into Nevada or Arizona. The interior temperature might spoil the goods.

Another consideration about using a self-driving car would be that the vehicle is normally aimed at carrying passengers. As such, the interior is designed and purposely constructed for passenger comfort and enablement. Tossing a care package into a self-driving car is perhaps a form of overkill in that you are using a vehicle devised for a different purpose.

That's not to say that using a self-driving car for carrying care packages is somehow inherently wrong. Just pointing out that depending upon the circumstance, a different form of self-driving vehicles might be more appropriate.

Consider for example those self-driving rolling bots.

You might have seen videos of those self-driving bots that go along on the sidewalk and deliver a sandwich or a pizza to someone at their house or dorm. That could be a care package delivery mechanism, assuming that the care package itself is small enough to fit into the storage bunk of the self-driving bot.

Another possibility is the self-driving delivery vehicles that kind of resemble cars but do not have any provision for carrying passengers. Instead, the interior is intentionally crafted to carry items such as groceries or other goods. It might make more sense to use a self-driving delivery vehicle to get your care package to its intended destination.

There are tradeoffs involved.

For many of the self-driving delivery vehicles, they are today usually being capped at relatively low speeds, perhaps in the range of 25 to 35 miles per hour. The slower speeds mean that the AI driving system has a somewhat easier job of driving the vehicle. Faster speeds require quicker actions to avoid getting into a collision or vehicle crash. There are little time available and fewer options as to maneuvering to avoid an untoward outcome.

Of course, sending a care package from Los Angeles to New York City via a vehicle that is going to only go at around 25 to 35 miles per hour is going to take a very long time to get there. Likewise, imagine trying to use a self-driving bot to do the same delivery and cruising at a top speed of say 5 mph, and you'd be a skeleton by the time the care package arrived.

All told, the point being that choosing the right type of self-driving vehicle will be essential when opting to use one to get your care package from point A to point B. There are differences in the pace or speed of travel, the vehicular accommodations for the care package, the costs of the traversal, etc.

Pretend that the care package is going a great distance, such as carting something across the USA.

What would occur if we used a human-driven vehicle for that delivery?

A human driver would need to take breaks for food, for resting, and the like. The driver would undoubtedly become weary of the driving task and perhaps increasingly be dangerous as a driver due to fatigue, pushing themselves to their cognitive and physical limits. The beauty of an AI driving system is that it needs no rest, no food breaks, and will otherwise be just as attentive when the driving begins and as when it ends.

Some are quick to bring up the fact that the self-driving vehicle will need to replenish its fuel during any lengthy trip. In that sense, the self-driving vehicle won't be able to continuously proceed and will have to take breaks from time to time.

Yes, indeed there is the refueling matter that needs to be taken into account.

The general rule-of-thumb is that self-driving vehicles will usually be EV's and therefore the refueling consists of getting charged up at a charging station. Right now, few charging stations allow for an automated means of connecting the vehicle with the charging pump. This means that a human would need to be at the charging station and willing to physically undertake the connecting action.

In the future, anticipate that a self-driving vehicle can pull up to a charging station and readily connect to a charging pump, doing so without any human intervention needed. There are efforts too of exploring whether EVs can essentially recharge while in motion, using the roadway as a means of receiving charging, or possibly have another vehicle come alongside and provide charging while both are in motion.

One additional concern about today's self-driving cars and other such vehicles is that they tend to require extensive pre-mapping before being able to navigate in a given locale. These are specialized 3D and HD maps that are created for the AI driving system. They aren't the everyday maps that you or I would use to normally get around.

The crux here is that this implies that your care package might not be able to reach the destination that you've specified.

Assume that you are sending the self-driving car to your pal that lives in a small town in the Midwest. The odds are that the town has not already been pre-mapped for use by the self-driving car. This could mean that you either aren't going to be able to use the self-driving car to get there, or it might need to end its journey at a nearby city that has been pre-mapped for use by self-driving vehicles.

That could be a sticking point.

Meanwhile, there are efforts underway to try and reduce this need for a pre-mapped indication of locales. The hope is that an AI driving system could adequately drive in areas that it has little prior detailed descriptions of. Using only the same kinds of GPS maps that humans use, the AI driving system would be able to navigate safely and properly. When that comes to fruition, you can pretty much assume that the self-driving vehicle could reach just about any reachable destination.

Well, let's put a big caveat on that last point about reachability.

One major hurdle that will last for a long time involves going off-road versus remaining on-road.

By and large, most AI driving systems are aimed at driving while on a conventional road, whether it be composed of asphalt, concrete, or even packed down dirt. Going off-roading is a different animal altogether. Sure, you can expect that this will ultimately be devised, so I'm just cautioning that for the near-term the focus is for navigating on developed roads or staying on-road.

Your first thought might that you would almost always be sending a care package to someone that has a street address and can be entirely reached while staying on-road. In that case, this off-road versus on-road limitation does not matter much to you.

That off-road aspect though might be important to others.

**Conclusion**

Returning to the earlier indication about sending a care package to your offspring while they are attending camp, that's a handy example of how off-roading might enter into the picture.

There are roads likely leading up to the camp entrance since that's probably how the kids were transported there, to begin with. Once at the camp, the remainder of the location might be only suitable for hiking or for off-road vehicles that can cope with the rigors of an outdoor region.

I would bet that your camp-going child would gladly scramble to the front receiving area of the camp to grab up their care package. Just make sure that you include bona fide goodies. Though a few pairs of clean socks might be handy, the odds are that any delectable food or mouthwatering snacks would get a much more welcoming reception.

But, hey, either way, you have demonstrated that you care, and that's what counts. In that case, your child will have fond memories of camp, and especially remember the day that the self-driving vehicle arrived with those heartwarming and scrumptious goodies.

Fond memories are made at summer camp, that's for sure.

# CHAPTER 28
# RETIRE THE KEYS AND SELF-DRIVING CARS

Most of us take for granted that we can drive a car.

The driving act seems to be ostensibly trivial. You get behind the wheel, turn on the engine, put your foot on the gas, and away you go. During a driving journey, you need to avoid hitting things and you are required to generally obey all traffic laws.

That about sums things up.

The thing is, there is a tremendous amount of cognitive effort and physical coordination effort that goes into properly driving a car. Watch any newbie teenage driver and you can see how the seemingly effortless task of driving a car entails a huge amount of rapt attention. The young driver will probably grip the steering wheel as though their life depended upon it.

Well, come to think of it, indeed their life and the lives of others are in fact dependent upon a capacity to appropriately drive a car.

Cars are a life-or-death type of gambit.

Each time that you drive a car, you are making a bet. The bet is that you will not get hit by other cars and nor will you strike other cars (along with averting hitting pedestrians, lampposts, etc.). What's on the line is your life, the life of your passengers, and the lives of those other nearby drivers, their passengers, and any pedestrians in the vicinity of your car.

At some point, for most of us, the cognitive acumen needed to safely drive a car will likely wane. Likewise, the eye-to-hand coordination will potentially fade too. We all must face the potential reality that we might eventually reach a point in life that driving a car is no longer a suitable task to be performed.

Assuredly, you might be able to sit in that revered driver's seat, but when it comes to driving the vehicle and doing so with the utmost driving care, this is something that might no longer be feasible.

They refer to this as *retiring your keys*.

If you have a loved one that has reached a point that it is time to have them retire their keys, the realization of this circumstance can be a tough pill to swallow. We all grow up with the notion that driving a car is a sign of being independent, being able to choose your own destiny, altogether coming and going as you please.

Traditionally, young adults have dreamed of the day that they can finally drive a car. This is a signal of maturity and more so a chance to showcase their freedom. It is nearly unimaginable that someday you would need to hand over your keys and no longer be a car driver.

The angst that goes into discussing the topic with someone that seems to be in need of retiring their keys can be overwhelming. How will the person react? Will they take the broached subject as an insult or perhaps perceive it to be an outright attack upon their fluidity? A wide range of emotions will come to the forefront, that's for sure.

At the same time, it is somewhat like allowing a ticking time clock to be on the verge of producing a calamity. Perhaps you've witnessed the person driving and thought to yourself that at any moment, they are going to ram into someone. Think of the results that could cut off someone else's life.

And consider too the impact to the life of the person doing the driving. The driver might get killed by veering off the road or failing to notice that a truck was stopped ahead and blocking traffic. There are innumerable ways that a driver that no longer has sufficient driving capacity can get themselves and others into very dire situations.

The loss of a sense of independence is but one of the factors that come to play. Another is the seeming admission by the person that they are no longer of sufficient facility to drive. The person retiring their keys might also be concerned that they will no longer be able to travel. Without a car at the ready, they could become entirely homebound and rarely if ever get over to the grocery store or out to the mountains for enjoying local wooded hikes.

You can add into the mix that many people simply enjoy the act of driving. They don't need to be driving anywhere in particular. There is a visceral and joyful feeling that comes from steering a car and making it go from here to there. By retiring your keys, you are presumably giving up that act of enjoyment.

Retiring the keys is filled with a wide array of difficulties and rarely a straightforward event.

Sometimes, those trying to get someone to retire their keys will offer that anytime the person needs a ride, they are happy to provide a ride for them. This is certainly heartfelt and helpful. At the same time, it can be very hard to arrange logistically. Being on call at any time of the day or night, and getting over to provide a lift, well, this can strain the best of relationships.

The advent of ridesharing or more aptly called ride-hailing has provided a new avenue for dealing with the car key retirement conundrum. The person that is no longer driving can merely use an app to request a lift. The odds are reasonably high that they will get a ride, assuming that they live in an area that is relatively popular for ride-hailing services.

Someone that lives in an area absent of ride-hailing will find themselves unable to readily get a ride whenever they might wish. There is also the potential qualm about the driver of the ride-hailing service and what they might say or do regarding the passenger that is no longer able to drive themselves. As such, some ride-hailing services offer customized rides that are specifically tailored toward particular segments of riders, though this often comes at a heightened price.

Do not though give up hope on this vexing problem of retiring the keys.

In many ways, the advent of self-driving cars can help soften the blow and might aid demonstrably in shifting someone from being a strident car driver to becoming a happy passenger. Keep in mind too that there are those exasperated drivers that have come to realize that driving is no longer the most joyful of tasks for them. They continue to drive because they do not know of any viable alternative that seems sufficiently agreeable to them.

The question to consider is this: *Does the advent of AI-based true self-driving cars provide a viable alternative for those that are in need of retiring their keys?*

Time to unpack the matter and see.

**Self-Driving Cars And Retiring Your Keys**

For Level 4 and Level 5 true self-driving vehicles, there won't be a human driver involved in the driving task.

All occupants will be passengers.

The AI is doing the driving.

One aspect to immediately discuss entails the fact that the AI involved in today's AI driving systems is not sentient. In other words, the AI is altogether a collective of computer-based programming and algorithms, and most assuredly not able to reason in the same manner that humans can.

Why this added emphasis about the AI not being sentient?

Because I want to underscore that when discussing the role of the AI driving system, I am not ascribing human qualities to the AI. Please be aware that there is an ongoing and dangerous tendency these days to anthropomorphize AI. In essence, people are assigning human-like sentience to today's AI, despite the undeniable and inarguable fact that no such AI exists as yet.

With that clarification, you can envision that the AI driving system won't natively somehow "know" about the facets of driving. Driving and all that it entails will need to be programmed as part of the hardware and software of the self-driving car.

Let's dive into the myriad of aspects that come to play on this topic regarding retiring the keys of a human driver. The emphasis here will be on the potential allure of using a self-driving car in lieu of being the driver oneself per se, but I'll also tell it like it is, covering both the sunshiny facets and the more dour ones.

As a mindful word of prudence, even though there are plenty of advantages to letting the AI driving system undertake the chore of driving, there is still no debating the fact that the person riding in the vehicle is no longer actually at the wheel. As such, for some that are intricately and emotionally tied to driving, the aspect of using a self-driving car is not necessarily going to overcome the sting of not being a driver themselves.

That being said, we can dive into the self-driving car aspects and showcase why the use of a self-driving vehicle might be a reasonably attractive alternative to being a driver or in some instances might seem an outright and unabashed better choice than having to drive a car.

Okay, so a person that has retired their keys will want to have a semblance of freedom of movement akin to when they could just go out to their own car and get into the driver's seat. The notion is that you can go for a drive whenever you wish. Furthermore, you can pretty much drive wherever you want to go.

For self-driving cars, they will likely be available on a ride-hailing or ridesharing basis, similar to how human-driven cars today are listed for available use. Using an app, the person seeking a ride will indicate their originating location and their destination preference, and then a self-driving car will be dispatched to the person. Again, akin to when using human-driven ride-hailing, there might or might not be any available vehicles or they might not be nearby to the indicated origination spot. Those are all still the same considerations.

One slightly different aspect entails the boundary or scope of where the self-driving cars being used are able to go.

Level 4 self-driving cars are set up by the automaker or self-driving tech maker to work based on an Operational Design Domain (ODD). The ODD indicates the constraints or limitations associated with that particular brand or model of a self-driving car. For example, it could be that the fleet of self-driving cars being utilized are only able to drive in sunny weather and are not prepared to drive in rain or snow. This all depends upon how the maker of the self-driving car has put together the self-driving capabilities.

Another constraint encompasses the geographical region that the self-driving car is prepared to drive in. Usually, an area that is going to be utilizing Level 4 self-driving cars is pre-mapped by the automaker or self-driving tech maker. These specialized and very detailed maps are typically required for the AI driving system to properly navigate in that locale.

The bottom line is that if a person requests to be picked up and the origination location is outside the defined ODD, the request would be denied since the AI driving system is not readied to drive in that locale. Likewise, if the destination that is specified is outside the geographical scope, the request would be denied since the self-driving car won't be able to navigate to the desired endpoint.

You could argue that the same could be said about human drivers, namely that they are somewhat based on geographical boundaries. If you ask an Uber or Lyft driver to take you from say Los Angeles to San Francisco, they are likely to turn down the request. The reason for turning you down is not though because the human is unfamiliar with either location, but instead simply due to the notion of going beyond the scope of where the driver is willing to go (albeit, there are many famous stories of riders that offered such a large sum of money that the driver found the choice irresistible).

In any case, gradually the Level 4 ODDs will be established in more and more geographical areas. This would then reduce the chances of the self-driving car not being a viable option for use.

We can reasonably assume for the moment that the person that has retired their keys is merely interested in relatively routine driving trips, such as to the local grocery store or a nearby park. The odds are that a self-driving car operating in a general locale would be able to accommodate those kinds of requests. My point is that we should not necessarily get hung up on the question of where the self-driving car is readied to go. This is certainly a consideration, and yet it in many cases would be an unlikely roadblock to making use of a self-driving car by someone that has retired their keys.

Lo and behold, let's imagine that the person has requested a self-driving car and it arrives to pick them up.

The person gets into the self-driving car and settles inside as a passenger. There is no other human in the vehicle since there isn't a human driver at the wheel. This could be a nice and comforting aspect for some riders. Rather than having to carry on awkward pleasantry conversations with a driver, the passenger can just go for a ride and not need to engage in sappy dialogue.

I realize that some riders relish being able to have conversations with the driver of a ride-hailing car. This might be one of the few person-to-person chats they have during their day. With self-driving cars, there is likely to be an interactive AI system akin to an Alexa or Siri. This could provide a bit of an interactive discussion for the rider.

Another possibility is that most self-driving cars will be equipped with electronic communications and contain interior LED display screens, along with microphones and stereo speakers, thus allowing for remote communications while riding inside a self-driving car. For example, suppose that the person that has retired their keys wants to chat with a loved one and tell them that they are on their way to see them. Just as you could possibly use a smartphone to do that kind of remote dialoguing, you could use the capabilities within the self-driving car to so.

I've previously predicted that we are likely to see a new job role emerge of the self-driving car go-along that will ride in self-driving cars to assist others. This person is not doing the driving. They are more akin to say a chaperon or a momentary companion during a riding journey. This can be useful for situations whereby the rider is not quite able to get into and out of the vehicle on their own, and thus this other person rides along to assist with entry and exit from the vehicle. When requesting a self-driving car for a ride, you would presumably indicate whether you want to have a ride-along person or not. An added fee would likely apply.

There are many other instances of desiring a ride-along person.

The most notable possibly being the case of having children ride alone inside a self-driving car.

Yes, since there isn't a human driver in the vehicle, this means that self-driving cars can transport a child or children and there won't be any adult supervision inside the car. A parent might be too busy and cannot go with their offspring. Some parents are undoubtedly going to be concerned about the child riding alone. In that case, the request might be for an adult ride-along that has been properly trained and certified for providing such an accompanying role.

Pretend for the moment that the self-driving car contains just the person that has retired their keys.

One concern by loved ones is that if the rider unexpectedly has a health issue, perhaps sudden heart palpations, there is no one else in the vehicle to assist (again, there isn't a human driver). There are various proposed ways to deal with these predicaments. For example, the AI driving system might be monitoring the interior of the vehicle, using inward-facing cameras and microphones, and if the person yells out for help, the AI could immediately contact 911. The odds are too that most self-driving cars will also have an emergency button that can be pressed by a rider.

There is also the notion that the fleet operator will have remote agents that can come onto the interior screen and see or discuss with the rider the nature of the emergency. This can be helpful, though obviously, the remote agent cannot directly physically render aid.

A remote operator could potentially reroute the self-driving car to the nearest hospital. Note that I've indicated this would be a rerouting. I mention this due to the qualm that some fleets are anticipating allowing a remote operator to take over the driving, which I've emphatically said is a bad idea (see my discussion at **this link here**).

Besides rerouting to a hospital, another possibility would be to route the self-driving car to rendezvous with an ambulance or paramedics. Suppose that a hospital is a thirty-minute drive away haul, while there is an ambulance that perchance is roaming around and within a two-minute driving distance. The AI driving system could be instructed to meet up with the ambulance, thus allowing medical responders to right away proffer assistance to the rider.

### Conclusion

For some riders, it can be a relief to not have to be at the wheel. They are happy to have someone else do the driving. There is a notable caveat in that they don't necessarily want to bother other people about having to drive them around, and nor deal with the complications of arranging for a ride.

The nice thing about a self-driving car is that you no longer are bothering a human. It is just the AI doing the driving.

In addition, self-driving cars are likely to be available 24x7. There is no need for the AI driving system to take any vacation or avoid working at off-hours. You just submit a request for a ride, whenever you so desire, and a self-driving car will be soon coming to your door (well, as mentioned, it depends upon where you live and where self-driving cars are being deployed).

Some self-driving car tryouts are taking place in retirement communities. This is a handy place to use self-driving cars because the speed limits are usually lower than on regular streets and highways.

There also tends to be less ruckus in the streets and lessened traffic.

I bring this up because of another crucial and yet not realized factor about a willingness to switch away from driving and instead be a passenger inside self-driving cars. If you live in an area that has very few drivers, and everyone has accepted the use of self-driving cars, the notion of going without your driver's license is no longer much of an issue. A big difficulty arises when others around you are driving, and you are the only one that is not.

In a retirement community, the odds are likely that many would have given up their driving and be satisfied with using a self-driving car or self-driving shuttle instead. This means that it is easier for others living there to do likewise.

Jumping forward in time, imagine that after self-driving cars become ubiquitous, nearly the entire populace would be using self-driving cars and only a smattering of holdouts would still be driving. When that happens, the retiring of the keys would be a relative nonissue.

On top of that, it could be that almost no one opts to drive to begin with. This suggests that there is no longer any notion of retiring the keys, based on the straightforward rationale that since you never got car keys to start with, you'll never need to retire them and won't ergo miss having them.

That day is a long way off in the future, sorry to say. Begrudgingly, the retiring of the keys is going to continue to be a gut-wrenching matter. Stay strong. The allure of self-driving cars will eventually play out and the retiring of keys won't be so onerous.

Keep that in mind and perhaps be hopeful that the future gets here soonest possible.

# CHAPTER 29
# INDUSTRIAL REVOLUTION AND SELF-DRIVING CARS

Just about everyone has heard of the Industrial Revolution and how it changed everything.

Fewer know that we have presumably been through several iterations or progressive versions of the Industrial Revolution. Depending upon which research you wish to accept, there have been three *industrial revolution instances* and we are either in, on the cusp of, or heading fervently toward the fourth one.

The purported latest iteration is officially referred to as the Fourth Industrial Revolution, or some prefer to note it cannily as simply Industry 4.0. Since Industry 4.0 isn't potentially cool enough per se, there is also the further shortened notation of stating that it is I4.0.

And you can go even shorter and use just I4.

If you want to impress your friends and strangers too, you can try mentioning I4 and see what they say. The odds are that unless they perchance realize you are contextually discussing the iterations of the Industrial Revolution, they will probably think you are mentioning a model of an automaker's particular car or perhaps referring to an interstate highway. Probably easiest to stick with Industry 4.0 and only switch to saying I4.0 or I4 when amongst fellow colleagues and debating the ins and outs of this presumed latest iteration of the Industrial Revolution.

The crux of Industry 4.0 is that it contains a grab bag of leading-edge high-tech, including Artificial Intelligence (AI) based systems, robotics, Internet of Things (IoT), smart sensors, Augmented Reality

(AR), quantum computing, and the like. This is a veritable smorgasbord of any kind of digital technology and might encompass the proverbial kitchen sink, as it were, in terms of the profusion of advanced machinery to be included.

Another crucial element of Industry 4.0 is that the value chain is intended to be made faster and better through the use of digitalization. Within companies, Industry 4.0 means that internal processes are connected and integrated, doing so via computer-based digitalization. Likewise, the same connectivity and integration go with the suppliers, customers, and other partnering elements in the value chain. This is generally known as vertically and horizontally integrating the value chain.

To what end is the Fourth Industrial Revolution trying to take us?

In theory, this Industry 4.0 is supposed to provide a slew of benefits when it comes to making and distributing products and goods. That would be good all around.

The cost to produce items is said to be reduced, leading commensurately to lowered prices for consumers or at least heightened profits for makers. The goods being produced will be tailored to consumers and not quite so mass-produced and no longer excessively vanilla flavored, allowing for those individualistic one-off customizations at an affordable price. Low-volume production will also become more feasible. You won't have to have gobs of orders for a product to warrant getting the items produced. Etc.

For those that are insiders about the Fourth Industrial Revolution, they typically would mention the emergence of Massively Distributed Manufacturing (MDM) as an integral part of the I4.0 equation or evolution.

What does Massively Distributed Manufacturing portend?

You likely are already familiar with the notion of *centralized* manufacturing, which ostensibly consists of making a product in essentially one place or locale. Something is produced in a large-scale facility and then shipped out to those desirous of the item produced. This is sometimes tongue-in-cheek considered the *castle* mentality or mindset of how to make a product (all must come to the mighty castle or palace).

It is as though a fortress is in one spot and that all have to come and eventually arrive there to be involved in the manufacturing process for the particular product at hand. Suppliers need to send all of the needed inputs to that manufacturing site (i.e., the castle). When finished goods are ready to go, they have pushed out the backdoor and sent along on their way.

In contrast, we might set up a *distributed* approach to manufacturing.

Rather than centralizing the whole shebang, we could have part of the manufacturing done in location A, and something else done in location B, and so on. This distributed manufacturing means that there isn't just the one castle involved. The work and processing are distributed amongst various locales.

You cannot immediately proclaim that centralized is necessarily better or worse than decentralized, and nor that decentralized is necessarily better or worse than centralized. Tradeoffs make the choice a significant one and are worthwhile to figure out. You might be wisest to choose centralized manufacturing in some cases. You might be most astute to go with distributed manufacturing in some cases. Neither one wins in a hands-down always-right runoff (though, just to mention, an argument is made by some that the distributed approach can be construed as a form of democratization of manufacturing and ought to be heralded accordingly, as will be further mentioned momentarily).

The idea of distributed manufacturing via an Industry 4.0 perspective is that you can distribute or set up manufacturing in many geographically dispersed places. These can be small-scale in size. By a proper and digitized means of connecting and integrating the multiple and distributed manufacturing sites, you can achieve the same kind of heightened volume that a single large-scale manufacturing site might attain.

We'll add the word "massively" to the notion of this distributed manufacturing and do so to emphasize that this doesn't just have to be a few handfuls of dispersed locales. If this is done well, you could have dozens, hundreds, maybe thousands of distributed manufacturing sites and they all will ultimately be doing things that are coordinated and ostensibly seamless. For sites that are considered small-scale, they are typically referred to as micromanufacturing sites.

If you are especially curious how the democratization topic gets intertwined, consider that people heretofore had to perchance live near the centralized manufacturing facility to actively participate in the production process. In this MDM approach, people living in scattered locations throughout a country or region of the world would be able to participate. Jobs for those that live just about anywhere might be made feasible.

The MDM aspect has a somewhat hidden factor that many do not give much attention to, namely the shipment of goods.

A product that you might purchase from a centralized manufacturing facility on the East Coast would need to be transported all the way across the country to the West Coast if that is where you lived. Imagine instead that the product was manufactured in your local state or county. The distance traveled to get the item would be relatively short in comparison. You could get the product sooner, assuming all else being equal. The cost associated with the product could be lessened if it had normally included the shipping cost.

These factors are widely touted therefore as an overall advantage of trying to produce goods as closest possible to where they will be utilized or nearest to their points of use. Ergo, the excitement for and push toward Massively Distributed Manufacturing.

Now that we've brought up the subtle but essential subtopic about shipping or transportation-related to manufacturing, this opens the door to talking about my favorite topic which is Autonomous Vehicles (AVs).

Moving items from place to place is usually done by a human-driven vehicle of one kind or another.

This of course is not necessarily always the case, since you might have within a manufacturing facility an assembly line robotic-like conveyance system that moves in-process items around and there is no human hand involved. You might also have specialized AVs that are purpose-built for shunting around items within a highly controlled environment. Painted lines for example might clearly be marked on the floors and there are oftentimes guardrails or coned-off areas that the simplistic AVs are programmed to go.

Let's focus on getting stuff from one manufacturing facility to another.

We are herein interested in inter-transit more so than the intra-transit without a specific facility. How are we going to get items from manufacturing locale A to say our manufacturing locale B? Assume that those locations are miles upon miles away from each other. Furthermore, assume that the use of public roadways will be required, and we don't luckily have exclusively private pathways to traverse on.

One aspect of transit entails going from a manufacturing site to another one. We can also consider the transit required of a supplier sending raw materials or partially finished goods or other items to a manufacturing site. There are plenty of transit needs that will arise. Another would be the transit of getting the completed product to the intended points of use.

Autonomous vehicles could be a boon for undertaking that massive amount of transit needs for massively distributed manufacturing (that sounds catchy).

We could use self-driving cars, self-driving trucks, self-driving drones, self-driving planes, self-driving ships, self-driving submersibles, and all manner of self-driving variations of vehicular systems. They are considered autonomous, or some say fully autonomous if they do not need a human driver or human pilot at the wheel.

A scenario involving the use of AI-based true self-driving cars will serve handily here as a convenient means to explain how this might work.

Before we get into the scenario, it might be helpful to clarify what is meant by AI-based true self-driving cars.

**Self-Driving Cars And Massively Distributed Manufacturing**

For Level 4 and Level 5 true self-driving vehicles, there won't be a human driver involved in the driving task.

All occupants will be passengers.

The AI is doing the driving.

One aspect to immediately discuss entails the fact that the AI involved in today's AI driving systems is not sentient. In other words, the AI is altogether a collective of computer-based programming and algorithms, and most assuredly not able to reason in the same manner that humans can.

Why this added emphasis about the AI not being sentient?

Because I want to underscore that when discussing the role of the AI driving system, I am not ascribing human qualities to the AI. Please be aware that there is an ongoing and dangerous tendency these days to anthropomorphize AI. In essence, people are assigning human-like sentience to today's AI, despite the undeniable and inarguable fact that no such AI exists as yet.

With that clarification, you can envision that the AI driving system won't natively somehow "know" about the facets of driving. Driving and all that it entails will need to be programmed as part of the hardware and software of the self-driving car.

Let's dive into the myriad of aspects that come to play on this topic.

Suppose there is a micromanufacturing site nearby your hometown.

They make widgets. And about twenty miles from that site there is an associated manufacturing site that also makes widgets. Turns out they make a ton of widgets. Furthermore, they are part of a larger collective that could be considered a massively distributed manufacturer and are spread throughout the country.

We'll refer to the micromanufacturing site that is closest to your hometown as Widget Site 1. The other site that is approximately twenty miles away will be labeled as Widget Site 2.

One day, a manager at Widget Site 1 realizes that they are running low on essential supplies that go into making their widgets. Fortunately, Widget Site 2 has an oversupply and willingly will provide the components to Widget Site 1. This is an ongoing reciprocal arrangement, akin to a classic of scratch my back and I'll scratch yours.

The normal approach would be to have someone working at Widget Site 1 get into a car and drive over to Widget Site 2. Upon getting the needed components loaded into the vehicle, the employee would then drive the materials back over to Widget Site 1. The drive time for this journey is about an hour, plus another half hour to load and unload the vehicle.

The Widget Site 1 manager has to use the precious and limited labor at the manufacturing facility to do this chore. It takes a person that could be working actively in the manufacturing process and instead turns them into a delivery driver. In addition, there are of course the usual risks that are entailed in making such a drive, wherein the person could get regrettably entangled in a car crash or other calamity during the driving chore.

This is where self-driving cars step into the picture.

The manager at Widget Site 1 dispatches one of the self-driving cars that the manufacturing firm owns. Without any need for a human driver, the autonomous vehicle drives over to Widget Site 2. At Widget Site 2, someone loads the components into the vehicle and then signals that it can proceed back to Widget Site 1. If anything goes awry during the driving journey, the AI driving system will automatically alert the manager at Widget Site 1.

Notice that this allows Widget Site 1 to continue working without any disruption by having had to send an employee on this necessary errand. This also avoids any potential issues of the person getting mired in a car accident or similar concern. The AI driving system will do as instructed and drive as expeditiously as feasible to get the materials and return them. No lunch breaks are needed.

A human driver might be tired and not fully attentive to the driving task. A human driver could get waylaid during this chore, perhaps opting to make some side stops to get coffee or do some other non-related errand. And so on.

Now that we've covered that singular example, let's up the ante, as it were.

Imagine that daily trips are being made back and forth between Widget Site 1 and Widget Site 2. There could be lots of good reasons for a frequent series of trips. Multiply all those trips times the amount of labor that would have been required, along with the risks of injury or calamity while on the road, and the resultant total becomes notable.

Thus, on a once-in-a-blue-moon trip basis it might not seem especially significant, but if you multiply things out and are doing this daily, perhaps amounting to thousands of trips per year, it all adds up. The firm reduces the excess cost of labor used for the delivery chore. The firm uses the labor toward the act of manufacturing and doesn't need to deplete the labor pool by these side trips. Plus, there is lowered risk for the humans that would have been doing the driving.

You can zoom further out and take a sizable macroscopic view.

Pretend that there are dozens of these widget-making manufacturing sites, scattered throughout the US. They are all willing to share with each other as needed. Getting items from one location to another could be quite onerous and costly.

Via the use of autonomous vehicles such as self-driving cars, self-driving trucks, and the like, they can be sending items to each other without the labor required to do so. Another factor is that those lengthier trips would normally necessitate the drivers taking breaks, sleeping overnight and not driving 24x7, etc.

With self-driving vehicles, the AI driving system can operate all of the time. There is no need for breaks or sleep. Of course, refueling of the vehicle would likely be required. Currently, the refueling does tend to involve a human at the pump that connects the fuel to the vehicle, though the latest capabilities are doing away with this aspect and the pump will automatically extend and connect to the AV.

**Conclusion**

In a sense, a silent and unnoticed army of self-driving vehicles are bound to become an integral part of Industry 4.0, including as a means of physically interconnecting those MDM sites. The belief is that AVs will run at a lower cost per mile than would the comparable human-driven vehicle. Ergo, there is a multitude of cost savings that will arise.

Some envision an eerie sight of all these self-driving cars and self-driving trucks driving around without any human driver inside. There is no doubt that it will take some getting used to seeing, and at first, the whole shebang will be quite a spectacle. After a while, the odds are that we will all take the matter in stride and the use of AVs for tasks like this will become the new normal.

Do not mistakenly think this will be some Utopian-like future.

You can assume that there will be issues, such as:

- How will humans that once relied upon driving as their money-making role be able to make a living?
- Will self-driving vehicles be subject to difficulties that would not normally confront a human-driven vehicle?
- Might hackers be able to take over self-driving vehicles and

wreak havoc accordingly?
- What happens if a human-driven vehicle crashes with a self-driving vehicle?
- On and on.

You can add those considerations to a long list of the issues that are not yet fully known about the emergence of the Fourth Industrial Revolution.

Presumably, once we figure out those answers, we'll be ready to proceed to Industry 5.0, the next iteration after the vaunted Industry 4.0, and enter into the Fifth Industrial Revolution (seems like we can keep on counting up as we go).

Well, to be cool, let's just say I5.

# CHAPTER 30
# BEHAVING BADLY AND SELF-DRIVING CARS

Humans can be troubling.

How so?

Consider your daily commute.

The odds of coming across a driver that is doing something untoward is seemingly quite high. You might be minding your own business, calmly driving along, and out of the blue, another driver does something quite wacky.

On a daily basis, most of us will observe a car that swerves across all lanes of traffic to make a panicky turn that they had failed to prepare for. We will likely see drivers that cut off other cars and force those poor souls into having to hit their brakes or make a sudden maneuver to avoid rear-ending the imposing vehicle. There is a solid chance that you'll come across a driver that crazily rolls through a stop sign and confounds both pedestrians and nearby cars that are underway.

The variety and volume of wayward drivers are astronomical.

Yet we typically take most of the foul driving in stride and just assume that it is the way of the world.

You would love to report the driver to someone and make sure the vile driver gets sternly rebuked, possibly even have their driver's license revoked. Get those miscreants off the road, your mind screams. But the reality is that the fleeting act of those careless drivers is not readily converted into them getting nailed for their unruly driving.

Unless a police car happens to come along and witness the outlandish and likely illegal driving, the whole shebang boils down to your word against theirs (and they would seem unlikely to freely admit to their driving transgression).

When a car gets into a crash or collision, this can be an occasion whereby a driver that is doing rotten driving can potentially get noticed. Of course, the odds are they will defend to the teeth that it was either purely an accident as though nothing could have been done to prevent the pileup, or they are bound to claim they weren't at fault and somebody else was. This all translates into the odds being unfortunately low that even after getting into a car wreck that they will get summarily dinged for being a lousy driver.

There is a bit of difference between someone that on a one-time basis makes a bad driving choice versus someone that drivers terribly all of the time. The thing is, you might not have any means of knowing which is which. A driver that cuts you off might be the type of person that does this to everyone and always, or it could be a driver that made an honest mistake and regrets profusely the intrusion.

In California and similar to many other states, their respective Department of Motor Vehicles (DMVs) have various complex rules about designating a driver as negligent with regard to the driving task or potentially incompetent at driving. A lot of hoops have to be jumped through to get somebody onto that list. If you perchance come across a driver that you believe is negligent or incompetent, you pretty much have an extremely slim chance of adding their name to that bad driver's compilation (it will take a massively persistent effort with tons of unshakable evidence).

Besides the everyday response of having to grit your teeth and put up with a badly behaving driver, you could consider taking more overt action. For example, you could potentially call 911 to report the driver. This would seem prudent if you genuinely believe the driver is a roadway hazard and a ticking time clock that might soon crash into other innocent drivers and pedestrians.

Making the decision to contact 911 is not an easy one.

You don't want to waste the time of the police. You don't want to be that type of person that makes superfluous calls to 911. You don't want to send the police on a potential wild goose chase. There are a ton of bona fide reasons to not call 911. Presumably, you would only use the 911 option as a last resort in the sense that you fully believe there is an imminent and possibly deadly situation brewing.

It is tough to be a Good Samaritan.

Another possibility involves trying to warn other traffic about the disruptive driver.

You might honk your horn or flash your headlights, doing so to alert drivers nearby. This can backfire on you, simply due to the somewhat obvious aspect that you are drawing attention to you, rather than to the car that you believe is being improperly driven. Other drivers will think you have a screw loose. This might cause them to overlook the dangerous driver. You have somewhat shot your own foot, leading to the bad driver continuing along, and meanwhile, there are a bunch of wary drivers probably eyeing you like a hawk.

You could try to do something about the troublesome driver.

Perhaps position your vehicle in front of the miscreant to get them to slow down or stop. I can emphatically say this, decidedly do ***not*** take those kinds of actions. Your desire to rectify the situation could readily worsen things considerably. The other driver might react in a fit of road rage. Drivers coming upon the two of you won't know what led to the altercation. And some of those other cars are likely going to end up in a conflagration with the two of you during the potentially deadly tangling.

Most authorities including the police would sternly say that you should not try to engage in a dogfight between cars. You would be better off staying back from the bad driver and report the situation to the police. Again, as mentioned earlier, you don't do this at the drop of hat, and reserve such direct reporting only when things are relatively dire.

One aspect that probably goes through your head is the wonderment of what is going through the noggin of the other driver. Why did that person make that nutty driving move? Are they completely witless? Was there some reason to drive so badly?

We all make use of something referred to as the "theory of mind" when we mull over what another driver is doing. The notion is that you try to imagine what is in that person's mind. It could be that the person has a perfectly rational basis for making a bad move. On the other hand, perhaps the person is intoxicated. Maybe they are angry because of something that happened at work that day. We try to put ourselves into the shoes of the other driver and figure out what is going on in their mind.

Suppose you are behind a driver that surprisingly hits their brakes and yet you don't see any discernable reason for doing so. A few moments later, you see a dog that was hidden from view and had been in the middle of the street, for which the driver opted to go to a screeching halt to avoid. You are likely to feel somewhat sheepish that your first thought was that the person was a lunatic. That being said, there is some concern that they could have caused a car crash and perhaps might have handled the predicament with more aplomb.

Anyway, this takes us back to the earlier point that you might not know from a single instance whether the driver is altogether bad or whether it was an ad hoc one-off situation. Sometimes you need to observe the other car over a sizable distance and detect numerous clues that accumulate into a more strident case that the driver is a maniac at the wheel.

Shifting gears, consider that the future of cars consists of self-driving cars. These AI-based true self-driving cars are driven by an AI driving system. No human is at the wheel.

There are a lot of myths and misconceptions about self-driving cars.

Some pundits seem to declare that the beauty of self-driving cars is that they will never ever do anything wrong while on the roadway. They will be perfect drivers. In addition to strictly driving in a legal fashion, you will apparently never need to worry about a self-driving car that perhaps cuts you off, or stops in the middle of the road, or does anything else that a wayward human driver might do.

Those that spew out such nonsense are living in a dream world. The kind of perfect driving that they envision is either akin to a Utopian society that I assure you won't become reality, or they are perhaps conflating those putt-putt cars at the theme parks with driving in the real world.

My point is that self-driving cars will indeed drive badly, from time to time, and though it hopefully will be a rarity, it is certainly not going to be a big fat zero. Anyone that throws around the word "never" is taking an outsized risk of being readily proven wrong by even the occurrence of one such instance. In that way, they are absolutely out to lunch since there will be at least one (and a lot more).

This is especially the circumstance right now as the use of self-driving cars is being tried out on our public roadways whilst in the midst of still being devised and readied for open-ended use. You might have heard or read the brouhaha the other day about a self-driving car that got immersed in a construction zone and took driving actions that could be described as undesirable.

No one was hurt, and you should be mindful that this was a case assuredly not worthy of outstretched headlines and hand wringing. Save that for the problems associated with cars that aren't at all self-driving and yet being portrayed outrageously as though they are.

I'd like to forgo discussing the false self-driving cars or ones that are clearly not self-driving and focus herein solely on the AI-based true self-driving cars.

The intriguing question is this: *Will the advent of AI-based true self-driving cars entail having the AI driving system at times drive badly, and if so, what should you do about it as a nearby driver in a human-driven vehicle?*

Before jumping into the details, I'd like to clarify what is meant when referring to true self-driving cars.

**Self-Driving Cars And Behaving Badly**

For Level 4 and Level 5 true self-driving vehicles, there won't be a human driver involved in the driving task.

All occupants will be passengers.

The AI is doing the driving.

One aspect to immediately discuss entails the fact that the AI involved in today's AI driving systems is not sentient. In other words, the AI is altogether a collective of computer-based programming and algorithms, and most assuredly not able to reason in the same manner that humans can.

Why this added emphasis about the AI not being sentient?

Because I want to underscore that when discussing the role of the AI driving system, I am not ascribing human qualities to the AI. Please be aware that there is an ongoing and dangerous tendency these days to anthropomorphize AI. In essence, people are assigning human-like sentience to today's AI, despite the undeniable and inarguable fact that no such AI exists as yet.

With that clarification, you can envision that the AI driving system won't natively somehow "know" about the facets of driving. Driving and all that it entails will need to be programmed as part of the hardware and software of the self-driving car.

Let's dive into the myriad of aspects that come to play on this topic.

Imagine that you are driving along and perchance a self-driving car is ahead of you. The autonomous vehicle seems to be abiding by the lawful rules of driving. There is nothing out of the ordinary taking place, other than this is a self-driving vehicle and there is no human driver at the wheel.

As an aside, I realize it might seem unusual to be near a self-driving car while on the public roadways, but this is relatively common in select locales. On a daily effort of driving around in the Silicon Valley and San Francisco area, you would perhaps be surprised to know that you are bound to regularly encounter a self-driving car in traffic. For some human drivers in that region, the appearance of a self-driving car has become an altogether ho-hum matter and accepted as the norm. You can expect that this will inevitably be the case throughout the country.

Back to our saga.

The self-driving car ahead of you is coming up to a part of town that has some quite wicked streets that are replete with potholes, wide cracks, faded street markings, etc. Turns out that as you get closer to those bad spots, you notice a road crew is doing some roadway repair work. Thank goodness, finally, the city is fixing this mess.

There is an electronic display board flashing a warning that you are soon entering into a construction zone. Red cones have been placed to guide traffic around the workers. The proper path through this zone is somewhat confusing, but human drivers are determined to proceed and are maneuvering and jockeying for position to navigate the morass.

The self-driving car seemed to at first figure out where to go. It moved over into the narrowed open lane. Unfortunately, the cones have been shoved around by other passing vehicles, and the AI driving system appears to now be confused. It starts to shift out of the open lane, then stops, then shifts back into the lane, then pops out of it. Finally, the self-driving car comes to a standstill.

The self-driving car has become a blockage and is straddling the only open lane. Human-driven cars are sitting behind self-driving cars and waiting for the AI driving system to figure out what to do. Patience is thin, anger and angst are brewing. Some of the waiting drivers lean on their horns. Other cars begin to veer directly into the construction area to try and make their way around the halted self-driving car.

You are also pinned behind the self-driving car. There is no ready means to proceed forward. You would need to either go head-to-head into oncoming traffic or try to sneak into the construction area and endanger the road crew.

Is this an instance of a self-driving car behaving badly?

You could certainly say so.

The AI driving system has abruptly stopped the vehicle, doing so in a precarious spot that entails an active roadway with numerous cars and lots of ongoing traffic. In theory, self-driving cars are not supposed to do this. The overall general requirement or preference is that if a self-driving car is going to halt, it does so in a manner that offers a so-called Minimal Risk Condition (MRC).

Some might try to argue that the self-driving car is not threatening anyone per se. It did not try to run anyone down. It did not nearly sideswipe another car or rear-end another vehicle. As such, the case could be made that though the act of coming to a dead stop in an active lane is undesirable, it does not rise to a level of notable concern.

A retort would be that the self-driving car has landed into an illegal driving action. This breaks the touted myth that self-driving cars will never drive illegally. Furthermore, by blocking traffic, the self-driving car is clearly in the wrong and impeding the flow of traffic. Worse still, human drivers are now going out of their way to circumvent the stopped self-driving car, and are likely to get into dangerous postures as they do so (well, one realizes that this could be construed as the fault of those human drivers, though there is fault to be laid at the feet of the self-driving car too).

What should you do, if anything, about the self-driving car that has unexpectedly and wrongly halted like this?

Suppose a human driver had done the same thing.

If so, you would probably be yelling at the driver to get the heck out of the way. Unfortunately, for most of today's self-driving cars, there is no means to proffer external instructions or advice to the AI driving system (see my column for how this might take place with more advanced AI driving systems).

You would also likely be thinking about what the driver is thinking about. This goes back to my mentioning a "theory of mind" whereby you try to guess what other drivers are doing via what is going on in their noggin. For self-driving cars, you are unlikely to have any means of reasonably guessing at what the AI driving system is undertaking. Your best guess is that perhaps like any computer that sometimes gets overloaded and freezes up, maybe that's what has happened with the self-driving car (a plethora of possibilities exist).

Another aspect would be to consider contacting the company that makes or operates the self-driving car. Perhaps the fleet operator doesn't realize the predicament of the self-driving car. In theory, they should, and the AI driving system should have sent out an alert to the fleet operator, though this might or might not have been included in the system capabilities, plus there is a chance that the vehicle is in a place that has little or no viable electronic communications to be broadcast out.

Even if the self-driving car did send out an alert, you would have no means of knowing that it had done so. In other words, perhaps a team has been dispatched to come and aid the self-driving car toward getting back underway. That team might be many minutes away and therefore you would be stuck there and not aware that help is coming. All that you would see is that the self-driving car is unmoving and blocking traffic, dangerously so.

One would hope that at least the self-driving car would invoke its emergency flashers as a signal to others that it is halted. This might happen, or it might not happen. There is a chance that the AI driving system hasn't derived that the situation is deserving of using the emergency flashers. Another possibility is that the emergency flashers can only be activated by a remote agent of the fleet. And so on.

On a related note, the odds of your being able to contact someone about the self-driving car is also confounded because few of the self-driving cars are outwardly well-marked with appropriate contact info. I've repeatedly emphasized that self-driving cars should have those bumper stickers or similar markings that state how to call, text, or make contact with a fleet operator or whoever can cope with that self-driving car when it has gone afoul.

Meanwhile, for those crazy daredevils that often try to take matters into their own hands, someone may try to come up to the rear bumper and push the self-driving car out of the way. Bad idea! As earlier stated about messing around with human-driven cars, you should not be messing around with self-driving cars either.

Okay, after considering all those options, you could potentially call 911. Per the prior discussion, the calling of 911 is supposed to occur only in the direst of traffic settings.

Does this constitute such an instance?

Given the potential for either the nearby roadway crew getting hit or for human-driven cars to ram into each other, a solid case could be made that this warrants a 911 call.

The rough thing is that the self-driving car might suddenly start moving again before any 911 emergency services arrive. It could be that a remote agent has communicated with the AI driving system and indicated where the AI should drive the car too. By the time the emergency services get there, the self-driving car could be long gone.

**Conclusion**

The focus in this brief exploration was a self-driving car that got itself stuck into a dour position, doing so of its own volition.

This reflects that the AI driving system is inadequate and has not been sufficiently programmed to handle some rather common situations that are nonetheless framed as edge or corner cases by some AI developers (there is a great deal of debate about what constitutes a rare or oddball driving scene versus what should be construed as every day expected).

The key here is that you cannot try to blame the AI as though it is the AI per se, i.e., the AI being sentient. It is not sentient. You have to look at the automaker or self-driving tech firm that has devised the AI driving system and hold them responsible for what their technology and vehicle are doing. Do not shrug your shoulders and wave your hands that this is somehow just the vagaries of AI.

Keep in mind too that a slew of other situations can readily reveal the foibles or weaknesses of the AI driving system (at least with respect to that particular version, for that specific make and model, and should not be generalized to all self-driving cars). The saga provided is a somewhat tame or tepid instance.

Worse cases will undoubtedly arise.

You also need to take into account that there will be malfunctions of an automotive nature, beyond the AI driving system itself. A tire can suffer a blowout on a self-driving car. The under-the-hood mechanical elements of a self-driving car can bust or break.

Some seem to think that a self-driving car will not ever be subject to the same physical and mechanical breakdowns of human-driven cars, but this a ridiculous and foolish assumption.

Right now, the few self-driving cars on the roadways are being nightly pampered with tiptop maintenance service and ergo unlikely to have any mechanical issues while underway. This might not be the case once there are thousands upon thousands of self-driving cars on our roadways.

That about wraps things up.

As a recap, human drivers are known to behave badly. We don't yet seem to widely realize that self-driving cars can behave badly too, which we need to realize can and will happen, and therefore be prepared to respond appropriately.

Always be prepared is a handy motto.

# APPENDIX

# APPENDIX A
# TEACHING WITH THIS MATERIAL

The material in this book can be readily used either as a supplemental to other content for a class, or it can also be used as a core set of textbook material for a specialized class. Classes where this material is most likely used include any classes at the college or university level that want to augment the class by offering thought provoking and educational essays about AI and self-driving cars.

In particular, here are some aspects for class use:

- Computer Science. Studying AI, autonomous vehicles, etc.
- Business. Exploring technology and it adoption for business.
- Sociology. Sociological views on the adoption and advancement of technology.

Specialized classes at the undergraduate and graduate level can also make use of this material.

For each chapter, consider whether you think the chapter provides material relevant to your course topic. There is plenty of opportunity to get the students thinking about the topic and force them to decide whether they agree or disagree with the points offered and positions taken. I would also encourage you to have the students do additional research beyond the chapter material presented (I provide next some suggested assignments they can do).

# RESEARCH ASSIGNMENTS ON THESE TOPICS

Your students can find background material on these topics, doing so in various business and technical publications. I list below the top ranked AI related journals. For business publications, I would suggest the usual culprits such as the Harvard Business Review, Forbes, Fortune, WSJ, and the like.

Here are some suggestions of homework or projects that you could assign to students:

a) Assignment for foundational AI research topic: Research and prepare a paper and a presentation on a specific aspect of Deep AI, Machine Learning, ANN, etc. The paper should cite at least 3 reputable sources. Compare and contrast to what has been stated in this book.

b) Assignment for the Self-Driving Car topic: Research and prepare a paper and Self-Driving Cars. Cite at least 3 reputable sources and analyze the characterizations. Compare and contrast to what has been stated in this book.

c) Assignment for a Business topic: Research and prepare a paper and a presentation on businesses and advanced technology. What is hot, and what is not? Cite at least 3 reputable sources. Compare and contrast to the depictions in this book.

d) Assignment to do a Startup: Have the students prepare a paper about how they might startup a business in this realm. They must submit a sound Business Plan for the startup. They could also be asked to present their Business Plan and so should also have a presentation deck to coincide with it.

You can certainly adjust the aforementioned assignments to fit to your particular needs and the class structure. You'll notice that I ask for 3 reputable cited sources for the paper writing based assignments. I usually steer students toward "reputable" publications, since otherwise they will cite some oddball source that has no credentials other than that they happened to write something and post it onto the Internet. You can define "reputable" in whatever way you prefer, for example some faculty think Wikipedia is not reputable while others believe it is reputable and allow students to cite it.

The reason that I usually ask for at least 3 citations is that if the student only does one or two citations they usually settle on whatever they happened to find the fastest. By requiring three citations, it usually seems to force them to look around, explore, and end-up probably finding five or more, and then whittling it down to 3 that they will actually use.

I have not specified the length of their papers, and leave that to you to tell the students what you prefer. For each of those assignments, you could end-up with a short one to two pager, or you could do a dissertation length paper. Base the length on whatever best fits for your class, and the credit amount of the assignment within the context of the other grading metrics you'll be using for the class.

I mention in the assignments that they are to do a paper and prepare a presentation. I usually try to get students to present their work. This is a good practice for what they will do in the business world. Most of the time, they will be required to prepare an analysis and present it. If you don't have the class time or inclination to have the students present, then you can of course cut out the aspect of them putting together a presentation.

If you want to point students toward highly ranked journals in AI, here's a list of the top journals as reported by *various citation counts sources* (this list changes year to year):

- Communications of the ACM
- Artificial Intelligence
- Cognitive Science
- IEEE Transactions on Pattern Analysis and Machine Intelligence
- Foundations and Trends in Machine Learning
- Journal of Memory and Language
- Cognitive Psychology
- Neural Networks
- IEEE Transactions on Neural Networks and Learning Systems
- IEEE Intelligent Systems
- Knowledge-based Systems

# GUIDE TO USING THE CHAPTERS

For each of the chapters, I provide next some various ways to use the chapter material. You can assign the tasks as individual homework assignments, or the tasks can be used with team projects for the class. You can easily layout a series of assignments, such as indicating that the students are to do item "a" below for say Chapter 1, then "b" for the next chapter of the book, and so on.

a) What is the main point of the chapter and describe in your own words the significance of the topic,

b) Identify at least two aspects in the chapter that you agree with, and support your concurrence by providing at least one other outside researched item as support; make sure to explain your basis for disagreeing with the aspects,

c) Identify at least two aspects in the chapter that you disagree with, and support your disagreement by providing at least one other outside researched item as support; make sure to explain your basis for disagreeing with the aspects,

d) Find an aspect that was not covered in the chapter, doing so by conducting outside research, and then explain how that aspect ties into the chapter and what significance it brings to the topic,

e) Interview a specialist in industry about the topic of the chapter, collect from them their thoughts and opinions, and readdress the chapter by citing your source and how they compared and contrasted to the material,

f) Interview a relevant academic professor or researcher in a college or university about the topic of the chapter, collect from them their thoughts and opinions, and readdress the chapter by citing your source and how they compared and contrasted to the material,

g) Try to update a chapter by finding out the latest on the topic, and ascertain whether the issue or topic has now been solved or whether it is still being addressed, explain what you come up with.

The above are all ways in which you can get the students of your class involved in considering the material of a given chapter. You could mix things up by having one of those above assignments per each week, covering the chapters over the course of the semester or quarter.

As a reminder, here are the chapters of the book and you can select whichever chapters you find most valued for your particular class:

Companion Book By This Author

***Advances in AI and Autonomous Vehicles: Cybernetic Self-Driving Cars***

*Practical Advances in Artificial Intelligence (AI) and Machine Learning*

by

Dr. Lance B. Eliot, MBA, PhD

Chapter Title

1 Genetic Algorithms for Self-Driving Cars
2 Blockchain for Self-Driving Cars
3 Machine Learning and Data for Self-Driving Cars
4 Edge Problems at Core of True Self-Driving Cars
5 Solving the Roundabout Traversal Problem for SD Cars
6 Parallel Parking Mindless Task for SD Cars: Step It Up
7 Caveats of Open Source for Self-Driving Cars
8 Catastrophic Cyber Hacking of Self-Driving Cars
9 Conspicuity for Self-Driving Cars
10 Accident Scene Traversal for Self-Driving Cars
11 Emergency Vehicle Awareness for Self-Driving Cars
12 Are Left Turns Right for Self-Driving Cars
13 Going Blind: When Sensors Fail on Self-Driving Cars
14 Roadway Debris Cognition for Self-Driving Cars
15 Avoiding Pedestrian Roadkill by Self-Driving Cars
16 When Accidents Happen to Self-Driving Cars
17 Illegal Driving for Self-Driving Cars
18 Making AI Sense of Road Signs
19 Parking Your Car the AI Way
20 Not Fast Enough: Human Factors in Self-Driving Cars
21 State of Government Reporting on Self-Driving Cars
22 The Head Nod Problem for Self-Driving Cars
23 CES Reveals Self-Driving Car Differences

***This title is available via Amazon and other book sellers***

Companion Book By This Author

***Self-Driving Cars:***
***"The Mother of All AI Projects"***

by Dr. Lance B. Eliot, MBA, PhD

Chapter Title



***This title is available via Amazon and other book seller***

Companion Book By This Author

***Innovation and Thought Leadership on Self-Driving Driverless Cars***

by Dr. Lance B. Eliot, MBA, PhD

Chapter Title



***This title is available via Amazon and other book sellers***

Companion Book By This Author

***New Advances in AI Autonomous Driverless Cars Self-Driving Cars***

by Dr. Lance B. Eliot, MBA, PhD

Chapter Title



***This title is available via Amazon and other book sellers***

Companion Book By This Author

***Introduction to Driverless Self-Driving Cars***

by Dr. Lance B. Eliot, MBA, PhD

Chapter Title



***This title is available via Amazon and other book sellers***

Companion Book By This Author

***Autonomous Vehicle Driverless Self-Driving Cars and Artificial Intelligence***

by Dr. Lance B. Eliot, MBA, PhD

Chapter Title



***This title is available via Amazon and other book sellers***

Companion Book By This Author

***Transformative Artificial Intelligence Driverless Self-Driving Cars***

by Dr. Lance B. Eliot, MBA, PhD

Chapter Title



***This title is available via Amazon and other book sellers***

Companion Book By This Author

***Disruptive Artificial Intelligence and Driverless Self-Driving Cars***

by Dr. Lance B. Eliot, MBA, PhD

Chapter Title



***This title is available via Amazon and other book sellers***

Companion Book By This Author

***State-of-the-Art***
***AI Driverless Self-Driving Cars***

by Dr. Lance B. Eliot, MBA, PhD

Chapter Title



***This title is available via Amazon and other book sellers***

Companion Book By This Author

***Top Trends in***
***AI Self-Driving Cars***

by Dr. Lance B. Eliot, MBA, PhD

Chapter Title



***This title is available via Amazon and other book sellers***

Companion Book By This Author

## *AI Innovations and Self-Driving Cars*

by Dr. Lance B. Eliot, MBA, PhD

Chapter Title



***This title is available via Amazon and other book sellers***

Companion Book By This Author

***Crucial Advances for***
***AI Self-Driving Cars***

by Dr. Lance B. Eliot, MBA, PhD



***This title is available via Amazon and other book sellers***

Companion Book By This Author

***Sociotechnical Insights and AI Driverless Cars***

by Dr. Lance B. Eliot, MBA, PhD

Chapter Title



***This title is available via Amazon and other book sellers***

Companion Book By This Author

***Pioneering Advances for AI Driverless Cars***

by Dr. Lance B. Eliot, MBA, PhD

Chapter Title



***This title is available via Amazon and other book sellers***

Companion Book By This Author

***Leading Edge Trends for AI Driverless Cars***

by Dr. Lance B. Eliot, MBA, PhD

Chapter Title



***This title is available via Amazon and other book sellers***

Companion Book By This Author

***The Cutting Edge of***
***AI Autonomous Cars***

by Dr. Lance B. Eliot, MBA, PhD

Chapter Title



***This title is available via Amazon and other book sellers***

Companion Book By This Author

***The Next Wave of AI Self-Driving Cars***

by Dr. Lance B. Eliot, MBA, PhD

Chapter Title



***This title is available via Amazon and other book sellers***

Companion Book By This Author

***Revolutionary Innovations of AI Self-Driving Cars***

by Dr. Lance B. Eliot, MBA, PhD

Chapter Title

Companion Book By This Author

***AI Self-Driving Cars***
**Breakthroughs**

by Dr. Lance B. Eliot, MBA, PhD

Chapter Title



***This title is available via Amazon and other book sellers***

Companion Book By This Author

***Trailblazing Trends for***
**AI Self-Driving Cars**

by Dr. Lance B. Eliot, MBA, PhD

Chapter Title



***This title is available via Amazon and other book sellers***

Companion Book By This Author

***Ingenious Strides for***
**AI Driverless Cars**

by Dr. Lance B. Eliot, MBA, PhD

Chapter Title



***This title is available via Amazon and other book sellers***

Companion Book By This Author

***AI Self-Driving Cars Inventiveness***

by Dr. Lance B. Eliot, MBA, PhD

Chapter Title



***This title is available via Amazon and other book sellers***

Companion Book By This Author

***Visionary Secrets of***
***AI Driverless Cars***

by Dr. Lance B. Eliot, MBA, PhD

Chapter Title

Companion Book By This Author

***Spearheading***
***AI Self-Driving Cars***

by Dr. Lance B. Eliot, MBA, PhD

Chapter Title



***This title is available via Amazon and other book sellers***

Companion Book By This Author

***Spurring***
***AI Self-Driving Cars***

by Dr. Lance B. Eliot, MBA, PhD

Chapter Title

Companion Book By This Author

***Avant-Garde***
***AI Driverless Cars***

by Dr. Lance B. Eliot, MBA, PhD

Chapter Title



***This title is available via Amazon and other book sellers***

Companion Book By This Author

***AI Self-Driving Cars Evolvement***

by Dr. Lance B. Eliot, MBA, PhD

Chapter Title

Companion Book By This Author

***AI Driverless Cars Chrysalis***

by Dr. Lance B. Eliot, MBA, PhD

Chapter Title



***This title is available via Amazon and other book sellers***

Companion Book By This Author

***Boosting***
***AI Autonomous Cars***

by Dr. Lance B. Eliot, MBA, PhD

Chapter Title



***This title is available via Amazon and other book sellers***

Companion Book By This Author

***AI Self-Driving Cars Trendsetting***

by Dr. Lance B. Eliot, MBA, PhD

Chapter Title



***This title is available via Amazon and other book sellers***

Companion Book By This Author

***AI Autonomous Cars Forefront***

by Dr. Lance B. Eliot, MBA, PhD

Chapter Title



***This title is available via Amazon and other book sellers***

Companion Book By This Author

***AI Autonomous Cars Emergence***

by Dr. Lance B. Eliot, MBA, PhD

Chapter Title



***This title is available via Amazon and other book sellers***

Companion Book By This Author

***AI Autonomous Cars Progress***

by Dr. Lance B. Eliot, MBA, PhD

Chapter Title



***This title is available via Amazon and other book sellers***

Companion Book By This Author

## *AI Self-Driving Cars Prognosis*

by Dr. Lance B. Eliot, MBA, PhD

Chapter Title



***This title is available via Amazon and other book sellers***

Companion Book By This Author

***AI Self-Driving Cars***
***Momentum***

by Dr. Lance B. Eliot, MBA, PhD

Chapter Title



***This title is available via Amazon and other book sellers***

Companion Book By This Author

***AI Self-Driving Cars Headway***

by Dr. Lance B. Eliot, MBA, PhD

Chapter Title



***This title is available via Amazon and other book sellers***

Companion Book By This Author

***AI Self-Driving Cars Vicissitude***

by Dr. Lance B. Eliot, MBA, PhD

Chapter Title



***This title is available via Amazon and other book sellers***

Companion Book By This Author

***AI Self-Driving Cars***
***Autonomy***

by Dr. Lance B. Eliot, MBA, PhD

Chapter Title



***This title is available via Amazon and other book sellers***

Companion Book By This Author

***AI Driverless Cars Transmutation***

by Dr. Lance B. Eliot, MBA, PhD

Chapter Title

Companion Book By This Author

***AI Driverless Cars Potentiality***

by Dr. Lance B. Eliot, MBA, PhD

Chapter Title



***This title is available via Amazon and other book sellers***

Companion Book By This Author

***AI Driverless Cars Realities***

by Dr. Lance B. Eliot, MBA, PhD

Chapter Title



***This title is available via Amazon and other book sellers***

Companion Book By This Author

***AI Self-Driving Cars***
***Materiality***

by Dr. Lance B. Eliot, MBA, PhD

Chapter Title



***This title is available via Amazon and other book sellers***

Companion Book By This Author

***AI Self-Driving Cars Accordance***

by Dr. Lance B. Eliot, MBA, PhD

Chapter Title



***This title is available via Amazon and other book sellers***

Companion Book By This Author

***AI Self-Driving Cars***
***Equanimity***

by Dr. Lance B. Eliot, MBA, PhD

Chapter Title



***This title is available via Amazon and other book sellers***

Companion Book By This Author

***AI Self-Driving Cars Divulgement***

by Dr. Lance B. Eliot, MBA, PhD

Chapter Title



***This title is available via Amazon and other book sellers***

Companion Book By This Author

***AI Self-Driving Cars Consonance***

by Dr. Lance B. Eliot, MBA, PhD

Chapter Title



***This title is available via Amazon and other book sellers***

Companion Book By This Author

***Revelatory AI Self-Driving Cars***

by Dr. Lance B. Eliot, MBA, PhD

Chapter Title



***This title is available via Amazon and other book sellers***

Companion Book By This Author

***Edifying AI Self-Driving Cars***

by Dr. Lance B. Eliot, MBA, PhD



***This title is available via Amazon and other book sellers***

Companion Book By This Author

***Apprising AI Driverless Cars***

by Dr. Lance B. Eliot, MBA, PhD

Chapter Title



***This title is available via Amazon and other book sellers***

Companion Book By This Author

***Improving AI Self-Driving Cars***

by Dr. Lance B. Eliot, MBA, PhD

Chapter Title



***This title is available via Amazon and other book sellers***

Companion Book By This Author

***Improving AI Self-Driving Cars***

by Dr. Lance B. Eliot, MBA, PhD

Chapter Title



***This title is available via Amazon and other book sellers***

# ABOUT THE AUTHOR

Dr. Lance B. Eliot, Ph.D., MBA is a Stanford Fellow and a globally recognized AI expert and thought leader, an experienced executive and leader, a successful serial entrepreneur, and a noted scholar on AI, including that his Forbes and AI Trends columns have amassed over 4.5+ million views, his books on AI are frequently ranked in the Top 10 of all-time AI books, his articles are widely cited, and he has developed dozens of advanced AI systems.

He currently serves as the CEO of Techbruim, Inc. and has over twenty years of industry experience including serving as a corporate officer in billion-dollar sized firms and was a partner in a major consulting firm. He is also a successful entrepreneur having founded, ran, and sold several high-tech firms.

Dr. Eliot previously hosted the popular radio show *Technotrends* that was also available on American Airlines flights via their in-flight audio program, he has made appearances on CNN, has been a frequent speaker at industry conferences, and his podcasts have been downloaded over 100,000 times.

A former professor at the University of Southern California (USC), he founded and led an innovative research lab on Artificial Intelligence. He also previously served on the faculty of the University of California Los Angeles (UCLA) and was a visiting professor at other major universities. He was elected to the International Board of the Society for Information Management (SIM), a prestigious association of over 3,000 high-tech executives worldwide.

He has performed extensive community service, including serving as Senior Science Adviser to the Congressional Vice-Chair of the Congressional Committee on Science & Technology. He has served on the Board of the OC Science & Engineering Fair (OCSEF), where he is also has been a Grand Sweepstakes judge, and likewise served as a judge for the Intel International SEF (ISEF). He served as the Vice-Chair of the Association for Computing Machinery (ACM) Chapter, a prestigious association of computer scientists. Dr. Eliot has been a shark tank judge for the USC Mark Stevens Center for Innovation on start-up pitch competitions and served as a mentor for several incubators and accelerators in Silicon Valley and in Silicon Beach.

Dr. Eliot holds a Ph.D. from USC, MBA, and Bachelor's in Computer Science, and earned the CDP, CCP, CSP, CDE, and CISA certifications.

# ADDENDUM

## ***Improving AI Self-Driving Cars***

*Practical Advances in Artificial Intelligence (AI) and Machine Learning*

By

Dr. Lance B. Eliot, MBA, PhD

---

For supplemental materials of this book, visit:

**www.ai-selfdriving-cars.guru**

For special orders of this book, contact:

**LBE Press Publishing**

Email: LBE.Press.Publishing@gmail.com

Made in the USA
Monee, IL
07 May 2022

96037225R00223